Non-State Social Protection Actors and Services in Africa

For millions of Africans, the social situation is dire. Over half of the population of sub-Sahara Africa does not have access to improved sanitation facilities, and about a quarter are undernourished. If factors such as armed conflicts in the region, the impact of climate change, or the widespread presence of a broad range of infectious agents are considered, it shows a large number of Africans living in very fragile circumstances, highly vulnerable to any kind of shock or rapid change. Small, informal community groups deliver the majority of social protection services in Africa, but most of these are disqualified from official recognition, support, or integration with state systems because they do not "fit" the modern management model of accountability. The studies in this book challenge that verdict.

This book outlines insightful and valuable research generated by teams of established scholars. It is divided into nine studies exploring the governance of non-state actors in Ethiopia, Ghana, Kenya, Senegal, Tanzania, and Uganda. It examines the numerous self-help groups and their effectiveness and argues that if the modern management model is right, why do so many Africans avoid interacting with it? The book provides a warning against undermining what is possibly the single greatest social protection resource throughout Africa in the name of "reform", and suggests that the modern welfare establishment needs to adapt to (and learn from) self-help groups – not the other way around.

Non-State Social Protection Actors and Services in Africa will be of interest to donors, policymakers, practitioners, and students and scholars of African Studies, social policy, and politics.

Nicholas Awortwi is Director of Research Partnership for African Social and Governance Research (PASGR), a pan-African organisation based in Nairobi, Kenya.

Gregor Walter-Drop is Managing Director of the Center for Area Studies at the Free University of Berlin, Germany.

African Governance

1 **Traditional Institutions in Contemporary African Governance**
   Edited by Kidane Mengisteab and Gerard Hagg

2 **Non-State Social Protection Actors and Services in Africa**
   Governance Below the State
   Edited by Nicholas Awortwi and Gregor Walter-Drop

Non-State Social Protection Actors and Services in Africa
Governance Below the State

Edited by Nicholas Awortwi
and Gregor Walter-Drop

LONDON AND NEW YORK

First published 2018
by Routledge
2 Park Square, Milton Park, Abingdon, Oxon OX14 4RN

and by Routledge
711 Third Avenue, New York, NY 10017

Routledge is an imprint of the Taylor & Francis Group, an informa business

© 2018 selection and editorial matter, Nicholas Awortwi and Gregor Walter-Drop; individual chapters, the contributors

The right of Nicholas Awortwi and Gregor Walter-Drop to be identified as the authors of the editorial material, and of the authors for their individual chapters, has been asserted in accordance with sections 77 and 78 of the Copyright, Designs and Patents Act 1988.

All rights reserved. No part of this book may be reprinted or reproduced or utilised in any form or by any electronic, mechanical, or other means, now known or hereafter invented, including photocopying and recording, or in any information storage or retrieval system, without permission in writing from the publishers.

Trademark notice: Product or corporate names may be trademarks or registered trademarks, and are used only for identification and explanation without intent to infringe.

British Library Cataloguing-in-Publication Data
A catalogue record for this book is available from the British Library

Library of Congress Cataloging-in-Publication Data
A catalog record for this book has been requested

ISBN: 978-1-138-05962-7 (hbk)
ISBN: 978-1-315-16116-7 (ebk)

Typeset in Times New Roman
by Apex CoVantage, LLC

Contents

List of figures   vii
List of tables   viii
List of abbreviations   x
List of contributors   xiii
Foreword   xxi
Preface   xxiv
Acknowledgements   xxvi

1 **Governance below the state: non-state social protection services in Africa**   1
NICHOLAS AWORTWI AND GREGOR WALTER-DROP

2 **Governance characteristics and policy relevance of informal social protection services in Ethiopia: when the state is willing but not able**   25
AMDISSA TESHOME, ADANECH DUTU, KASSA TESHAGER, AND TEREFE ZELEKE

3 **Governance of non-state social protection services in Ghana: communication as an accountability mechanism in mutual aid organisations in Wassa**   44
ELLEN BORTEI-DOKU ARYEETEY, STEPHEN AFRANIE, DANIEL DOH, AND PAUL ANDOH

4 **Social protection and citizenship rights of vulnerable children: a perspective on interventions by non-state actors in western Kenya**   55
AUMA OKWANY AND ELIZABETH NGUTUKU

5 **Governance mechanisms of burial societies in western Uganda** 72
NARATHIUS ASINGWIRE, DENIS MUHANGI, ROSE B. NAMARA, AND MARGARET KEMIGISA

6 **Hedging against vulnerability: associational life as a social insurance strategy by the poor in the central region of Ghana** 87
AKOSUA K. DARKWAH, MAVIS DAKO-GYEKE, AND EDWARD NKETIAH-AMPONSAH

7 **Women's economic empowerment in Kenya: lessons from non-state social protection actors and services in the Nyanza region** 104
AKINYI NZIOKI AND WINNIE MWASIAJI

8 **Governance of non-state social protection initiatives for addressing gendered poverty in Uganda: beyond counting of women on governance committees?** 117
FLORENCE KYOHEIRWE MUHANGUZI

9 **Governance dynamics in the provision of community-based social protection services in Tanzania** 135
ADALBERTUS KAMANZI, EMMANUEL NYANKWELI, AND AUMA OKWANY

10 **Conclusion and implications for public policy and governance theory: possible but different** 151
NICHOLAS AWORTWI AND GREGOR WALTER-DROP

Index 163

Figures

2.1	The location of the study areas	31
2.2	Services delivered by non-state actors	34
2.3	Non-state actors' services delivery by geographic location (urban vs. rural)	35
4.1	Range of services	58
4.2	Impact of interventions	65
5.1	Type of services provided by burial societies (%)	76
5.2	Beneficiary assessment of organisational performance in terms of quality of services received	80
7.1	Number of non-state actors mapped by district (county)	108

Tables

1.1	The number of non-state social protection actors	10
1.2	Types of non-state social protection actors	11
1.3	Types of social protection services provided by non-state social protection actors	12
1.4	Funding sources for non-state social protection actors	13
2.1	Some Millennium Development Goal indicators (1995–2011)	27
2.2	Types of non-state actors in research sites	32
2.3	Forms of informal social protection providers	32
2.4	Geographical coverage of informal social protection providers	33
2.5	Services provided by informal non-state actors	34
2.6	The types of beneficiaries covered by informal non-state actors (N = 519)	36
2.7	Perceptions of beneficiaries on service provision	36
2.8	Presence of organisational structures and operational rules	37
2.9	Accountability mechanisms in informal organisations	38
3.1	Breakdown of mutual organisations selected for the in-depth analysis	48
3.2	Forms of reporting	49
5.1	Report card results of members' perceptions of their organisation and leaders	81
6.1	Determinants of associational membership (full sample)	95
6.2	Determinants of associational membership (by gender)	96
6.3	Effect of associational intensity on monetary benefits	97
7.1	Registered women's groups by membership and contribution	105
7.2	Women's ability to make decisions as a result of non-state actors social protection programmes	112
8.1	Sex composition of members in senior decision-making positions in non-state actors in the study districts	127
9.1	Sources of funds for non-state social protection services	142
9.2	Selection of leaders	143

9.3	Service affordability	146
9.4	Service availability	147
10.1	Governance indicators: Ibrahim Index of African Governance, 2015	155
10.2	Presence of non-state actors in the six countries	155
10.3	Types of social protection services provided by non-state actors	156
10.4a	Economic and social welfare indicators	156
10.4b	Economic and social welfare indicators	157

Abbreviations

ACPF	African Child Policy Forum
ADR	Alternative Dispute Resolution
AIDS	acquired immune deficiency syndrome
ARVs	antiretroviral
AU	African Union
CBO	community-based organisation
CCB	community capacity building
CPR	common pool resources
CPRC	Chronic Poverty Research Centre
CT-OVC	cash transfer for orphaned and vulnerable children
DfID	Department for International Development
DRT	development research training
EC	European Commission
FBO	faith-based organisation
FDRE	Federal Democratic Republic of Ethiopia
FGD	focus group discussion
FGM	female genital mutilation
GDP	Gross Domestic Product
GII	Gender Inequality Index
GLSS	Ghana Living Standards Survey
GOK	Government of Kenya
GoU	Government of Uganda
GPRS	Growth and Poverty Reduction Strategy
GTP	Growth and Transformation Plan
HDI	Human Development Index
HIV	human immunodeficiency virus
IDIs	in-depth interviews
IDP	internally displaced people
IGA	income-generating activity

ILO	International Labour Organisation
INGOs	international non-governmental organisation
ISPOs	informal social protection organisations
KNBS	Kenya National Bureau of Statistics
KNCHR	Kenya National Commission for Human Rights
LACCDP	Lower Ambira Community Child Development Programme
LCDs	Least Developed Countries
LEAP	Livelihood Empowerment Against Poverty
MCB	Ministry of Capacity Building
MDG	Millennium Development Goal
MKUKUTA	Tanzania's National Strategy for Growth and Poverty Reduction
MoH	Ministry of Health
NCG	Nordic Consulting Group
NDP	National Development Plan
NGO	non-governmental organisation
NSA	non-state actor
NSSP	non-state social protection
NSSPA	non-state social protection actor
OECD	Organization for Economic Co-operation and Development
OLS	Ordinary Least Square
OVCs	orphans and vulnerable children
PAMSCAD	Programme of Action to Mitigate the Social Cost of Adjustment
PAPRO	Patience Pays Professional Organisation
PASDEP	Plan for Accelerated and Sustained Development to End Poverty
PASGR	Partnership for African Social and Governance Research
PEAP	Poverty Eradication Action Plan
PRSP	Poverty Reduction Strategy Programme
PSNP	Productive Safety Net Programme
SACCOs	Savings and Cooperative Credit Schemes
SAP	Structural Adjustment Programmes
SGDs	Sustainable Development Goals
SID	Society for International Development
SNDES	Senegal's National Strategy for Social and Economic Development
SP	social protection
STEP	Strategies and Tools against Social Exclusion and Poverty
UN	United Nations
UNCTAD	United Nations Conference on Trade and Development

UNICEF	United Nations Children's Fund
UNRISD	United Nations Research Institute for Social Development
VIFs	Variance Inflation Factors
WEF	Women's Enterprise Fund
WHO	World Health Organisation
YDEF	Youth Development Enterprise Fund

Contributors

Stephen Afranie holds a Ph.D. in Sociology and has had fourteen years teaching experience in sociology in the areas of industrial sociology and sociology of industrial relations, introduction to sociology and social anthropology, and sociology of rural development in the Department of Sociology at the University of Ghana. He is a former deputy director for the Centre for Social Policy Studies (CSPS) in the university and is currently a senior lecturer at the Centre. Dr. Afranie has led and participated in many social and policy researches including the Non-State Actors (NSAs) and Accountable Social Protection in child protection and livelihoods in Ghana for PASGR, Orphans and Vulnerable Children study in Ghana for UNICEF, Child Marriage study in Ghana for World Vision, and Master Card Foundation's sponsored Youth Save Ghana Experiment research project (a multi-national study evaluating the impact that access to savings accounts can have on youth developmental outcomes).

Paul Andoh has a background in sociology and worked as an Assistant Research Fellow at the Centre for Social Policy Studies, University of Ghana, where he taught courses in Social Policy and Public Policy Analysis. His research interests cover community development issues, well-being of vulnerable groups, juvenile delinquency and education. He is presently completing his Ph.D. research at the School of Social Science, University of Queensland, Australia. He has authored and co-authored articles in peer reviewed journals and has been a lead researcher as well as researcher in a number of contract research activities on inclusive education, working school children, orphaned and vulnerable children, community resettlement, social protection, and alternative livelihoods in mining communities in Ghana.

Ellen Bortei-Doku Aryeetey is an associate professor of sociology at the Centre for Social Policy Studies in the College of Humanities at the University of Ghana. She holds a Ph.D. in sociology from Michigan State

University, Michigan, USA. She has taught and conducted research, as well as engaged with policymakers, development practitioners, and development partners, in a wide range of areas in the field of social development. Her research and publications have focused on social policy studies across the life course, community development in farming and fishing communities, gender relations, and policymaking institutions.

Narathius Asingwire (Ph.D.) is an associate professor of social policy at Makerere University, College of Humanities and Social Sciences. Between 1998 and 2011, he was chair of the Department of Social and Social Administration, Makerere University. For over 25 years, he has been involved in several research projects as a principal investigator and team leader. His areas of interest include social policy reforms in Eastern Africa and their impact on social service provisioning. Additionally, he has served as a consultant for government ministries, departments, and agencies, as well as national and international agencies both bilateral and multi-lateral.

Nicholas Awortwi (Ph.D.) is the director of research for Partnership for African Social and Governance Research (PASGR), a pan-African organisation based in Nairobi, Kenya. Prior to that, Nicholas was a senior lecturer in development management at the International Institute of Social Studies (ISS) of Erasmus University, the Hague, the Netherlands, and a visiting senior lecturer at F.H.R Lim A Po School of Public Administration & Governance, Paramaribo in Suriname, and Nsamizi Training Institute of Social Development, Uganda. He is among the leading authors of decentralisation and local governance issues in Africa and provided expert advice to Commonwealth Secretariat, United Nations Capital Development Fund, and United Nations Development Programme. He has 30 publications on decentralisation, local governance and public management in internationally refereed journals and books.

Mavis Dako-Gyeke completed her Master's Degree in Clinical Social Work at Ohio State University in Columbus, Ohio, USA, and Doctor of Philosophy Degree at Texas Woman's University in Denton, Texas, USA. She previously taught at Texas Woman's University and currently teaches courses at both undergraduate and graduate levels at the Department of Social Work, University of Ghana. At present, she is the Head of the Department of Social Work and her research interests include experiences of orphaned and vulnerable children, social protection, migration and gender issues. She has conducted funded research and consultancy projects in the areas of her research interest for UNICEF, Partnership for African Social and Governance Research (PASGR), United Nations Development Programme (UNDP) and Canada-Africa Research Exchange Grants (CAREG).

Contributors xv

Akosua K. Darkwah (Ph.D.) is currently a senior lecturer in the Department of Sociology at the University of Ghana, Legon. In addition to her work as an academic in the Department of Sociology, she is currently the director of the Centre for Gender Studies and Advocacy at the University of Ghana. Her primary area of research interest is to investigate the myriad ways in which global economic policies and practices affect the nature and quality of work opportunities available to Ghanaian women.

Daniel Doh is a social policy analyst and researcher. His research interests are in social protection, policy actors, ageing & vulnerability, child protection, policy evaluation, and institutions of governance. He is a trainer in research methodology and has trained several methods short courses for PASGR. He has carried out numerous researches as a consultant as well as principal investigator including: principal investigator for *Qualitative Impacts of the LEAP Cash Transfer Programme in Ghana*, funded by *UNICEF Ghana*; co-principal investigator in *Non-State Actors and Accountable Social Protection in Ghana*, funded by *PASGR*; lead researcher in *Monitoring of Conditionality Compliance of the LEAP Cash Transfer Programme in Ghana*; principal consultant in *Monitoring of natural resource governance: Assessment of challenges in policy and practice as a result of the multi-stakeholder Ghana Dams Dialogue,* for IIED, UK. He worked as a Research Fellow at the Centre for Social Policy Studies, University of Ghana. He has just completed his Ph.D. (social sciences) at the Edith Cowan University, Western Australia.

Adalbertus Kamanzi holds a Ph.D. in development studies, Radboud University, Nijmegen, Netherlands. He has worked as lecturer in the Department of Development Studies at the University of Dodoma, Tanzania. He is currently a research fellow at the Institute of Rural Development Planning, Dodoma, Tanzania, and an online tutor at the Virtue University of Uganda for the course Development Discourses: Theory and Practice. He has specialised in qualitative research on issues pertaining to people's livelihoods. He has been involved in a number of research activities with different research institutions, among them Organisation for Social Science Research in Eastern and Southern Africa (on gender issues, 2006–2011), Lake Victoria Research Initiative – VICRES (on a multidisciplinary research approach to dealing with environmental issues, 2006–2009), EDI Ltd (on economic issues, 2004 until this date), and some other researches and capacity-building activities with the local development organisations in the Kagera region. He has written widely on development-related issues, particularly on gender issues, development studies, HIV/AIDS, micro-finance, politics, and development cooperation.

Margaret Kemigisa (Ph.D.) is an independent development consultant in Uganda. She holds a Ph.D. in public health and policy from the University of London (London School of Hygiene and Tropical Medicine), and her Ph.D. research focused on social networks and the prevention of HIV/AIDS in Uganda. Her professional career spans fifteen years that comprise a mixture of national and international assignments with governments and Civil Society Organisations (CSOs). Most of this has centred on research, including monitoring and evaluation assignments in varied fields such as HIV and AIDS, education, agriculture, gender, social protection and governance structures. She is also an experienced trainer and facilitator and has undertaken leadership, administrative and coordination roles in several of my assignments.

Denis Muhangi (Ph.D.) is a social scientist and policy analyst currently employed at Makerere University, Department of Social Work and Social Administration. He completed his Ph.D. studies at Queens University of Belfast in the UK in 2009. His Ph.D. research focused on government-NGO partnerships in HIV/AIDS response in Uganda. His research experience covers a wide range of social and economic fields, but is particularly in the areas of HIV/AIDS, social protection, OVC, health care, education, and water and sanitation. He has published some of his work in these areas. His other fields of interest include social policy reform, social services design and delivery, and institutional development. He was among the researchers who in 2012 to 2013 undertook studies on the features and governance of non-state social protection in Uganda.

Florence Kyoheirwe Muhanguzi (Ph.D.) is a senior lecturer at the School of Women and Gender Studies, College of Humanities and Social Sciences, Makerere University, Kampala Uganda. She holds a Ph.D. in gender studies from the University of Cape Town, South Africa and is currently teaching and supervising research projects for students in both undergraduate and postgraduate programmes. Her area of interest is gender-focused research in the fields including women's health and sexuality, reproductive health, women's rights, social protection (SP), and adolescent girls' well-being. She is a gender trainer and activist who promotes the status of women, girls, and boys.

Winnie Mwasiaji is Senior Assistant Director in the State Department for Social Protection. She has over ten years' experience in social protection policy and programming. She has led the Kenya team in several activities around rethinking the social protection policies, strategies, programming and linking policy makers, practitioners and researchers in the

Contributors xvii

evolvement of social protection in Kenya. She conceptualized, initiated and supported the development of social protection systems in Kenya including the single registry system and the National Social Protection Policy. She is currently serving as the vice chairperson of the Community of Practice for conditional and unconditional cash transfer – Anglo phone, Africa Chapter.

Rose B. Namara (Ph.D.) is a senior lecturer and Head of Research at the Uganda Management Institute, the leading government training institution in management studies in Uganda. She has 17 years of experience in development work, social research, monitoring and evaluation, and has served as a consultant in diverse fields such as programme development, strategic/corporate planning, policy analysis, poverty and gender analysis, and partnership development. She has spent a large part of her career offering technical support to non-governmental organisations and government department in Uganda, Rwanda and Botswana. Namara has a doctorate in development studies from the Institute of Social Studies (ISS), The Hague and her research focused on NGOs, poverty reduction and social exclusion in Uganda with a focus on poverty reduction policies and National Agriculture Extension programmes.

Elizabeth Ngutuku is a Ph.D. candidate at the International Institute of Social Studies of Erasmus University, Rotterdam in the Netherlands. Her doctoral research focuses on dominant representations of child poverty in Kenya against the lived experience of children. She was the executive director of Nascent Research and Development Organization in Kenya and Uganda from 2008–2015. Her research interests are in critical studies of childhood and youth, and she has undertaken various research projects in this area in Kenya, Uganda, Ethiopia and Tanzania. She has co-authored a book and book chapter and published several articles.

Edward Nketiah-Amponsah is a senior lecturer at the Department of Economics, University of Ghana. He holds Bachelor of Arts and Master of Philosophy degrees in Economics from the University of Ghana. He also holds a Ph.D. with Specialization in Development and Health Economics from ZEF, University of Bonn, Germany. His research interests include the economics of maternal and child healthcare utilization, health seeking behaviour, applied microeconometrics, social protection, poverty and welfare analyses. He currently teaches Public Sector Economics and Health Economics at the undergraduate and graduate levels, respectively. He has published in *Journal of Developing Societies*, *International Journal of Social Economics*, *Development Southern*

Africa, Cost Effectiveness and Resource Allocation, Health Economics Review, BMC Health Services Research, International Journal of Equity in Healthcare, Environmental Health Perspectives, Human Resources for Health, Journal of Applied Economics and *PLoS ONE*, among others.

Emmanuel Nyankweli holds a Ph.D. in Development Studies, AISSR-University of Amsterdam, the Netherlands and is currently an associate professor and Deputy Director of Higher Education at the Ministry of Education, Science and Technology, Tanzania. For the past twelve years, he worked at the Institute of Rural Development Planning, Dodoma where he taught various courses in project planning and management, project management theories and practices, agricultural development planning, strategic planning and integrated rural development planning for both undergraduates and postgraduates. He also worked as a visiting lecturer at St. John's University of Tanzania, Mazengo Campus, Dodoma, where he lectured in Population and Development, Public Policy, Gender and Development as well as Social Conflict Management and Resolutions for Postgraduates in Development Studies. His research interests are on the China-Africa trade relations, climate change and environment, African mineral resource economies and governance of non-state socio-protection services.

Akinyi Nzioki holds a Ph.D. in anthropology and is currently the executive director and chief consultant at the Centre for Land, Economy and Rights of Women. Her area of specialization includes gender and development policy analysis. She is a member of the Association of African Women in Research and Development, Development Alternatives for Third World Women, and the Associated Country Women of the World.

Auma Okwany is a faculty member of the Social Policy and Development Programme at ISS of Erasmus University, Rotterdam in the Netherlands. She is a core teaching member of the MA in child and youth studies at the institute and has convened the postgraduate diploma in children youth and development at the institute for the last five years. Her teaching and research interests (including publications) centre on the relationship between policy, practice, and theory in childhood and youth more broadly and in education reform efforts in particular with a focus on factors that define exclusion for disadvantaged groups. In addition to teaching and research, she is involved in several externally funded projects. She is coordinating the operations research of a three-year project on comprehensive sexuality for young people in Ethiopia and Uganda funded by the Dutch government and implemented by Save the Children Netherlands and USA. She is also a co-coordinator of the three-year project funded by MasterCard Foundation titled Righting the Future: South-South Collaboration and Capacity Building for Universalizing Secondary Education for Girls in Africa. She has degrees from Indiana University (USA), University of New Brunswick (Canada), and Kenyatta University (Kenya).

Kassa Teshager is a citizen of Ethiopia. At present, he is Deputy Director for Research and Community Service and an Assistant Professor at Ethiopian Civil Service University. In this position, he lectures, consults, and conducts research on value chains, land, livelihoods, social protection, sustainable development, etc. He holds a B.A. in Development Management from Ethiopian Civil Service University, an M.A. in Local and Regional Development from International Institute of Social Studies, Erasmus University, and a Ph.D. in Development Studies from University of South Africa. He has published widely in the areas of development. His area of research includes Rural Development, Agriculture, Rural Livelihoods, Food Security, Social Protection, Value chain Analysis, Local Economic Development, Urban and Rural Poverty Alleviation, Private Sector Development, NGOs, Local Government and Governance.

Amdissa Teshome is an independent consultant based in Addis Ababa, Ethiopia, with 30 years of work experience in Ethiopia and clients including USAID, World Bank, DfID, Intergovernmental Authority on Development, and NGOs. He specializes in food security programming and policy, and he has reviewed and evaluated aspects of the Productive Safety Net Programme and Household Asset-Building Programme in Ethiopia, and remains very engaged with the strategies and activities of these programs. He is also a very experienced reviewer and evaluator of agriculture and food security programs in Ethiopia. He was the country coordinator of the Future Agricultures Consortium and worked closely with the Ministry of Agriculture to facilitate policy dialogues on extension systems, farmer organisations, SP, and climate change. He has designed and delivered trainings for NGOs in Ethiopia on gender equity and sensitivity, and much of his support to program design, review, and evaluation has included gender analysis.

Gregor Walter-Drop holds a Ph.D. in political science at the University of Bremen. Subsequently, he worked in the start-up team of the Hertie School of Governance and developed its curriculum. He moved on to an assistant professorship at Freie Universität Berlin in 2006. Since 2010, he has been serving as managing director of the Collaborative Research Center 700, "Governance in Areas of Limited Statehood", hosted at Freie Universität Berlin. Since 2014, he has directed the Center for Area Studies at Freie Universität. He has specialized in international relations and has published and taught in the fields of globalization, governance, limited statehood, and foreign policy analysis.

Terefe Zeleke (M.A.) studied regional and local development at Addis Ababa University, Ethiopia, and is a lecturer at Ethiopian Civil Service College (ECSC), Institute of Public Management and Development Studies.

Foreword

The inability of several African states to ensure inclusive social protection (SP) for all their citizens in spite of the fact that these are often enshrined in constitutional and legal mandates between states and citizens represents one of the key deficiencies and limitations of statehood on the continent. It not only undermines one of the basic principles and obligations of citizenship but also erodes key elements of what constitutes citizenship. This deficit and breach of national "social contracts" is best illustrated by states' delivery of social welfare and the growth of articulate and coherent social policy that recognizes and values all players, particularly non-state social protection actors (NSSPAs).

In recent times, African governments have made noteworthy progress in prioritising and integrating SP in constitutional and policy commitment, to ease the pains of the structural adjustment programmes of the previous two to three decades, and to meet the more recent Millennium Development Goals (MDGs) 2000–2015, now Sustainable Development Goals (SDGs) 2016–2030. Nevertheless, the gap between rights and reality remains a chasm – about 90 per cent of Africa's poorest and most vulnerable are yet to be provided for in any form of state SP scheme. Lack of resources and narrow institutional aptitude – "limited statehood" – are widely (but not always accurately) presented as the main obstacles to inclusive SP.

This book – based on empirical studies in 30 districts across six sub-Saharan African countries – illustrates how NSSPAs have responded to citizens' vulnerability in a well-planned, governed, and coordinated manner. Most notably, the small, informal membership-based and membership-financed community organisations have covered for state default in many SP services. The potential of these organisations in the field of SP has been, up to now, largely insufficiently recognized by the state and in academic research. Yet NSSPAs are at the forefront – in initiative, scale, and scope – of grassroots delivery of SP services including cash transfers, micro-credit, health insurance, and care for orphans, elderly people, and physically impaired. They are vibrant, nimble, responsive, and knowledgeable, even as they operate beneath the radar of formal authorities and conventional research.

The case studies in this book challenge the failure to acknowledge organic forms of SP simply because they emerge from marginalised spaces and groups that use less elegant forms of management and accountability.

It is clear that many African states are not the key responders to poverty, disability, and many other social vulnerabilities of their citizens. NSAs, even without recognition or support, are already playing a much more active role. An extensive and an all-encompassing SP system does not exist and is unlikely to evolve without them.

This book suggests a range of policy options to harness their potential for micro-level response to poverty and vulnerability. In addition, it evaluates the theoretical implications of this form of "governance below the state". While the six countries are no doubt democratically governed, the absence or weakness of the state in (not) providing SP to the overwhelming majority of citizens has not led to a vacuum, but welfare services have, necessarily, taken a different form.

The Partnership for African Social and Governance Research (PASGR) commissioned the study to enable empirical investigations of non-state social protection (NSSP) in Africa to provide better understanding of "governance from below" in areas of limited statehood. Knowing the limitation of policy traction in the SP sector, PASGR intends to use the findings to inform policy through the innovative research-policy engagement approach (Utafiti Sera). The Utafiti Sera-Kiswahili phrase for research-policy community model supports a community of researchers and policy actors working together to ensure that appropriate and negotiated actions occur through debates, policy design, administrative, and civic actions around a policy problem for which there is research evidence. PASGR aims to use *Utafiti Sera* to engage varied policy actors to ensure that states recognise NSAs as partners in providing SP services and integrate them in national planning and budgeting while also providing support through training, networking, and engagement with devolved governments.

PASGR, established in 2011, is an independent, non-partisan, pan-African, not-for-profit organisation located in Nairobi, Kenya. Currently engaged in 13 African countries, PASGR works to enhance research excellence on themes of governance and public policy that contribute to the overall well-being of all African people. In partnership with individual academics and researchers, higher education institutions, think tanks, civil society organisations, businesses, and policy communities, both in the region and internationally, PASGR supports the production and dissemination of policy-relevant research, designs and delivers suites of short professional development courses for researchers and policy actors, and facilitates the development of collaborative higher education programmes. Our vision is "a vibrant African social science community addressing the continent's public policy issues".

It is in pursuit of this vision that we firmly hold the hope and commitment that studies such as this will continue to contribute evidence for robust policy debates and effective policy uptake on Africa's development process, SP trajectories, and social policy.

Tade Akin Aina
Executive Director, PASGR
January 2017

Preface

Africa is hitting new heights in democratic process, macro-economic growth, and constitutional commitment to social welfare. However, the continent lacks the financial and institutional capacity – and/or the political will – to honour its pledges to the poor and vulnerable. About 90 per cent of all citizens, many of whom are desperately poor and vulnerable, do not have access to even meagre state support. While international attention has searched for state remedies to state shortfalls, the poor themselves have taken a different route.

They have improvised, organised, delivered, and governed their own collective social protection (SP) services in forms and shapes often below the official radar. Based on empirical studies in 30 districts in Ethiopia, Ghana, Kenya, Senegal, Tanzania, and Uganda, this book illustrates how – in the context of limited statehood – localised self-governance by small, informal, and community-level organisations has delivered more SP to more needy people than all state programmes combined.

The greatest irony is this: self-help systems are denied any state support (or even recognition) because they do not conform to modern systems of accountability. Yet their traditional, informal, and unconventional character is precisely why they work to the benefit of their members. They may not be perfect, but their highly localised and homespun groupings and methods in fact make them more accountable, not less. They are probably a best fit. They could be the primary channel of government support, using meagre state resources more efficiently and effectively than the state itself.

The greatest danger is this: If states try to reform community-based organisations (CBOs) through regulation, they will dissent or disobey or disband. If they are encouraged (and enabled) to conform voluntarily through skills support and practical incentives, then no "enforcement" will be necessary. Their traditional practices persist because they work; they deliver the optimum cost benefit with the skills, time, materials, and funds, which they are able to mobilise.

Preface xxv

The studies in this book draw attention to the need for an all-encompassing SP policy beyond the current donor-funded and state-run cash transfer programmes that cover only a tiny fraction of the poor. They show policymakers the potential of community-based mechanisms to expand SP programmes in Africa affordably. Government welfare departments struggling against inadequate human resources, funding constraints, and an exponential increase in the number of those in need, have a potential ally in non-state social protection actors (NSSPAs).

SP is not an ivory tower theory; it is a grassroots reality. And that is where the informal groups live. Self-organising SP services in areas of limited statehood help explain how – in the absence of government – governance is possible. Even good governance! Below the state, people actively seek to govern themselves on their own collective terms. Their organisations and membership behaviour are structured by flow of information, resources, and accountability. They axiomatically work to be the best they can be (not a common trait in state institutions).

Great care should be taken not to undermine CBOs' informal governance methods, which make them uniquely capable of knowing and responding to community and member needs with extreme accuracy and cost efficiency. Any edict, which imposes rigid conventional governance mechanisms on self-help groups, could be destructive, with significant political and welfare risks. The CBO system is not broken. It does not need to be fixed. It is the rest of the national SP services system that needs to change: in its perception of informal governance mechanisms, in its respect for the essential importance of trust traditions, and in its willingness to engage CBOs – supportively – on a case-by-case community level for any intervention.

Poor-to-poor financing of SP is a reminder that a successful community may not necessarily be dominated by worthy individuals nor a benevolent state, but people who see themselves in each other's eyes. Left to their own devices, the poor will organise, connect to one another, and coordinate their action. The social contract between the state and the poor is replaced by a functional contract between the people themselves. Just as bureaucratic institutions try to control human behaviour to ensure state goals, so do mutual trust, peer pressure, and informal mechanisms enable small organisations to organise services for their members in an orderly manner, without the support – or the encumbrance – of the state. At the community level, if the state is absent, there is not anarchy. There is governance without the state.

Nicholas Awortwi
Gregor Walter-Drop

Acknowledgements

The Partnership for African Social and Governance Research (PASGR) was established in 2011 to strengthen graduate-level education and enrich the teaching and practice of social science research for public policy in Africa. The governance of non-state social protection (NSSP) services and actors was the first major policy study facilitated by the organisation. It was commissioned in 2012 in response to prioritisation of SP by African governments, the donor community, and regional bodies such as the African Union (AU).

The authors of this book acknowledge the support of PASGR's founding executive director, Joseph Hoffman, and his board of directors, for selecting the theme. The determination and encouragement of Prof. Tade Aina, the current executive director of PASGR, has been a crucial catalyst through his regular reminders of PASGR's commitment to African scholarly work and recognition of endogenous and innovative mechanisms many Africans adopt in response to challenges. Through this leadership, publication has become a key component of PASGR's modus operandi.

The studies also benefited from the contribution of three resource persons: Prof. Gregor Walter-Drop, managing director of DFG Collaborative Research Centre 700, Free University Berlin; Prof. Sam Wangwe of Economic and Social Research Foundation (ESRF), Dar es Salaam; and Ms. Catalina Gomez, an independent researcher from Brazil.

Special thanks are due to the many reviewers who guided the selection of chapters and to all the authors who reviewed adapted versions of their original papers amid teaching loads and academic engagements. Director of Research Dr. Nicholas Awortwi and Research Coordinator Dr. Darlison Kaija led the PASGR team during the development of the framework paper, implementation, and assignment of resource persons and peer reviewers. Mrs. Pamellah Lidaywa organised research meetings and coordinated and collated different versions of the reports and chapters. The research programme received support from all PASGR staff, especially Dr. Beatrice Muganda, Dr. Pauline Ngimwa, Ms. Cynthia Mugo, and Femi Balogun.

Gavin Bennett gently edited the final texts for language flow and clarity and offered some useful thoughts on reasoning.

This book was produced in the context of a multi-country study on the "governance of non-state social protection in Africa", generously supported by the UK Department for International Development (DfID) through the PASGR. The views herein are those of the authors and do not necessarily represent those held by PASGR or DfID.

1 Governance below the state
Non-state social protection services in Africa

Nicholas Awortwi and Gregor Walter-Drop

Introduction

Recent achievements of African countries in both macro-economic growth and democratic governance are commendable. The new dawn in Africa is celebrated. *The Economist*, in its 2013 headline "Africa Rising", depicts the changing narratives in contrast to a decade ago when the heading was "Hopeless Africa" (Economist, 2000, 2013). Some 19 of the 30 fastest growing economies in 2014 were African countries. Democratically, in 1989 there were only five countries in Africa (Botswana, Senegal, Mauritius, the Gambia, and Zimbabwe) practicing multi-party politics. By the end of the millennium, virtually all countries had shifted from military or single-party to multi-party systems of democratic government, but what does that major transformation mean to ordinary people who need support in times of economic and social vulnerability?

For millions of Africans, the social situation is dire. Of the 54 African nations, 34 are on the UN's list of Least Developed Countries (LDCs) (UNCTAD, 2013: XIV). The criteria combine indicators of wealth, human assets, and economic vulnerability. On an individual level, these aggregate statistics translate – among other things – into poverty, malnutrition, and health risks. About half of the population in sub-Sahara Africa has to live off less than US$1.25 a day (UN, 2014); about a quarter of the population is undernourished (UN, 2014), and about 70 per cent do not have access to improved sanitation facilities (WHO/UNICEF, 2013). If factors such as armed conflicts in the region, the impact of climate change, or the widespread presence of a broad range of infectious agents (including Ebola or HIV) are considered, clearly a large number of Africans live in very fragile circumstances and are highly vulnerable to any kind of shock or rapid change; their social situation and even their lives are acutely endangered. They need social protection (SP)[1] to help them survive economic and social shocks. Although it is said that a rising tide lifts all boats, recent advances have not provided respite to many poor people because growth has not been inclusive enough in wage employment and higher incomes (McKinsey Global Institute, 2012; World Economic Forum, 2014). While much attention is drawn to an emerging middle class in Africa, there are signs that even their continuous income rise is not guaranteed, and they could easily fall back to poverty.

Concerted efforts to extend state SP in Africa are a recent phenomenon in the wake of constitutional and legal reforms since the end (hiatus?) of the Cold War, democratic resurgence in the 1990s, programmes to mitigate the social cost of economic structural adjustment, and the Millennium Development Goal (MDG) agitation to make poverty history. These trends led many African countries to incorporate SP (in one form or another) in their legal systems. "Access to social security", for instance, became a constitutional right in Angola, Burkina Faso, Eritrea, Ethiopia, Kenya, Mali, Nigeria, South Africa, and Uganda. Some are even more detailed and grant more specific rights such as access to health care, food, water, education, sickness benefits, and old-age pensions.[2] A decade later, several governments have given SP high priority in numerous public policy documents, poverty reduction papers, and, more specifically, developed national SP policy documents as strategies to combat poverty and vulnerability. These include Ghana's 2008 "National Social Protection Strategy", Senegal's 2010 "Strategie Nationale de Protection Sociale en Maurritanie", the "National Social Protection Policy of Ethiopia, 2012", and Rwanda's 2011 "National Social Protection Strategy".

In countries emerging from armed conflict (for example, Rwanda, Sierra Leone, and Ivory Coast) and post-election violence (Kenya), SP has been incorporated in a whole range of recovery programmes. Regional bodies such as the African Union (AU) recognise the importance of SP (AU, 2004, 2010), and the international donor community has also focused on SP policies and programmes (see e.g. OECD, 2009; UNICEF, 2008, 2012, 2013; ILO, 2012; EC, 2010, 2012). The coming into effect of Sustainable Development Goals (SGDs) in 2016 will reinforce the process, as target 1.3[3] of the SDGs is devoted to SP (UN, 2015: 8).

A growing number of studies show that extending state social support to poor and vulnerable groups is economically positive: it contributes to building human, financial, and physical assets, which contribute to general growth (World Bank, 2012; Barrientos and Niño-Zarazua, 2011; Shepherd et al., 2004). To specific vulnerable groups in society such as the working poor, orphans, people with disability and elderly, SP is essential to safeguard their consumption standards, without which they are unable to survive let alone build their human and financial assets for the future. Those in micro-enterprises, such as vendors and informal sector workers for whom everyday life is at best a struggle, need SP interventions to mitigate their risk and vulnerability.

So far, state SP coverage has not reached the majority of citizens. Estimates suggest that about 90 per cent of the population in sub-Saharan Africa's low-income economies is not covered by any state SP scheme (vanGinneken, 2003: 277). In Ethiopia, the national social insurance (pension) programme covers only 1.8 per cent – those gainfully employed in government, parastatals, and private sector (The Federal Democratic Republic of Ethiopia, 2012). According to de Laiglesia (2011: 1), only 26.1 per cent of the working population has access to old-age coverage; only 17.1 per cent are insured against employment injury, and just 1.1 per cent have unemployment insurance. Even constitutional SP rights exist mostly on paper. As Fombad aptly put it, "No region in the world appears to endure so much disparity between people's rights and their realisation as Africa" 2013: 6).

The reasons are not elusive. The incorporation of certain rights into a reformed constitution or the drafting of a strategy paper in itself is not going to compel the state to act. Implementation depends, *inter alia*, on fiscal constraints; even if redistribution was politically feasible, the necessary funds have to be generated. While growth of gross domestic product (GDP) has been positive over the past decade, it is not necessarily adequate to absorb universal or wholesale-targeted redistribution without risking economic regression. The International Labour Organisation (ILO) calculates the initial annual cost for a basic SP package – including universal basic old age and disability pensions, basic child benefits, universal access to essential care, and social assistance/100 days employment scheme – at between 3.7 and 10.6 per cent of GDP for a number of low-income countries in 2010 (Barrientos, 2010: 140). Given the low levels of GDP in many sub-Saharan countries, the leeway for redistribution is limited.

There is also the issue of institutional and bureaucratic capacity. In most African states, employment is predominantly informal, making it difficult to administer job-related social security schemes. In Tanzania, for example, state social security covers only those in formal employment (6 per cent) (Republic of Tanzania, 2003). Further, the design and administration of SP schemes is – from a bureaucratic perspective – a formidable task that many countries do not have the institutional infrastructure to handle. As Nino-Zarazua (2010: 22) concludes,

> Limitations in capacity to formulate, deliver and evaluate (cash) transfer programmes are a key constraint in many low-income countries in sub-Saharan Africa.

Then, even if fiscal and bureaucratic challenges can be overcome, the effective guarantee of any rights depends on the will of the political and administrative elite. Only if civil society actors are powerful enough to hold governments accountable, to organise protest, or to fight lawsuits will rights be realised . . . and progressively assured. South Africa, where civil society actors successfully fought time and again for the implementation and extension of the SP system, is a case in point (Devereux, 2010: 13). However, the strength of civil society across Africa varies significantly, and the situation in South Africa is an exception. Consider Ethiopia, which passed a law in 2009 curtailing non-governmental organisation (NGO) activities. So add to the obstacles "the structural weakness of civil society in many African States" (Carbone, 2005).

These considerations lead to a veritable dilemma: in the poorest and weakest countries, the need for SP is particularly high, but these are also where the state appears least likely to offer support. The state budget is besieged, so institutional and bureaucratic capacity is weak, civil society serves different interest groups, and the poor go to the back of the queue. In other words, state SP systems are particularly unlikely to emerge and to function where they are needed most. And yet, discussions and research on SP in Africa have mostly focused on state and donor programmes (not non-state potentials) despite the fact that state and donor coverage is so greatly outweighed by overall need.

Policy focus beyond the state-run schemes is warranted. People must and do find other means of protecting themselves. Many – nay, the majority – have survived through some form of NSSP. However, too little is known about these mechanisms. Even the scope of their existence is unclear.

While the government of Kenya estimates that there are more than 300,000 non-state social services groups nationally (Republic of Kenya, 2011: 11), figures from Ethiopia's Ministry of Justice indicate around 3,000 NGOs providing SP services (Rahmato et al., 2008: 5), and an ILO/Strategies and Tools against Social Exclusion and Poverty (STEP) census from 2004 found 150 not-for-profit SP organisations registered in Senegal, fewer than 40 in Cote d'Ivoire, even fewer in Cameroon, and around 10 each in Chad and Mauritania (Coheur, 2004: 10). Given the cultural parallels across Africa, the figures indicate how little is actually known about non-state providers of SP. This anomalous variation in numbers (and the complete absence of statistics from many countries) underscores the need for a more systematic study (PASGR, 2012). This book offers an analysis of non-state social protection (NSSP) actors and services.[4] The countries covered are no doubt democratically constituted, with government elected by the people and with well-defined territory. However, much of what the citizens organise in responses to risks and vulnerabilities are below the state radar.

Governance below the state: a theoretical framework of policy relevance

The enormous disparity between rights and reality is captured by the concept of "governance" under the conditions of "limited statehood".[5] According to Krasner and Risse, limited statehood exists in

> those areas of a country in which central authorities (governments) lack the ability to implement and enforce rules and decisions and/or in which the legitimate monopoly over the means of violence is lacking.
>
> (Krasner and Risse, 2014: 549)

By this definition, many countries – not only in Africa – exhibit areas of limited statehood. Borzel and Risse (2010: 119) indicated that this is what countries as disparate as Brazil, Indonesia, Somalia, and China have in common. There are many areas in Brazil, Indonesia, Pakistan, Afghanistan, and Somalia where the state has no monopoly over the means of violence. In China, though the state is able to control most parts of its territory, the central government lacks the capacity to enforce its own laws, particularly environmental protection. So limited statehood does not apply only to failed and failing states' limited abilities to enforce their own decisions because of insufficient administrative, political, and economic resources. In Africa, the concept of limited statehood may apply to almost all countries. On the one hand, there are zones of armed conflict where states cannot uphold the monopoly of force. On the other hand, many African states face severe challenges with rule implementation and enforcement. On the Bertelsmann Transformation Index, the average value for the indicator "basic administrative structures" for African countries hovers at 50 per cent (by far the lowest of any world region).[6] In fact, there are significant parts of Africa – Kinshasa, for example – where the respective state is barely present beyond the capital. The edge of town is in a sense the border of the country. In fact, even inside capitals there are areas were the state is barely present. Urban slums such as Kibera and Mathare in Nairobi, and Old Fadama derogated as "Sodom and Gomorrah" in Accra offer examples of areas of limited statehood at the very heart of a territorial state.

Limited statehood can also have a sectoral form, where a state lacks the ability to implement and enforce its rules in a particular policy field. SP constitutes such a sector in almost all of Africa. African states find themselves – to varying degrees – unable (or unwilling) to guarantee the rights they grant citizens and incapable of effectively passing, implementing, and/or enforcing related legislation.

Limited statehood does not mean that there is no governance. "Governance" should not be conflated with "government". The World Bank is notably guilty of this misrepresentation, as it describes the actions of government as governance, hence its normative assessment of good governance (World Bank, 1989) is a standard for the behaviour of government. A more nuanced picture conceives governance as the interaction of state-society-market relations. The Partnership for African Social and Governance Research (PASGR), for instance, considers its own governance research in this perspective. The relationship between state and society goes far beyond centralised hierarchical "command and control" approaches (see, for example, Pierre and Peters, 2000). PASGR aligns with the definition introduced by Risse, with governance meaning "institutionalised modes of social coordination to produce and implement collectively binding rules, or to provide collective goods" (Risse, 2011: 9). Such governance may not link to the state at all. In the absence of government (the legitimised representative of the state), people can and do organise their collective goods and services. This decoupling of "governance" and "government" is particularly useful when analysing areas of limited statehood. In the context of state weakness, it becomes especially interesting to see the forms and shapes governance can take, with, without, above, next to, or below the state. As Risse concludes,

> Limited statehood does not equal the absence of governance, let alone political, social, or economic order. State weakness does not simply translate into the absence of political order, rule-making, or the provision of basic services.
>
> (Risse, 2011: 9)

And what is more, governance in the context of limited statehood is much more than a residual category. In fact, empirically, there is no clear linear relationship between statehood and governance at all (Lee et al., 2014). In other words, it is possible that in weak states, the level of governance (in the sense of effective service provision) can be much higher than one would expect. This begs the question: if governance is not provided by the state, then who is providing it and what does it look like?

In tackling this question, significant attention has already been paid to the role of external (usually international) state or non-state actors (NSAs) in areas of limited statehood. This ranges from the analysis of the role of international interventions (Lake and Fariss, 2014) via public-private partnerships between state and NSAs from donor and recipient countries (Beisheim et al., 2014; Beisheim and Liese, 2014), various forms of philanthropy (Aina and

Moyo, 2013), all the way to the role of multi-national corporations (Hönke and Thauer, 2014). Less attention has been paid to "governance from below" in areas of limited statehood: governance by domestic NSAs. Theoretically, we would expect at least two types of this form.

On the one hand, there are national or local NGOs. They can play the role of advocates trying to make government provide social services (e.g. South Africa). Alternatively, NGOs can act as service providers themselves, and thus they become governance actors (Amutabi, 2006). This line of reasoning is familiar from the literature of development cooperation (see e.g. Brüntrup-Seidemann, 2011), though less so in the field of SP.

On the other hand, governance from below can take the form of local self-governance on the basis of small community-level organisations. What comes to mind here is the seminal work by the late Elinor Ostrom on "governing the commons" (Ostrom, 1990; Thompson, 2000). Note, however, that SP differs significantly from the management of common pool resources (CPR). In SP, the "resources" themselves have to be generated and collected. To borrow from Lowi's (1972) classic distinction, whereas the management of CPRs is about regulatory politics, the local self-governance of SP is about redistributive politics – something not obvious in the context of poor and highly vulnerable communities. Thus empirical investigations of NSSP in Africa can also improve our understanding of "governance from below" in areas of limited statehood.

Reflecting on the limited SP reach of African states, are mainstream definitions of the subject really applicable? The academic literature and various policy documents on the topic provide a multitude of definitions that pitch SP as state or public action (African Union, 2008). Most useful here is a definition that does not focus on the state as a provider or regulator of SP and instead focuses on the nature of the services being provided while allowing for advocacy. This book follows the work by Devereux and Sabates-Wheeler (2004), who, in turn, extend an earlier concept developed by the ILO. According to this, SP describes

> all public and private initiatives that provide income or consumption transfers to the poor, protect the vulnerable against livelihood risks, and enhance the social status and rights of the marginalised; with the overall objective of reducing the economic and social vulnerability of poor, vulnerable and marginalised groups.
> (Devereux and Sabates-Wheeler, 2004: 9)

Devereux and Sabates-Wheeler distinguish between four types of services (note this typology is ordered, starting with a narrower, traditional concept of SP as "emergency support" and progressing via risk reduction towards personal and political change):

- *Protective services* "come to the rescue" of vulnerable people in crisis. This reactive service includes food aid, cash transfers, disability benefits, single-parent allowances, social pensions for the elderly poor, etc.
- *Preventive services* "reduce the risk" of life shocks and avoid negative coping strategies. Examples include mutual health insurance, welfare associations, burial groups, etc.
- *Promotive services* seek to "improve livelihoods" to help make the poor more self-sufficient. These include micro-finance, income-generating activities (IGAs), and skills training, etc.
- *Transformative services* aim at "changing cultures and social structures" that lead to inequality. Examples include collective action for workers' rights, affirmative action, human rights for disadvantaged groups, and minimum wage rules, etc.

Based on these conceptual considerations, this book outlines the study of NSSP in Africa as an example of "governance from below" in areas of limited statehood.

Non-state social protection in African countries

Case selection and method

To analyse governance of non-state SP services in Africa, full studies by eight teams were carried out in Ethiopia, Ghana, Kenya, Tanzania, and Uganda, and data was also gathered in Senegal. These countries have a combined population of about 250 million people – one-quarter of the total population of Africa. All of them have significant parts of their population who are living in severe poverty, or on less than US$1.25 a day, or vulnerable to severe poverty (Malik 2013). All are to be found in the lower third of the Human Development Index (HDI). There is, however, some variation. Economic conditions are most difficult in Ethiopia (global HDI rank 173 out of 187), followed by Uganda (161), Senegal (154), Tanzania (152), Kenya (145), and Ghana (135). Despite this variation, it can be safely assumed that in all of them, the need for SP is high.

In all six study countries, SP is grounded in national programmes – embedded in the Constitution or national policy documents which commit the state to provide some form of SP to citizens. This includes Ethiopia's Growth and Transformation Plan (GTP), Tanzania's National Strategy for

Growth and Poverty Reduction (MKUKUTA), Uganda's Poverty Eradication Action Plan (PEAP), Senegal's National Strategy for Social and Economic Development (SNDES), Kenya's Vision 2030, and Ghana's Growth and Poverty Reduction Strategy (GPRS). In addition, these countries have national SP strategy documents reflecting, in part, a changed political and economic context since the early 1990s (de Haan, 2014). However, in all six countries, enormous social risks persist, and they all thus exhibit limited statehood in SP.

The studies were conducted at the administrative district level where the state (presence of government) is weak and where responsibilities transferred to sub-national governments are hardly performed. The poor delivery of services by local governments has required NSAs to step in. The districts were chosen on an "easy case selection principle" where demand for SP was particularly high and where statehood was rather weak. Selection criteria were as follows:

- the presence of poverty and vulnerability as well as the presence of specific vulnerable groups such as orphans and other vulnerable children, street beggars, persons with disabilities, elderly persons, and persons living with HIV including those affected by AIDS;
- areas prone to natural calamities – e.g., drought, flooding, food insecurity, and areas recovering from conflict;
- poor infrastructure, remoteness, and reach of government services.

The studies covered both rural and urban districts as a control on any significant difference between them (which turned out not to exist).

The first phase mapped non-state social protection actors (NSSPA) and their services through data from the national registration offices, where information was found to be incomplete and out of date. However, based on these leads, the research teams used a snowball approach whereby one NSSPA led to others until all the communities in a district were covered. The mapping documented the profiles of NSSPAs, their characteristics, the nature of services they provide, their scope and reach, the types of beneficiaries, and their governance, management, and funding mechanisms. Mapping was followed by in-depth analyses of sampled NSSPAs and their beneficiaries. The study used simple structured and semi-structured interviews and focus group discussions to collect data from beneficiaries, leaders, and managers. Selection of cases for in-depth study sought a representative cross-section of NSSPAs working with different categories of vulnerable groups and a mix of formal and informal actors.

Number and types of non-state social protection actors

Table 1.1 summarizes the mapping results. About 7,000 NSSPAs were identified in the 30 districts under investigation – on average about 230 per district. Using a crude proportional estimate from the sampled adult population,[7] the studies suggest that, in the six countries combined, there could be as many as 760,000 NSSPAs. On average, there are about 250 persons per NSSPA and somewhat fewer in Ethiopia and Uganda.

More than three-quarters of these NSSPAs are fairly young, having been formed between 2000 and 2012 – arguably in response to increasing risks. It is apparent that NSSPAs are widespread in areas where corresponding state services are weak or absent and where poverty indicators are high. While there are too many variables for direct correlation between levels of distress and NSSPA prevalence, it is not surprising that Ethiopia, with an HDI rank of 173, has more NSSPAs per population than Ghana with an HDI ranking of 135. Some 8 per cent of all NSSPAs are small community-based organisations (CBOs; see Table 1.2). These CBOs take specific forms such as the following:

- rotational savings and credit associations
- burial groups
- women's groups and youth groups
- welfare associations
- family and neighbourhood associations
- home town/ethnic associations
- farmers' groups and trade (e.g. dressmakers) associations, etc.

Fewer than 10 per cent of CBOs are affiliated with NGOs. The role of district-level and national-level NGOs is comparatively small, and INGOs are

Table 1.1 The number of non-state social protection actors

Country	Total number of districts in the country	Number of districts sampled	Adult population in the sampled covered in the district	Total NSSPAs identified in the sampled districts	Crude estimate of national total	Ratio of population per NSSPA
Ghana	170	9	370,162	992	18,738	373
Kenya	300	7	392,899	865	37,071	452
Tanzania	169	2	388,161	426	35,997	911
Senegal	46	3	46,629	210	3,220	222
Uganda	112	5	171,175	1,180	2,6432	146
Ethiopia	770	4	387,962	3,313	637,752	117
Total	**1,567**	**30**	**1,756,988**	**6,986**	**759,210**	**251**

Table 1.2 Types of non-state social protection actors

Type of organization	Share across all countries
Community-based organisations (CBOs)	87.2%
Faith-based organisations (FBOs)	2.8%
National-level NGOs	3.2%
District-level NGOs	4.7%
International NGOs (INGOs)	2.1%
Total	100%

Source: Field data, 2012

(quantitatively) almost insignificant in comparison with CBOs. The predominance of CBOs indicates high participation by the poor in organising groups, pooling resources, and helping each other in difficult situations. The basic principle of CBO operation is that it is the business of the collective to look after the individual – a principle that resonates with needs throughout sub-Saharan Africa (Adesina, 2010). Under conditions of limited statehood, small, local, CBOs of different types proliferate to deliver SP services in addition to activities undertaken by NGOs that operate from the district, national, or international level. The poor and vulnerable organise and support one another with services that individually they cannot obtain.

Types of social protection services

Most NSSPAs offer multiple services that can be type classified (Devereux and Sabates-Wheeler, 2004). Table 1.3 summarizes findings in the study countries.

CBOs have traditionally provided protective services – relief and humanitarian support in times of specific hardship. Because their help for the poor is funded by the poor, much of this support is in kind, including shelter construction, nursing for the sick, grave digging, providing equipment and cooking for burial ceremonies, agricultural labour and inputs, and food. CBOs are now increasingly active in development work, with services in health, education, micro-finance, water and sanitation, agriculture, and economic empowerment. For instance, burial groups in Uganda began by providing "hospitality money" for widows, widowers, and orphans during funerals, but some now run more general-purpose savings and loan schemes for members. All the country studies show that CBOs are already leading providers of both protective and preventive services, and increasingly deliver promotive services (e.g. IGAs). However, they lack the scale and influence to be transformative, which is a vital strategy for issues such as gender equality. The prime channel for transformative action is NGOs,

Table 1.3 Types of social protection services provided by non-state social protection actors[1]

Type of Service	Ethiopia	Uganda	Senegal	Tanzania	Kenya	Ghana	Average
Protective (%)	65.0	41.3	49.0	7.8	30.4	15.6	34.85
Preventive (%)	7.0	18.4	45.0	22.5	21.3	28.3	23.75
Promotive (%)	57.0	63.2	54.0	90.8	41.6	54.1	60.1
Transformative (%)	2.0	5.9	8.0	1.4	3.0	2.0	4.38

Source: Field data, 2012
[1] Many NSSPAs offer multiple types of services, thus the column sums are over 100.

which have stronger resources, reach, and leverage. However, their cultural knowledge is least complete, and their activism is politically sensitive; in some countries (such as Ethiopia), it is purposefully restricted.

Funding, membership, and beneficiaries

Most of the funds for SP services come from the poor themselves in the form of membership dues. CBO members join voluntarily and must pay a regular subscription fee – usually US$1 to US$10 annually – and meet other case-by-case requirements for membership, especially regular attendance at group meetings. On average, CBOs run an annual operational budget of US$3,800–10,000. Of those mapped, 90 per cent do not have external funding. The majority do not have legal status, formal credentials, or staff skills to secure funding from international donors and governments. Nevertheless, the studies show that these self-help groups use their funds with extreme efficiency; they have no overhead or intermediary costs; they agree and enforce affordable contribution levels; they know what services are most needed, and they deliver support directly to specific beneficiaries. They blend cash, material, and social support in the most practical way. Table 1.4 summarizes the funding sources of the NSSPAs.

NGOs can and do access funding from governments and international donors, and the larger their organisational footprint, the better their access. However, their grants tend to be project-based and short term, while SP services need to be adaptable and long term. Donors who finance NGO services usually dictate what those services should be. For instance, there are many NGOs providing SP services for orphans and other vulnerable children or the effects of HIV/AIDS because international funding is most abundant in those fields. The European Commission (EC; 2012) cautions that, over the past two decades, developing countries have witnessed a proliferation of bigger NSSPAs that do not constitute homogeneous groups or interests. Referring to studies in Mozambique and Nepal, the EC found that

Table 1.4 Funding sources for non-state social protection actors

Non-state actor	Funding sources (%)			
	Membership fee and internally generated funds	Government	International donors	Benevolent individuals
CBOs	92	4	1	3
District-wide NGOs	5	25	50	20
National NGOs	2	15	80	3
International NGOs	0	0	100	0

Source: Country studies field data, 2013

many NSSPAs (particularly NGOs) were actually "little more than personal enterprises and vehicles for receiving funds" (EC, 2012: 23), thus raising accountability issues and questioning NSSPAs' legitimacy. Many African governments also take this opportunistic approach. They developed SP policies only after international donors such as UNICEF and DfID started financing them. Many state SP programmes, especially cash transfer to the poor and elderly, are donor led; governments have embraced them because internal donors fund them (Awortwi and Aiyede, 2017).

The membership of CBOs ranges from 15 to 80 people with a skew (circa 60:40) in favour of women; the membership in NGOs is less relevant because their members and beneficiaries hardly overlap. CBOs comprise contributory members who have some ability to pay subscriptions and non-contributory members who have no means and subsist on the margins of society. While most beneficiaries of CBOs are contributory, the opposite is the case among NGOs and faith-based organisations (FBOs). Their beneficiaries are non-contributory and include widows, HIV/AIDS patients, street children, orphans and vulnerable children (OVCs), elderly people, and persons with disabilities, as well as the general community. Target groups are defined by donor imperatives or assessed needs, usually within geographical areas. In terms of the spatial spread of non-state SP, NGOs have the resources for a wider reach. CBOs operate only among their base communities.

Internal governance structures and connection to the state

Internal governance structures of NSSP organisations encompass how members and leaders exercise their roles and responsibilities, and what control and accountability mechanisms are in place to ensure organisational effectiveness in responding to the needs of beneficiaries and funders (Bassett et al., 2012: 6).

NSSPAs such as INGOs, NGOs, and FBOs have formal organisational structures and most (especially those with a larger footprint) are registered with the national government. Executive committees and boards of directors take the decisions; a "constitution" is their main internal policy document, sometimes with further manuals on standard operating procedures, and they have written records on financial, human resources, and asset management. These are the basis for upward accountability to supervisors and/or donors through reports to boards of governors, donors, and government agencies. NGOs tend to have an upward accountability structure because their survival depends on funds from (often distant) donors, but they are largely unaccountable at point of delivery. Consequently, these organisations are focused on rolling out "their" programmes, sometimes designed with little or no regard to local conditions. In the studies, many non-contributory members and communities were not informed about the selection of beneficiaries, the nature of interventions, or how the NGO's activity was supposed to sustainably address given vulnerabilities over time. Gender aspects, often related to culture, were not considered beyond numerical generalities. For most NGOs, participation of beneficiaries was limited to electing community volunteers as their representatives. SP programmes from these types of organisations are typically planned and implemented without the participation of those they aim to support.

The numerically dominant CBOs function in a very different way. Most do not have formal organisational structures. The demarcation of CBO "departments", reporting relationships, and chains of command are informal, variable, and difficult to specify. The unwritten rules are collectively agreed on in meetings or have simply evolved over time.[8] CBOs operate – often remarkably well – on the unwritten rules of reciprocity and the social support expected of every member. Most of them rely on volunteers and part-time workers to manage the day-to-day business. Mistakes and misunderstandings are common. Nevertheless, the CBO "staff/officials" are under the close and constant scrutiny of their members and communities. The protocols, though unwritten, are known and enforced. They are small enough that, within their sphere, everybody knows everybody else, personally and in detail; they are run by their members for their members. If funds are diverted, they defraud only themselves; they report downwards to their members, frequently and regularly. While there may be no pen and paper present at their weekly/monthly meetings, every member is there. Among CBOs who run revolving or credit schemes, group pressure exerts effective accountability. The majority of CBOs are not affiliated and do not collaborate or network. They are isolated and value the lack of interference above the lack of synergy. Consequently, most of them are not registered with the state. While this allows them to operate without the state controlling them, they forfeit any opportunity to receive support or to influence state decisions in areas where they operate. This is especially true of a multitude of small, local, and unregistered CBOs that do not have any legal identity.

Overview of the chapters

After this introductory chapter, there are eight case studies of five countries presenting in-depth analyses of governance mechanisms, characteristics, and performance.

Chapter 2: Governance characteristics of informal social protection actors in Ethiopia

Ethiopia has a rich history and is the only country in sub-Saharan Africa that was not colonised. After years of political upheavals in the 1970s and '80s, and economic hardships arising from vagaries of weather, famine, and worsening poverty in the mid-1980s, the country has achieved an upward trend. Since 2004, the economy has been growing at an average of 11 per cent per annum and poverty has reduced from 44 per cent in 1999 to less than 30 per cent in 2011. The country is stable and has a new constitution that guarantees every Ethiopian access to public health and education, clean water, housing, food, and social security. Yet despite the remarkable economic growth, political stability since 1994, and constitutional pronouncement in support of the poor, about half the population is vulnerable to the extent that a single major shock – such as inadequate rainfall or the fall in the price of farm products – could push them into poverty. The national social insurance (pension) programme covers only 1.8 per cent of those gainfully employed in the government, parastatals, and private sector (The Federal Democratic Republic of Ethiopia, 2012). Through the support of international donors, the government provides some SP programmes involving food security, household asset building, voluntary resettlement, national nutrition, urban housing and grain subsidies, and support to older persons and vulnerable children. However, with a population of more than 80 million and high incidences of vulnerability, these state programmes are just drops in the ocean. The majority of citizens rely on informal mechanisms to protect themselves. In Chapter 2, Teshome, Dutu, Teshager, and Zeleke analyse the governance characteristics of informal SP and support mechanisms embedded in Ethiopia's social institutions, and the services they provide to those who have little or no access to official state schemes. The analysis includes institutions such as Iddirs, Iqqubs, and religious, as well as other self-help groups. The study uses a sample of 31 informal SP organisations from a larger pool of 308 identified in two districts – one urban and one rural. These support livelihood, social services, welfare, and advocacy. Some provide small credit through pooled revolving funds, often enabling the poor to build assets. The study shows that these informal mechanisms are crucial to the survival of many and form the foundation of SP in Ethiopia. The study gives the government and donor agencies cause to go beyond recognition of these informal mechanisms to active support of them.

Chapter 3: Informal communication as accountability mechanisms in mutual aid organisations in social protection services in Ghana

Mutual aid groups have become a vital component of SP systems in Africa. They work best at grassroots level because of their small size, with members having strong affinity to the common goal of the group, sharing a common interest and assets, and using peer pressure to control members' behaviour. Mutuality and trust become the basis of a group's survival.

But how do mutual help groups communicate with their members to ensure that there is transparency, accountability, and satisfaction? In Chapter 3, Aryeetey, Afranie, Doh, and Andoh examine community-based mutual organisations in the western region of Ghana and show that while many have loose reporting structures, communication tends to be informal and without paper trails that enable verification and accountability. Yet this approach does not pose any threat to the organisation and management of the group.

Using in-depth qualitative interviews with 66 mutual aid groups from a general mapping of 635 NSSPAs in the Wassa areas, the study observed that the groups' face-to-face communication and the principles of mutuality, trust, and reciprocity were the necessary, preferred, and most effective ways for groups to deliver services with limited resources and achieve accountability with limited literacy. Potential donors should recognise that formal "checklist" documentation is not a necessary nor an appropriate condition for external support to impose.

Chapter 4: Non-state social protection and citizen rights of vulnerable children in western Kenya

The Constitution of Kenya (Republic of Kenya, 2010) guarantees all citizens social security as a right and commits the state to provide for those who are unable to support themselves and their dependents. The rights embrace

SP, health care, working conditions, and justice. However, where state outreach is limited, informal NSAs remain safety nets of "first resort". In Chapter 4, Okwany and Ngutuku examine the extent to which NSAs interventions are responsive to child vulnerability in western Kenya. The study examines the range of services NSAs provide and interrogates the ability of their governance and accountability structures to enhance or constrain the rights of vulnerable children.

Using a triangulation of methods – including a quantitative mapping of all NSAs in the study context, followed by an in-depth study of purposively selected child-focused organisations – the study reveals that, while children are the prime targets of interventions, their voices are conspicuously muted. The study highlights "age and generational relations" as crucial to understanding vulnerability and designing SP interventions. Current programmes deliver material support, without which many children would not survive, but lack a broader transformative agenda to enhance citizenship and address the roots – not just the symptoms – of child vulnerability. There is a need for the voices of children and caregivers to be heard.

Chapter 5: Governance mechanisms of burial groups in Uganda

Death in the family is so costly that the poor often have to sell assets to meet burial ceremony costs. In traditional systems where respect and dignity for the dead are imperative, burials can be laborious and extended rites that can impoverish a household. In many parts of Africa, burial societies have emerged as distinct self-help groups to ensure decent burial without ruination of the bereaved. The activities are both preventive and protective SP services. Chapter 5 by Asingwire, Denis, and Rose notes that in western Uganda, these societies have existed for decades, and, as they are more resilient than other voluntary organisations, some have diversified into addressing other SP needs. Burial groups may not have transformatively pulled their members out of poverty, but they have delivered a cushion that no other actor, government, or non-government, is providing. The foremost policy implication of this study is that efforts to strengthen the governance structures and processes in small and informal NSAs should build on their norms rather than displace them with presumptively "better" principles.

Chapter 6: Hedging against vulnerability: associational life as social insurance in Ghana

The costs of formal social insurance programmes are prohibitive for most citizens in Africa. Social insurance is therefore usually achieved through risk-pooling among self-help groups whose members support each other in times of shock and adversity. This informal "insurance" evaluates need on an undefined case-by-case basis and works for homogeneous communities with shared location, language, religion, etc. In Ghana, many citizens rely on affinity groups to hedge against adversity through membership associations that have well-defined rules and regulations to govern and sustain them. The number of associations that an individual joins is a risk-management strategy to reduce the probability of loss from idiosyncratic or covariate shocks. As in conventional financial hedging, individuals tend to join multiple associations to "spread" their cover. In Chapter 6, Akosua, Dako-Gyeke, and Nketiah-Amponsah investigate the non-monetary and monetary benefits of joining multiple non-state associations. Drawing on the life accounts of members in four communities in the Central Region of Ghana, the study assesses the benefits that members receive during emergencies. The study finds that the threshold of maximum financial benefit is to join two mutual organisations – not fewer, not more. However, non-monetary benefits increased on a "more memberships the better" basis. The chapter recommends awareness of the thresholds and highlights the importance of participating in group meetings to maximise personal returns.

Chapter 7: Women's economic empowerment groups in Kenya

More women than men are living in extreme poverty. Women face systemic and socio-cultural barriers that limit their access to equal opportunities for self-development. They are generally excluded from decision making on economic issues; they have limited access to means of production such as land, capital, and technology; they work on farms as free family labourers, and their work is both undervalued and underpaid. In Kenya, vulnerability to poverty of female-headed households is about 14 per cent – nearly three times the level for male-headed households (Republic of Kenya, 2012: 12). Consequently, many CBO and NGO programmes are aligned to women's needs. However, empirical studies on how these programmes ensure empowerment of women in households are lacking. In Chapter 7, Nzioki and Mwasiaji assess the gender contribution of the NSSP in Kenya's Nyanza region. The study question was whether SP services provided by non-state organisations empower women to make strategic life choices previously denied them. Using a sample of 35 NSAs in four districts, the study concludes that NSA programmes in SP are generally transformative, empowering poor women to take charge of their strategic and practical needs through IGAs and skills training. The paper recommends building on women's initiatives and recognising their active role as agents of change instead of seeing them as "beneficiaries" of handouts.

Chapter 8: Practical and strategic gender needs and non-state actors' response in Uganda

The 1995 Constitution of Uganda and directive principles of state policy provide for protection and promotion of the fundamental human rights of vulnerable groups such as children, elderly people, persons with disability, women, etc. The Constitution guarantees rights to social justice and economic opportunities such as access to education, food security, clean and safe water, decent shelter, pension, and retirement benefits, etc. It outlaws discrimination and obliges the state to take affirmative action in favour of groups marginalised on the basis of gender, age, disability, or any other reason created by history, tradition, or custom in order to redress imbalances. Some of these objectives and principles have been embedded in national gender policy documents. However, translation of policies into intervention programmes is weak. Today, about 93 per cent of the chronically poor are women. As the state is unable to reach the majority of women's groups, NSAs have increasingly responded to gender vulnerabilities. In Chapter 8, Muhanguzi examines SP services provided by NSAs in two districts and the extent to which they integrate a gender perspective in their governance mechanisms. The analysis focuses on the policies, laws and regulations (formal and informal), and women's participation in organisations' decision making. A gender analysis reveals that few NSAs have constitutions and policies informed by prior gender conditions or challenges that make women vulnerable. The study reveals that while organisations implement activities that target gender-specific vulnerabilities – such as women's poverty, hunger, and maternal health; social discrimination against women and children; sexual harassment; and gender-based violence – these services are largely protective and promotive. There is minimal transformative attention to women's strategic interests/needs. Most activities of informal SP groups are still rooted in the long-standing social culture that subordinates women.

Chapter 9: Governance dynamics of non-state social protection in Tanzania

CBOs have long been an indigenous coping mechanism in Tanzania. Traditional community groups were increasingly institutionalised after independence, particularly following the "communitarian" *Ujamaa* declaration in 1967. This system provided all sorts of services, ranging from burial support to collective farming, micro-credit for small business, health care, and education support. The economic squeeze that structural adjustment programmes (SAPs) imposed on the state in the 1980s made NGOs/CBOs even more central and essential.

Yet not much is written about NSA governance and management mechanisms and how they translate to services performance. In Chapter 9, Kamanzi, Nyankweli, and Okwany respond to this literature gap by presenting a study of NGO/CBO/SP governance dynamics. The chapter draws on data from a larger study conducted in two rural districts of Bukoba and the urban district of Dodoma (Tanzania's administrative capital). The study finds that some NSAs work on the principal-agent relationship and others on the principal-steward relationship. Those that deliver services funded by member contributions are "stewards" of the collective resources and needs. The members themselves are the "principals". This type of NSA (mostly CBOs) uses group solidarity, shared goals, obligatory participation, peer influence, and internal dispute settlement as its main governance mechanisms.

NSAs that generate funds from outsiders (mostly foreign donors and philanthropists) are effectively "agents" contracted by donor "principals" to provide SP programmes to the poor. These NSAs (mostly NGOs) use written agreements and/or memoranda of understanding to ensure accountability and have a series of monitoring mechanisms including regular visits to the people rendering services (sub-agents), ad hoc meetings, and evaluation reports. Clearly, the distinct "steward" and "agent" approaches use contrasting governance mechanisms and management styles.

Chapter 10: Conclusion, implications for public policy and governance concepts

The final chapter summarises findings, reaches general conclusions for governance theory, and draws implications for public policy. The chapter raises concerns about social justice (the poor depend on the poor) and recognises the vital contribution of NSAs towards the effective functioning of society (in the absence of state capacity/performance). The chapter draws the attention of policymakers to the potential of CBOs to expanding SP programmes. Government welfare departments struggling against inadequate human resources, funding constraints, and an exponential increase in the number of those in need have a potential ally in NSAs.

The chapter argues that self-organising SP services in areas of limited statehood help explain how – in the absence of government – governance is possible. Even good governance! Poor-to-poor financing of SP is a reminder that a successful community may not necessarily be dominated by worthy individuals, but people who see themselves in each other's eyes. Left to their own devices, the poor will organise, connect to one another, and coordinate their actions. The social contract between the state and the poor is replaced by a functional contract between the people themselves. Just as bureaucratic institutions try to control human behaviour to ensure state goals, so too do mutual trust, peer pressure, and informal mechanisms enable small organisations to organise services for their members in an orderly manner, without the support – or the encumbrance – of the state. At the community level, if the state is absent, there is not anarchy. There is governance without the state.

Notes

1 The term social protection is used widely to encompass social security, social welfare, safety nets, unemployment benefits, and pension schemes.
2 For a detailed summary of social security rights in African constitutions, compare the overview in Fombad, 2013: 13–15.
3 "Implement nationally appropriate social protection systems and measures for all, including floors, and by 2030 achieve substantial coverage of the poor and the vulnerable".
4 The study was facilitated by the PASGR based in Nairobi, Kenya, with funding from DfID.
5 This concept of "limited statehood" and "governance" was originally developed at the Collaborative Research Center (SFB) 700, funded by the German Research Foundation (DFG) and hosted at Freie Universität Berlin. See www.sfb-governance.com for more information.
6 Bertelsmann Transformation Index (BTI; see www.bti-project.org/bti-home/.) The BTI is based on reliability-checked expert coding. In this case, country experts are asked to evaluate the question "To what extend do basic administrative structures exist?"
7 We simply assume similar levels of vulnerability, a common culture of collective action, and sampled districts are representative for the country as a whole.
8 An example of an unwritten rule is a fine for missing a meeting without permission. Every member is expected to attend all meetings, and anyone unable to attend is expected to explain why, in advance, or face a fine. Latecomers are also fined, and the money collected is added to the group's account, which is then used to regulate its activities.

References

Adesina, J. (2010). *Rethinking the Social Protection Paradigm: Social Policy in Africa's Development*. Paper prepared for the conference 'Promoting Resilience Through Social Protection in Sub- Sahara Africa' organized by the European Union in Dakar, Senegal, 28–30 June, 2010.
African Union. (2004). *Declaration on Employment and Poverty Alleviation in Africa*. The African Union Extra-ordinary Summit on 'Employment and Poverty Alleviation in Africa' held in Ouagadougou, Burkina Faso, 3–9 September, 2004.
African Union (2008). *Social Protection in Africa: An Overview of the Challenges*. Prepared for the African Union by Viviene Taylor. Addis Ababa: AU.
African Union. (2010). *Declaration on Social Policy Action Towards Social Inclusion*. Draft, 2nd Session of the AU Conference of Ministers for Social Development, 21–25 November, Khartoum, Sudan.

Aina, T.A., and Moyo, B. (eds.). (2013). *Giving to Help, Helping to Give: The Context and Politics of African Philanthropy*. Dakar: Amalion Publishing.

Amutabi, M.A. (2006). *The NGO Factor in Africa: The Case of Arrested Development in Kenya*. New York: Routledge.

Awortwi, N., and Aiyede, E.R., (2017). *Politics, Public Policy & Social Protection in Africa*. London: Routledge Publishing.

Barriantos, A. (2010). *Social Protection and Poverty*. Geneva: UNRISD.

Barrientos, A., and Niño-Zarazúa, M. (2011). Financing social protection for children in crisis contexts. *Development Policy Review*, 29 (5): 603–620.

Bassett, Lucy; Giannozzi, Sara; Pop, Lucian; and Ringold, Dena. (2012). *Rules, Roles, and Controls: Governance in Social Protection with an Application to Social Assistance*. Background Paper for the World Bank 2012–2022 Social Protection and Labor Strategy, March 2012. Washington, DC: The World Bank.

Beisheim, Marianne, and Liese, Andrea. (eds.). (2014). *Transnational Partnerships: Effectively Providing for Sustainable Development?* Basingstoke: Palgrave Macmillan.

Beisheim, Marianne; Liese, Andrea; Janetschek, Hannah; and Sarre, Johanna. (2014). Transnational Partnerships: Conditions for Successful Service Provision in Areas of Limited Statehood. *Governance: An International Journal of Policy, Administration, and Institutions*, 27 (4): 655–673.

Börzel, T.A., and Risse, T. (2010). Governance Without a State: Canitwork? *Regulation and Governance*, 4 (2): 113–134.

Brüntrup-Seidemann, S. (2011). Actual and Potential Roles of Local NGOs in Agricultural Development in Sub-Saharan Africa. *Quarterly Journal of International Agriculture*, 50 (1): 65–78.

Carbone, Maurizio. (2005). Weak Civil Society in a Hard State: Lessons from Africa. *Journal of Civil Society*, 1 (2): 167–179.

Coheur, Alain. (2004). *The State of Development of Private Non-profit Social Protection Organizations*, International Social Security Association (ISSA), Technical Report 27. Geneva: ISSA.

De Haan, Arjan. (2014). The Rise of Social Protection in Development: Progress, Pitfalls and Politics. *European Journal of Development Research*, 26 (3): 311–321.

De Laiglesia, Juan R. (2011). *Coverage Gaps in Social Protection: What Role for Institutional Innovations?* Paper prepared for the International conference on Social Cohesion and Development, Paris 20–2 January, 2011.

Devereux, Stephen. (2010). *Building Social Protection Systems in Southern Africa*. Background paper commissioned by the European Report on Development 2010. Brussels: European Commission.

Devereux, Stephen, and Sabates-Wheeler, Rachel. (2004). *Transformative Social Protection*. IDS Working Paper No.232. Brighton: Institute of Development Studies.

The Economist. (2000). *Hopeless Africa*, 11 May 2000.

The Economist. (2013). *African Rising: A Hopeful Continent*, 2 March 2013.

European Commission (EC). (2012). *Social Protection in European Union Development Cooperation, Communication From the Commission to the European Parliament, the Council, the European Economic and Social Committee, and the Committee of the Regions*, COM (2012) 446. Brussels: European Commission.

European Communities. (2010). *Social Protection for Inclusive Development: A New Perspective in EU Co-operation with Africa*. San Domenicodi Fiesole: Robert Schuman Centre for Advanced Studies, European University Institute.

Fombad, Charles. (2013). An Overview of the Constitutional Framework of the Right to Social Security with Special Reference to South Africa. *African Journal of International and Comparative Law*, 21 (10): 1–31.

Hönke, Jana, and Thauer, Christian R. (2014). Multinational Corporations and Service Provision in Sub-Saharan Africa: Legitimacy and Institutionalization Matter. *Governance: An International Journal of Policy, Administration, and Institutions*, 27 (4): 697–716.

International Labour Organization (ILO). (2012). *Social Security for All Building Social Protection Floors and Comprehensive Social Security Systems: The Strategy of the International Labour Organization*. Geneva: ILO.

Krasner, Stephen D., and Risse, Thomas. (2014). External Actors, State-Building, and Service Provision in Areas of Limited Statehood: Introduction. *Governance: An International Journal of Policy, Administration, and Institutions*, 27 (4): 545–567.

Lake, David A., and Fariss, Christopher J. (2014). Why International Trusteeship Fails: The Politics of External Authority in Areas of Limited Statehood. *Governance: An International Journal of Policy, Administration, and Institutions*, 27 (4): 569–587.

Lee, Melissa M.; Walter-Drop, Gregor; and Wiesel, John. (2014). Taking the State (Back) Out? Statehood and the Delivery of Collective Goods. *Governance: An International Journal of Policy, Administration, and Institutions*, 27 (4): 635–654.

Lowi, Theodore J. (1972). Four Systems of Policy, Politics and Choice. *Public Administration Review*, 32: 298–310.

Malik, K. (2013). *Human Development Report 2013. The Rise of the South: Human Progress in a Diverse World*. United Nations Development Programme. New York: UN.

McKinsey Global Institute. (2012). *Africa at Work: Job Creation and Inclusive Growth*. Mckinsey Global Institute. Retrieved from: www.mckinsey.com/insights/africa/africa_at_work

Nino-Zarazua, Miguel; Barrientos, Armando; Hulme, David; and Hickey, Sam. (2010). *Social Protection in Sub-Saharan Africa: Will the Green Shoots Blossom?* Manchester, UK: Brooks World Poverty Institute, The University of Manchester.

Organization for Economic Co-Operation and Development (OECD). (2009). *Promoting Pro-Poor Growth: Social Protection*. Paris: OECD.

Ostrom, Elinor. (1990). *Governing the Commons: The Evolution of Institutions for Collective Action*. Cambridge, MA: Cambridge University Press, pp. 1–28.

PASGR. (2012). *Research Framework Paper: Features, Governance Characteristics and Policy Implications of Non-State Social Protection in Africa, Nairobi*. Retrieved from: www.pasgr.org/wp-content/uploads/2017/01/Features-governance-characteristics-and-policy-implications-of-non-state-social-protection-in-Africa_Synthesis-report.pdf

Pierre, Jon, and Peters, B. Guy. (2000). *Governance, Politics, and the State*. New York: St. Martin's Press.

Rahmato, Dessalegn; Bantirgu, Akalewold; and Endeshaw, Yoseph. (2008). *CSOs/NGOs IN Ethiopia: Partners in Development and Good Governance*. A Report Prepared for the Ad Hoc CSO/NGO Task Force, Addis Ababa.

Republic of Kenya. (2010) *The Constitution of the Republic of Kenya*, Nairobi: Government Printer.
Republic of Kenya, Ministry of Gender, Children, and Social Development. (2011). *Kenya National Social Protection Policy*. Nairobi. Government Printer
Republic of Kenya. (2010). *The Constitution of the Republic of Kenya*. Nairobi: Government Printer.
Republic of Kenya. (2012). *Kenya Social Protection Sector Review: Executive Report*. Ministry of State for Planning, National Development and Vision 2030. Nairobi: Government Printer
Republic of Tanzania. (2003). *The National Social Security Policy*. Dodoma: Ministry of Labour, Youth Development and Sports.
Risse, Thomas. (2011). "Governance in Areas of Limited Statehood: Introduction and Overview". In Thomas Risse (ed.), *Governance Without a State? Policies and Politics in Areas of Limited Statehood*. New York: Columbia University Press, pp. 1–35.
Shepherd, A.; Marcus, R.; and Barrientos, A. (2004). *Policy Paper on Social Protection*. DfID Paper on Social Protection.
The Federal Democratic Republic of Ethiopia (2012). *National Social Protection Policy of Ethiopia*. Ministry of Labour and Social Affairs, Addis Ababa, March 26.
Thompson Jr, Barton H. (2000). Tragically Difficult: The Obstacles to Governing the Commons. *Stanford Law School*, Working Paper 187: 241–278.
United Nations (UN). (2014). *The Millenium Development Goals Report 2014*. New York: United Nations.
United Nations (UN). (2015). *Transforming Our World: The 2030 Agenda for Sustainable Development*. New York: UN.
United Nations Children's Fund (UNICEF). (2008). *Social Protection in Eastern and Southern Africa: A Framework and Strategy for UNICEF*. New York: UNICEF.
United Nations Children's Fund (UNICEF). (2012). *UNICEF's Social Protection Strategy Framework*. New York: UNICEF.
United Nations Children's Fund (UNICEF). (2013). *Common Ground: UNICEF and World Bank Approaches to Building Social Protection Systems*. New York: UNICEF.
United Nations Conference on Trade and Development (UNCTAD). (2013). *The Least Developed Countries Report 2013: Growth with Employment for Inclusive and Sustainable Development*. New York: United Nations.
vanGinneken, Wouter. (2003). Extending Social Security: Policies for Developing Countries. *International Labour Review*, 142 (3): 277–293.
World Bank. (1989). *Sub-Saharan Africa. From Crisis to Sustainable Growth*. Washington, DC: The World Bank.
World Bank. (2012). *Managing Risk, Promoting Growth: Developing Systems for Social Protection in Africa*. Washington, DC: The World Bank
World Economic Forum. (2014). *Forging Inclusive Growth, Creating Jobs*. Abuja 7–9 May 2014. Retrieved from: www3.weforum.org/docs/AF14/WEF_AF14_Report.pdf
World Health Organization and UNICEF. (2013). *Progress on Sanitation and Drinking-Water: 2013 Update*. Geneva: WHO/UNICEF.

2 Governance characteristics and policy relevance of informal social protection services in Ethiopia

When the state is willing but not able

Amdissa Teshome, Adanech Dutu, Kassa Teshager, and Terefe Zeleke

Introduction

Ethiopia's economy has grown at an average of 11 per cent per annum for the past decade, reducing income poverty (below US$1.25 a day) from 44 per cent of the population in 1999 to about 29.6 per cent in 2011 (Federal Democratic Republic of Ethiopia, 2014; World Bank, 2015). In 1995, the transitional government adopted a new constitution that guarantees every Ethiopian access to public health and education, clean water, housing, food, and social security, pledging,

The State has the obligation to allocate ever-increasing resources to provide... public health, education and other social services and shall, within available means, allocate resources to provide rehabilitation and assistance to the physically and mentally disabled, the aged, and to children who are left without parents or guardian.

(Federal Democratic Republic of Ethiopia, 1995: Article 41 sections 4, 5)

Sections 6 and 7 add,

The state shall pursue policies which aim to expand job opportunities for the unemployed and the poor and shall accordingly undertake programmes and public work projects", and "shall undertake all measures necessary to increase opportunities for citizens to find gainful employment.

Although many social welfare programmes already existed, the government followed up the constitutional commitment with a series of public policies[1] and programmes related to Article 41. In 2012, the government developed the National Social Protection Policy document and, through the assistance of the international donor community, is implementing social protection (SP) programmes involving food security, household asset building, voluntary resettlement, national nutrition, urban housing and grain subsidies, and support to older persons and vulnerable children. The Food Security

Programme's Productive Safety Net Programme (PSNP) provides about 8.3 million chronically food-insecure households in 319 *woredas* with predictable cash and/or food transfers to smooth consumption (FDRE, 2012). Recently, the government has introduced a health insurance scheme for public-sector employees and community-based health insurance schemes for the informal sector.

SP programmes in Ethiopia must be understood in the context of widespread vulnerability. Some 50 per cent of those now statistically above the poverty line are only marginally so, and a single major shock (such as inadequate rainfall or fall in the prices of farm products) can push them into severe poverty. Further, more than 80 per cent of the population live in rural areas where the proportion below the poverty line is 30.4 per cent, compared with 25.7 per cent in urban areas. The SP policy document is a demonstration of government commitment to comprehensively tackling socio-economic vulnerabilities.

For a majority-poor population of more than 80 million people, state SP programmes are just drops in an ocean. For instance, the national social insurance (pension scheme) programme only covers 1.8 per cent of those gainfully employed in the government, state corporations, and private sector (FDRE, 2012: 11). Established in 1963, the state-organised contributory social insurance scheme provides benefits in old age, invalidity, and employment injury. The state health insurance addresses only public-sector employees, who are required to contribute part of their monthly salary as premium based on a unit cost of their medical benefit package, while the community-based health insurance scheme benefits people in the informal sectors who can contribute 11–15 Birr[2] per month (MoH, 2010). Those with social security and health insurance comprise about 7.2 per cent of the total workforce engaged in urban and rural areas (FDRE, 2012: 11). Private and charitable organisations, which employ less than 1 per cent of the national workforce, also provide some employment benefits (including a contributory provident fund) and may cover part or all of the health bills employees may incur. The overwhelming majority of the population are without access to any formal or state social security or health insurance (Dercon et al., 2006).

State capacity is limited not only in times of economic and social shocks but also in its ability to provide basic welfare services to citizens. The Constitution makes the state "willing", but does not make it "able". Less than 50 per cent of births are overseen by a skilled birth attendant; less than 30 per cent of Ethiopians use improved sanitation facilities (see Table 2.1).

State limitation does not mean there is a vacuum. Non-state actors (NSAs) have stepped in to fill the gaps and provide a variety of SP services to the poor and destitute at household, group and community levels. Non-state

Table 2.1 Some Millennium Development Goal indicators (1995–2011)

Some MDG indicators in Ethiopia	1995	2000	2005	2011
% of the population undernourished	64.5	53.5	45.4	37.1
Total net enrolment ratio in primary education (both sexes)	23.2	40.4	62.7	87.4
% of the population using improved drinking water sources	14	20	29	38
% of the population using improved sanitation facilities	3	8	14	21

Source: United Nations Statistics Division, updates as of 1 July 2014[1]
www.uneca.org/sites/default/files/PublicationFiles/mdg_report_2014_ethiopia_case_study.pdf

social protection (NSSP) organisations design and implement SP and services directly for the poor and also implement interventions designed by the state. For example, the implementation of the PSNP that is partly funded by international donors involves many NGOs and community organisations. Within the broad category of NSAs, there are numerous traditional support systems that act as the first line of defence against individual and community vulnerability and socio-economic shocks. These informal CBOs and their mechanisms have little or no connection with the state apparatus or agencies, but they enable the poor and excluded to protect themselves.

So who are these informal organisations and what services do they provide? What governance mechanisms are embedded in their operation? This chapter provides the findings of a study that asked these questions in Ethiopia. It describes various forms of informal social protection organisations (ISPOs), their scope and coverage, their governance arrangements, and how the government could support these organisations to complement and expand state services. The study was carried out in 2012–2013 in four areas, beginning with mapping of all NSAs and later an in-depth focus on 31 ISPOs and 274 beneficiaries.

Informal community-based social protection service providers in Ethiopia

There is an emerging body of policy and academic literature that explicitly recognises ISPO programmes and mechanisms in Ethiopia (Devereux and Getu, 2013; Hebo, 2013; Teshome, 2013; Verpoorten and Verschraegen, 2010). The ISPOs encompass arrangements and actions by an individual or group of individuals which are not formally regulated, but which do not necessarily contradict the laws and regulations of the nation (Oduro, 2010). These mechanisms enable transfers of assets and/or finances by individuals, families, clans, and associations. The principles of reciprocity, customary laws of social institutions, religious and cultural principles, community values, and collective action govern such transfers and other forms of support (De Coninck and Emily, 2008). Although such practices have been in existence for centuries, their modes of operation in response to poverty and vulnerability have not been legally recognised, institutionalised, or formally accepted by state bureaucracy, hence reluctance of the state to support them. In Ethiopia, the main institutions for such collective action at the community level are *Iddir*, *Iqqub*, *Mahiber/Senbete*, and self-help groups. According to Dessalegn (2008), at local level most people gain their social and economic benefits from these traditional organisations. Though precise figures are subject to debate, the Ministry of Capacity Building (2005) estimates that about 39 million people participate in *iddir*, some 21 million in *iqqub*, and about 9 million in a variety of self-help organisations. The services these organisations deliver certainly warrants policy attention.

Iddir

The tradition *Iddir* is established primarily to provide mutual aid or social insurance to its members, who are united by ties to families, friendship, or neighbourhood, or to an occupation (Teshome, 2008). *Iddir* has a very long history, and it is estimated that about 87 per cent of Ethiopians in urban centres and close to 70 per cent of people in rural areas belong to some type of *Iddir* in their community (Zewge, 2004). Among the most common *Iddir* services is provision of burial support when a member or a relative dies. Irrespective of the income level of that member, the *Iddir* ensures the bereaved member gets economic and social support to avoid destitution from the cost of providing a decent funeral (Pankhurst and Mariam, 2000). In recent times, some *Iddir* have transitioned from informal to semi-formal institutions, operating a system that has a clear leadership structure and keeps written records. Some have tried to register their status with local government, but the majority have not. An *Iddir's* funding comes from members' contributions. The chairperson, treasurer, and secretary elected by the members are responsible for managing activities and are accountable to the group.

Iqqub

Iqqub are traditional community-based savings and credit mechanisms in which like-minded individuals in a neighbourhood come together, agree to contribute a certain amount on a regular basis, and allocate the money on a lottery basis or according to the needs of an individual member. Any individual member can also make a request for group support. If the group considers support to be crucial for the survival of an individual member, he or she may be given priority for available resources. Some *Iqqub* have evolved to become a resource mobilisation strategy for members who want to start their own enterprises or existing micro-entrepreneurs who want to expand but lack the formal credentials to secure credit from formal banking institutions. Membership is usually based on pre-established social ties, same workplace or same trade, neighbourhood, ethnic background, etc. To join an existing *Iqqub*, a newcomer requires a positive testimony of two to six existing members regarding the person's creditworthiness, and the proposers act as guarantors. An *Iqqub* may start with 10 members and grow to 50 or more.

Mahiber/senbete

Mahiber are religious, usually Orthodox-based, members groups. During prayer meetings, they discuss their social and economic problems, and it is expected that members provide support to the needy if they can afford to. Members bring food and drinks to church to share a meal with the poor and discuss matters of common interest (Mogues, 2006). *Mahiber* are informal institutions involved in various community issues such as risk-coping, information, manpower and mechanisation, and conflict resolution. The aim is to promote social harmony among fellow believers, but *Mahiber* is also an instrument of mutual solace in times of grief. In its modern form, *Mahiber* is becoming a kind of alumni formed by educated people who attended the same school.

Self-help groups

There are many – and varied – self-help organisations that do not fit into any of the listed categories, but they do provide SP and welfare services. For example, one is based on the traditional "coffee ceremony", where a group of neighbouring women combine to set up a savings and credit scheme. The size of these groups is usually 20, primarily determined by manageability. Associations help their members in cash or in kind, in capacity building, and by sharing information (Dercon et al., 2006).

Other informal institutions, which are not the subject of this in-depth study, include *Debo* and *Gadaa*. *Debo* is a labour-sharing mechanism practiced mainly in agricultural areas. It pools labour to assist one or more individuals/households with building a house, land preparation, ploughing, and harvesting crops. The *Gadaa* is mainly practiced in pastoral areas of Oromia. The *AbaGadaa* (male head or governor of the *Gadaa*) changes every eight years to serve the community on economic, political, military, and social issues. The system assigns rights, obligations and responsibilities to all males in the society (Edossa et al., 2007). *Gadaa* coordinate response to shocks such as drought and conflict, through options of risk reduction, credit provision, information sharing, labour sharing, and conflict resolution services for members. Devereux and Sabates-Wheeler (2004) aptly categorise all SP in four different types of services:

a   emergency support or "protective" welfare services to assist, for example, the elderly, persons with disability, and orphans;
b   livelihood or "promotive" services involving, for example, income/employment-generating activities, micro-credit;
c   "preventive" social services such as education, health, and provision of utilities;
d   "transformative" services such as advocating education for all or elimination of female genital mutilation (FGM).

Any form of classification or typology suffers from at least some overlapping.

Case study of informal social protection actors and services

This study was carried out in four areas: Welmera (Oromia region), Shinile (Somali region), Addis Ketema (Addis Ababa), and Dire Dawa city. Welmera, 44 km to the west of Addis Ababa, has 24 rural *kebele* and 6 urban centres. The district has a population of circa 114,500 of which 82,800 are rural and 31,700 are urban. The population structure mirrors the national average in that the youth account for 44 per cent, the economically active 51.7 per cent, and the old age populations 4.3 per cent. The district suffers from chronic poverty, manifested in poor rural infrastructure, low productivity, high illiteracy rates, and prevalence of various illnesses. The rural communities profoundly depend on informal support mechanisms.

Shinile is 527 km east of Addis Ababa and 172 mm north-east of Jijiga, the capital of Somali Regional State. Based on the 2007 census, the district has a total population of 102,574, (55 per cent male). Shinile suffers from frequent drought, leading to food and water shortages and livestock and crop disease outbreaks (see Figure 2.1 for the study areas).

Addis Ketema is one of ten sub-cities of Addis Ababa. It is divided into ten local government zones (*kebele*) and has a population of 255,000. It is the sixth most populous suburb and the most densely populated, making it especially vulnerable to pollution, poor sanitation, congestion, and consequent disease. The sub-city is also subjected to high food prices.

Governance characteristics and policy 31

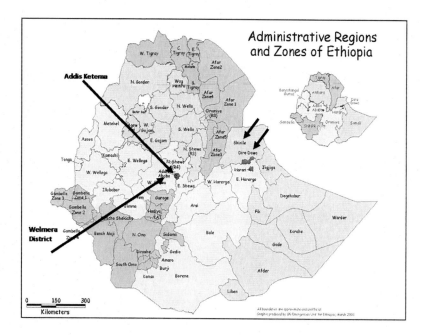

Figure 2.1 The location of the study areas.

Dire Dawa city has 12 urban *kebele* and is 505 km east of Addis Ababa. It has a population of 223,224 and suffers from occasional flooding and other risks and vulnerabilities similar to those of Addis Ketema.

Findings of the study

Mapping the forms and scope of informal non-state actors

The study's mapping identified 1,094 NSAs providing SP services (see Table 2.2). The urban centres (Addis Ketema sub-city and Dire Dawa city) have more than twice as many NSAs as the rural sites (Wolmera and Shinile).

Of the total NSAs, 47 per cent could be classified as ISPOs – mainly *Iddir, Iqqub*, or social networks. Their organisational structure was social networks defined by residential community and/or occupation. Table 2.3 shows the breakdown:

Among informal organisations, 57.6 per cent are *Iddir*, which serve as insurance mechanisms against death-related challenges (covering funeral expenses, taking care of guests/mourners, etc.). *Iqqub* address the financial challenges of their members and facilitate small savings against future

Table 2.2 Types of non-state actors in research sites

Types of non-state actor	Addis Ketema sub-city	Wolmera district	Dire Dawa city	Shinile district	Total
International NGOs	5	0	12	1	18
National & local NGOs	19	3	40	2	64
Business organisation	3	5	46	22	76
Faith-based organisation	0	2	10	7	19
Self-help groups	19	9	13	15	56
Informal CBOs	90	148	138	46	422
Semi-formal CBOs	10	0	58	1	69
Associations[1]	27	14	162	60	263
Cooperatives	13	1	27	20	61
Others	40	4	2	0	46
Total	226	186	508	174	1094

Source: Based on field survey data (2013)

[1] Associations include development associations, women associations, youth associations, HIV/AIDS associations, and professional associations

Table 2.3 Forms of informal social protection providers

Forms of informal CBOs	No of surveyed informal organisations	%
Iddir	299	57.6
Iqqub	85	16.4
Self-help groups	56	10.8
Religious: Mahiber/ Senbete/Jamaha	38	7.3
Others	41	7.9
Total	**519**	**100**

Source: Field data (2013)

contingencies. Self-help groups are formed to undertake some business activities that will allow members to generate income. *Mahiber Senbete/ Jamaha* are religious CBOs which strengthen social networks and discuss social affairs.

Many local officers estimated that there are 8–20 *Iddir* in a *kebele* (the smallest administrative unit), 10–15 *Iqqub*, and 5–10 *Mahiber/Jamaha*. Presently, there are about 15,000 rural *kebels* in Ethiopia, which computes to a significant number of ISPOs.

Rural-urban split in collective action to solve vulnerability challenges

The need for collective action against a common enemy – poverty and vulnerability – is ingrained in Ethiopians' way of life. Table 2.4 shows that IFPOS are widespread across both rural and urban areas.

Table 2.4 Geographical coverage of informal social protection providers

Forms of informal organizations	Urban (Dire Dawa)	Rural (Welmera)	Total
Iddir	176	123	299
Iqqub	39	46	85
Self-help groups	32	24	56
Religious Mahiber/ Senbet/jamaha	13	25	38
	39	2	41
Total	299 (57.6%)	220 (42.4%)	519 (100%)

Source: Field survey (2013)

In 2005, Ethiopia's Ministry of Capacity Building (MCB) estimated that 39 million people participate in *Iddir*, 21 million in *Iqqub*, and another 9 million in a variety of self-help organisations. Other studies suggest that about 87 per cent of Ethiopians in urban centres and close to 70 per cent in rural areas belong to *Iddir* (Zewge, 2004; Konjit, 2008). This study echoes those estimates and confirms that people provide more collective action in urban areas than rural, so reciprocity as a SP mechanism is ubiquitous. When people feel threatened by common challenges they respond with collective action irrespective of geographical location. The supposed rural-urban split in collective action is a myth (Awortwi, 2012; Berner, 1997; Hoefferth and Iceland, 1998).

Informal non-state social protection services

NSAs tend to provide multiple SP services rather than focus on a single speciality. They understand that poverty and vulnerability are multi-faceted and inter-connected. However, NSA services are more "protective" than "preventive" or "transformative" (see Figure 2.2).

Of 519 ISPOs, 65 per cent are providing protective services and 57 per cent are involved in the provision of livelihood services (promotive). Their involvement in preventive and transformative services is insignificant. The high involvement of ISPOs is to be expected, as that has been the role of traditional organisations (see Table 2.5).

Members of these organisations acknowledge the welfare services provided. In a focus-group discussion, the chairperson of Kebele 01 *Iddir* in Dire Dawa city stated,

> If there were no Iddir at the grassroots level, the burial responsibility would go to the government and it would have to allocate portions of the annual budget to bury poor citizens whose relatives cannot afford the cost of burial ceremony. Iddir have taken such burdens away from the government so the State has to recognise our role and give us the needed support.

34 Amdissa Teshome et al.

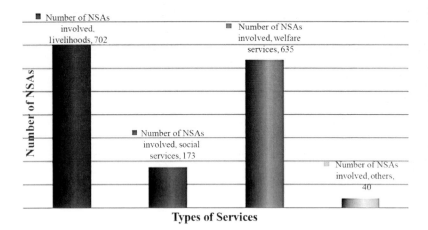

Figure 2.2 Services delivered by non-state actors.

Table 2.5 Services provided by informal non-state actors

Forms of informal NSAs	Livelihoods (promotive)	Social services (preventive)	Welfare (protective)	Advocacy (transformative)
Iddir	121	17	280	1
Iqqub	75	2	12	1
Self-help groups	41	8	20	1
Mahiber/ Senbete/ Jamaha	30	7	24	2
Others	31	–	1	3
Total	298 (57%)	34 (7%)	337 (65%)	8 (2%)

Source: Field survey (2013)

Informal organisations are gradually becoming active in promotive services, realising that income and livelihood activities – not charities – are the key to move people out of poverty sustainably. The poor themselves accept the axiom, "Give people a fish and you feed them for a day; teach people to fish and you feed them for a lifetime." Key informants indicated that, in recent times, ISPOs were actively involved in fundraising for development activities that the state initiated. Again, the type of social services does not differ by geography (see Figure 2.3).

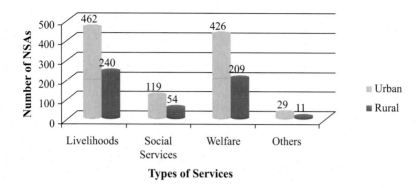

Figure 2.3 Non-state actors' services delivery by geographic location (urban vs. rural).

Charity work of informal social protection actors and beneficiaries' responses

A typical *Iddir* member contributes a registration fee of Birr 500 or more and pays a subscription of up to Birr 10 per month. In general, members contribute about 71 per cent of *Iddir* funds while internal income generation and external donations provide about 12 per cent and 17 per cent, respectively. So the objective of these informal actors is first to meet the socio-economic needs of their members who have contributed their dues and later to give charitable support to non-contributory community members. The charity work provides various forms of assistance to individuals and communities who do not have other means of survival. The main criterion for a non-contributing person to benefit is "being poor" in the assessment of the contributing members. Other criteria include being a permanent resident of the area, or unemployed, or elderly, or having evidence of asset depletion. Gender and degree of vulnerability (e.g. OVCs and widows) are also considered. So the informal actors apply well-defined means-testing criteria. Table 2.6 shows the magnitude and types of beneficiaries assisted by informal NSAs covered in the study areas.

Self-help groups identified in the study areas support 1,015 vulnerable people, while *Iddir* and *Mahiber/Senbete/Jamaha* assist 1,009 and 1,156, respectively – affirmation that informal actors play roles in solving the socio-economic problems of vulnerable people at the grassroots level. However, the government rarely recognises ISPOs' roles and operations, demands an unrealistically cumbersome and lengthy registration process, and rarely offers them a voice in policymaking on SP (Devereux and Getu, 2013; Hebo, 2013; Teshome, 2013).

Table 2.6 The types of beneficiaries covered by informal non-state actors (N = 519)

Types of beneficiaries targeted	Self-help groups	Iddir	Iqqub	Mahiber/ Senbete/ Jamaha	Total
Poor	380	42	84	481	987
Destitute people	118	194	–	18	330
Orphans and vulnerable children	243	253	5	81	582
People living with HIV/AIDS	75	98	51	–	224
Elders	75	122	15	19	231
Disabled people	46	101	17	10	174
Drought prone households	5	–	–	12	17
Informal sector workers	2	–	–	20	22
Youth	71	199	99	306	675
Victims of domestic violence	–	–	5	209	214
Total	1015	1009	276	1156	3456

Source: Field survey (2013)

Table 2.7 Perceptions of beneficiaries on service provision

Perception of household	Urban (Dire Dawa) (N = 66)			Rural (Wolmera) (N = 208)		
	Yes (%)	No (%)	Not sure (%)	Yes (%)	No (%)	Not sure (%)
SP services provided by informal NSAs are needed in the community in times of social and economic shocks. Without them, vulnerability would be extremely high and life precarious?	45.1	41.7	13.2	58.0	35.2	6.8
Informal social protection providers operate on the basis of all the poor rather than effectively maximizing the self-interest of organisational members?	65.6	27.0	7.4	82.2	12.3	5.5

Beneficiary groups included both men and women in close balance. In 7 of the 13 categories, the number of women beneficiaries exceeded the men. Overall, women targeted by NSAs accounted for 51.6 per cent of the beneficiaries. Household-level assessment of services provided by ISPOs indicated that about 45 per cent of respondents from Dire Dawa and 58 per cent from Welmera appreciated what they received from these organisations (see Table 2.7).

Governance structures of informal social protection mechanisms

The mapping survey generated ample data on how NSAs are governed, including the number of personnel by sex, whether or not the NSA has an organisational structure, who makes strategic decisions, and existence of rules and regulations. The staffing profile shows a clear male dominance – in line with traditional gender bias. Among the 519 ISPOs mapped, 52.6 per cent reported having an organisational structure that is not documented – they were able to describe the structure but could not show it. That is difficult for government or business organisations to work with. ISPOs' communication and reporting is verbal among members. They are not required by any formal body to report their performance or design their operational plan. Yet some 83 per cent of ISPOs do have operating rules that govern their activities, established through consensus (see Table 2.8).

Management or the executive committee usually make decisions on daily activities, but all members meet to take strategic decisions. In Mahiber/ Jamaha, all decisions are made at the general assembly of members. Either way, strategic decisions of ISPOs are participatory. Though many have not

Table 2.8 Presence of organisational structures and operational rules

Presence of organisational structure?	Self-help %	Iddir %	Iqqub %	Mahiber %	Others %	Total
Yes, organisational structure exists but is not documented	42.9	62.5	20	55.3	58.5	52.6
Not at all	57.1	37.5	80	44.7	41.5	47.4%
Total respondents	**56**	**299**	**85**	**38**	**41**	**519**

Presence of organisational rule?	Self-help %	Iddir %	Iqqub %	Mahiber %	Others %	Total
Yes, operating rule exists	87.5	88.3	57.6	76.3	97.6	83
No operating rule	12.5	11.7	42.4	23.7	2.4	17
Total respondents	**56**	**299**	**85**	**38**	**41**	**519**

Source: Field survey (2013)

Table 2.9 Accountability mechanisms in informal organisations

Informal organisations	Does your organisation produce progress reports?		Is your organisation's account internally audited?		Do you have systems that monitor the activities of the organisation?	
	Yes (%)	No (%)	Yes (%)	No (%)	Yes (%)	No (%)
Self-help (299)	76.8	23.2	78.6	21.4	89.3	10.7
Iddir (85)	75.3	24.7	87.6	12.4	76.3	23.7
Iqqub (56)	8.2	91.8	44.7	55.3	23.5	76.5
Mahiber/Jamaha (38)	52.6	47.4	57.9	42.1	94.7	5.3
Others (41)	63.4	36.6	65.9	34.1	82.9	17.1
Total	61.8	38.2	75.7	24.3	70.9	29.1

Source: Field survey (2013)

registered, as Table 2.9 shows, a high percentage of self-help groups, *Iddir*, and *Mahiber/Jamaha* prepare and communicate progress reports to their general assembly's when needed. Most *Iqqub* do not, as each member is aware of the amount contributed by and distributed to members on a weekly or monthly basis. When the last member receives an allocation, then the *Iqqub* is disbanded or the whole cycle is repeated.

Many ISPOs undertake internal audit (75.7 per cent) and have monitoring mechanisms (70.9 per cent). Thus most exercise the accountability mechanisms that contribute to effective performance (see Table 2.9). Some misuse of members' funds does occur and is more prevalent in rural areas where management skills are weakest and formal institutional arrangements are absent.

Interaction between informal organisations and the state is an important governance issue. Of 519 ISPOs mapped, only 32.8 per cent reported any form of interaction with state agencies in the past year. Where there was engagement, it mainly took place only at the district and *kebele* levels, which can do little to help ISPOs build their capacities or influence national policy on SP. The absence of interaction has led to little or no state recognition of the role of informal organisations.

In one of the focus group discussions, participants criticised the government:

> The informal community-based organisations are undertaking a lot of activities that ought to have been provided by the State. But the government has not facilitated us through institutional support. Thus, we are unable to get office accommodation; we also experience a lot of

bureaucratic hurdles to get a licence to engage in income-generating activities for ourselves and to support the poor.

The positive side is that informal NSAs are allowed to operate with minimum interference from government bureaucracy. Since these organisations are less involved in any advocacy activity, they are tolerated by government, unlike formal NSAs that are specifically and legally prohibited from engaging in advocacy. In Ethiopia, the law requires non-state organisations to register as foreign charities, Ethiopian charities, or Ethiopian residents' charities. Foreign charities are allowed to engage only in development activities without any advocacy space for sensitisation or rights campaigns. Ethiopian charities must generate 90 per cent of their project funds from local resources. They can participate in advocacy, sensitisation, and rights campaigns in addition to development activities. Ethiopian residents' charities are allowed to generate 90 per cent of their project funds from abroad but are restricted to development projects only. Informal organisations are not required to register, so any call for government recognition would have to weigh these pros and cons, and the apparent correlation between being "politically safe" and "politically unimportant". In recent times, *Iddir* have started to federate and form unions (even beyond Addis Ababa), which are required to register with a government office. Their aim is to enhance their recognition upwards to state and regional authorities. However, ISPOs such as *Iqqub*, *Mahiber*, and self-help groups are not changing their traditional status quo.

Conclusion and policy relevance

Ethiopia is a democratic and stable state that in recent times has made remarkable progress in human development. Studies now classify the country among the few "emerging, democratic developmental" states in Africa (Booth (ed.) 2015; Gagliardone, 2014). However, the state is unable to fulfil some of its constitutional responsibilities to citizens. One limitation is the provision of SP services – not by design but by resource constraints amid competing state budget demands and harsh climatic conditions that make vulnerability pervasive. As a result, NSAs, especially informal or CBOs, have responded in various ways to help the poor and vulnerable survive economic and social shocks. Without their presence, many of the poor might have fallen into helpless destitution.

The key conclusions from this study are as follows:

- Informal organisations such as *Iddir, Iqqub,* and *Mahiber/Senbete/Jamaha* are the first point of contact for the poor in times of social and economic shocks. When there are shocks in families and communities – illness, death of the bread winner in the household, harvest shocks – recourse to coping strategies are the natural response, and informal social arrangements become the first step. Protective services through collective action are not new. While the state has expanded its SP services, such programmes reach only a small number, and they do not respond to the diversity of needs. The poor understand the limitations of the state and reflexively rely on their traditional fall-back mechanisms for survival.

- Informal CBOs provide multiple services across the four typologies – protective, promotive, preventive, and (to a much lesser extent) transformative. This is in contrast to the conventional perception that informal NSAs are "welfarist" in nature – a kind of reciprocity network or gift-exchange arrangement as stated by Oduro (2010). The scope of operation of ISPOs is fluid and as diverse as the poor themselves (destitute, OVC, the elderly, people living with HIV/AIDS, women, and youth), meaning solutions to their social and economic challenges demand multiple approaches.

- Interaction between informal SP actors and the state is poorly developed. Government recognises and tolerates their existence, but that is all. These informal organisations have ample social capital, which the state could harness for micro-level action for poverty reduction. This should not be used as a way to regulate their activities but to strengthen the linkage between formal and informal SP. If this line of thinking was rooted in the SP policy process, Ethiopia could offer important lessons to other sub-Saharan African countries on how to develop a SP floor that is more responsive to the local context.

- Although the governance structures of informal organisations may not conform to normal business rules and management principles, that should not distract policymakers and practitioners – especially regional governments – from seeing them as important allies and complementary to SP services being provided by the state itself. What may be needed is for the government to be flexible enough to accommodate the (positive) peculiarities of informal organisations that have enabled the poor to survive.

- Not many ISPO members or beneficiaries can claim to have permanently moved out of poverty. They and their organisations are still vulnerable, though they have survived political, economic, and social turbulence over decades. State SP services that are discontinued because of inadequate funding could learn some lessons on survival and sustainability from these informal organisations.

Governance characteristics and policy 41

Finally, it must be understood that provision of welfare services is the role of the state and in Ethiopia's case that is guaranteed in the Constitution. The state is the principal duty bearer with the obligation to ensure that rights in the Constitution are fulfilled. NSAs play a supporting role. It is in the interest of the state to ensure that such roles are facilitated and maximised – not restricted and jeopardised.

Notes

1 This includes the National Women's Policy (2001), the National Youth Policy (2004), Poverty Reduction Strategy Programme (PRSP), the Development and Poverty Reduction Programme (SDPRP), the Plan for Accelerated and Sustained Development to End Poverty (PASDEP), Growth and Transformation Plan (GTP), etc.
2 1 birr = 0.05 US Dollar (2015)

References

Awortwi, N. (2012). The Riddle of Community Development: Factors Influencing Partnership and Management in 29 African and Latin American Communities. *Community Development Journal*, 48(1): 89–104. doi: 10.1093/cdj/bsr071

Berner, E. (1997). *Defending a Place in the City: Localities and the Struggle for Urban Land in Metro Manila*. Quezon City, The Philippines: Ateneo de Manila University Press.

Booth, D. (ed.). (2015). *Developmental Regimes in Africa*. Synthesis Report. London: ODI.

Coninck, J. De, and Emily, D. (2008). Social Protection Is Centuries-Old! Culture and Social Protection for the Very Poor in Uganda: Evidence and Policy Implications: In Social Protection for the Poorest in Africa. Compendium of papers presented during the International Conference on Social Protection, 8–10 September 2008, pp. 54–68.

Dercon, S.; De Weerdt, J.; Bold, T.; and Pankhurst, A. (2006). Group-based Funeral Insurance in Ethiopia and Tanzania. *World Development*, 34 (4): 685–703.

Dessalegn, R. (2008). "Civil Society Organisations in Ethiopia: The Challenge of Democracy from Below". In Z. Bahru and S. Pausewang (eds.), *Forum for Social Studies*. Uppsala: Nordiska Afrikainstiute and Addis Ababa, pp. 103–119.

Devereux, S., and Getu, M. (eds.). (2013). *Informal and Formal Social Protection Systems in Sub-Saharan Africa*. Addis Ababa: Organisation for Social Science Research in Eastern and Southern Africa (OSSREA).

Devereux, S., and Sabates-Wheeler, R. (2004). Transformative social protection. *UK: Institute of Development Studies*, Issue 01.

Edossa, D.C.; Awulachew, S.B.; Namara, R.E.; Babel, M.S.; and Gupta, A.D. (2007). "Indigenous Systems of Conflict Resolution in Oromia, Ethiopia". In B.C.P. Koppen, M. Giordano, and J. Butterworth (eds.), *Community-Based Water Law and*

Water Resource Management Reform in Developing Countries. London: CAB International, p. 146.

Federal Democratic Republic of Ethiopia. (1995). *The Constitution of the Federal Democratic Republic of Ethiopia*. Addis Ababa: Ministry of Finance and Economic Development.

Federal Democratic Republic of Ethiopia. (2004). *National Youth Policy. Addis Ababa: Ministry of youth, sports and culture*. Retrieved from: www.youthpolicy.org/national/Ethiopia_2004_National_Youth_Policy.pdf

Federal Democratic Republic of Ethiopia. (2012). *National Social Protection Policy of Ethiopia, Final Draft, Ministry of Labour and Social Affairs*. Addis Ababa: Ministry of Finance and Economic Development.

Federal Democratic Republic of Ethiopia. (2014). *Growth and Transformation Plan (GTP II)*. Addis Ababa: Ministry of Finance and Economic Development.

Gagliardone, I. (2014). New Media and the Developmental State in Ethiopia. *Africa Affairs*, 111 (451): 279–299.

Hebo, M. (2013). "Giving Is Saving: The Essence of Reciprocity as an Informal Social Protection Mechanism Among the Arsii Oromo, Southern Ethiopia". In S. Devereux and Melese Getu (eds.), *Informal and Formal Social Protection Systems in Sub-Saharan Africa*. Addis Ababa: Organisation for Social Science Research in Eastern and Southern Africa (OSSREA), pp. 9–42.

Hoefferth, S., and Iceland, J. (1998). Social Capital in Rural and Urban Communities. *Rural Sociology*, 63 (4): 574–598.

Konjit, F. (2008). "Civil Society in Kenya, South Africa and Uganda: Lessons for Ethiopia". In A. Taye and Z. Bahru (eds.), *Forum for Social Studies*. Uppsala: Nordiska Afrikainstiute and Addis Ababa, pp. 34–39.

Ministry of Capacity Building/MCB. (2005). *Civil Society Organisations Capacity Building Program (revised)*. Addis Ababa: Government of Ethiopia.

Ministry of Health/MOH. (2010). *Health Insurance in Ethiopia*. Addis Ababa: Government Ethiopia.

Mogues, T. (2006). *Shocks, Livestock Asset Dynamics and Social Capital in Ethiopia*. IFPRI DSDG Discussion Paper No. 38, August 2006.

Oduro, D. (2010). *Formal and Informal Social Protection in Sub-Saharan Africa*. Legon: Department of Economics, University of Ghana.

Pankhurst, A., and Mariam, D.H. (2000). "The Iddir in Ethiopia. Historical Development, Social Function, and Potential Role in HIVE/AIDS Prevention and Control". *Northeast African Studies*, 7 (2): 35–57.

Teshome, T. (2008). *Role and Potential of "Iqqub" in Ethiopia*. A project paper submitted to the school of graduate studies of Addis Ababa University in partial fulfilments of the requirements for the degree of Master of Science in accounting and finance school of graduate.

Teshome, A. (2013). "Informal and Formal Social Protection in Ethiopia". In S. Devereux and Melese Getu (eds.), *Informal and Formal Social Protection Systems in Sub-Saharan Africa*. Addis Ababa: Organisation for Social Science Research in Eastern and Southern Africa (OSSREA), pp. 95–120.

Verpoorten, R., and Verschraegen, G. (2010). "Formal and Informal Social Protection in Sub-Saharan Africa: A Complex Welfare Mix to Reduce Poverty and Inequality". In C. Suter (ed.), *World Society Studies*. Berlin: Lit Verlag, pp. 311–333.
World Bank. (2015). *Ethiopia's Great Run: The Growth Acceleration and How to Pace It*. Report No. 99399. Washington, DC: World Bank Group.
Zewge, A. (2004). "The New Roles of Iddirs in Dire Dawa". In Brian Pratt and Lucy Earle (eds.), *Study on Effective Empowerment of Citizens in Ethiopia, July 2004*. London: INTRAC, pp. 168–175.

3 Governance of non-state social protection services in Ghana
Communication as an accountability mechanism in mutual aid organisations in Wassa

Ellen Bortei-Doku Aryeetey, Stephen Afranie, Daniel Doh, and Paul Andoh

Introduction

Risks and livelihood shocks caused by ill health, accidents, unemployment, old age, etc., are more severe and life threatening to the poor. Vulnerability to poverty, destitution, or even death in instances of "simple" problems such as crop failure or death of a family member requires social protection (SP) as a safety net. That is the very meaning of SP: mechanisms to provide support to people who are vulnerable to chronic poverty, risks, and shocks.

Ghana's 1992 Constitution obliges the state to implement policies and programmes to address the social, economic, and educational imbalances in society. Under the Directive Principles of State Policy, the protection and promotion of all basic human rights and freedoms, including the rights of the disabled, aged, children, and other vulnerable groups, is guaranteed by the state (Article four of the 1992 Constitution). The African Union supports the need for governments to provide SP to their citizens (AU, 2010). The International Labour Organisation (ILO) strongly encourages countries to develop a national "social protection floor" that guarantees access to essential health for all; income security for children; support to the unemployed, underemployed, and poor; and income security for the elderly and disabled (ILO, 2011).

In practice, recommendations by regional bodies and international organisations are not often heeded by member states, for reasons including limited capacity to implement such policies and programmes. In the context of "limited statehood" – where the state does not have the capacity to deliver its constitutional responsibilities (Risse, 2011) – most citizens are left to their own devices. This is the case in the provision of SP services in many countries in Africa. For example, old-age pension in Ghana is provided to a small percentage of formal-sector employees – government workers and people who work for private sector organisations – who pay monthly state-scheme contributions. But that leaves about 80 per cent of the total population, who make a living in the informal sector, with no access to state social security (Osei-Boateng and Ampratwum, 2011). Typically, they rely on their own savings and/or fall back on non-state actors (NSAs), mutual organisations, and other coping strategies (ILO, 2012; Ellis, Devereux and White, 2009; Norton, Conway and Foster, 2001; Holzmann and Jorgensen, 2000).

Where the state is limited in financial capacity, or the knowledge and political will to provide comprehensive SP to all citizens, NSAs have stepped in to fill the gap, expand coverage, and deliver a range of innovative services. It is important to recognize a priori that African society has long recognised non-state mechanisms, especially the traditional informal sector, in the provision of welfare services. Until recently, the "extended family" system in Ghana was a dedicated provider of SP services to kin in times of need (Kumado and Gockel, 2003). With the gradual weakening of this system through urbanisation and globalisation, as well as the and high cost of living, mutual organisations have evolved to provide micro-level responses to individual and group vulnerability and risks.

Numerous groups from the same profession, social network, gender, tribe, old school, etc., are establishing mutual organisations to collectively "protect" their members. They provide a safety net and solidarity services and manage the group's collective resources and decision making.

The performance of mutual organisations relies on factors such as membership contributions, commitment to support each other, and their governance system (Bassett et al., 2012). Most community-based mutual organisations have loose and usually lateral reporting structures. This chapter posits that a non-hierarchical structure does not pose a threat to mutual organisations' survival or effective governance, because the underpinning principles of mutuality and trust hold individuals in the group together. This study examines the governance patterns of mutual organisations that provide SP services in the Western Region of Ghana.

- How do community-based mutual organisations, groups, and associations report their activities in a way that promotes accountability between the organisation's leadership and its members and beneficiaries?
- What factors drive the reporting systems and to what extent are members satisfied with the accountability mechanisms based on the nature of reporting?

The study was carried out in the Wassa area in the Western Region of Ghana. This chapter presents keynotes of that larger study conducted in 2013.

Accountability mechanisms in community-based mutual aid organisations

Accountability is an obligation to report on one's activities to a set of legitimate authorities. It is a control system by which officials or leaders declare and justify their plans of action, behaviour and results, and are sanctioned accordingly (Ackerman, 2004: 3). State and large business corporations have visible organisational structures characterised by clear roles and responsibilities, chains of hierarchy, impersonal relationships between individuals in the organisation, and formal communication channels. Such structures are fuzzy and informal in community-based mutual aid organisations in Ghana and much of Africa. Many provide SP services based on the principles of mutuality, cooperation, and trust.

The principles of mutuality and cooperation are the oldest of all strategies for solving collective action problems; they are arguably the very origin and definition of human society (Murray, 2012). In a liberal democratic system, citizens elect government and leaders to make public decisions regarding provision of public goods and services on their behalf. This includes the use of taxes to finance provisions. Thus policymakers become agents of the citizens. When dissatisfied with the performance of elected officials, citizens can vote them out. Mutual organisations, on the other hand, provide services to their members and work mainly on the basis of mutuality, trust, and stewardship – not the principal-agent relationship. If a member is dissatisfied with the performance or accountability of the organisation, s/he can withdraw personal membership – essentially vote himself/herself out. Mutuality is built around the traditional notion of reciprocity in social support service and has become popular in diverse policy settings (Mead, 1997; Ramia and Carney, 2010).

The accountability mechanisms of NSAs are a good basis for analysing the internal dynamics that facilitate the governance of such organisations. In the view of Norton, Conway, and Foster (2001), mutuality thrives on strong social networks, which are the basis on which small-scale mutual groups are formed. They are centred on factors such as kinship, community, religion, or occupation. Equally important is the principle of reciprocity, which is built around collective solidarity. At the community level, operations are usually guided by a common goal and relatively loose structure. Is that, or is it not, a formula for weak accountability?

Formal organisations systemize documentation of their activities; they collect data on the use of resources and the rationale for decision making, and provide feedback to members and clients. That's how they record, remember, and report. Informal mutual organisations rarely use written documents and rely instead on oral/face-to-face mechanisms to record, remember, and report – with the consensus bound by the principles of mutuality, trust, and reciprocity.

Non-state social protection actors in Wassa

NSAs, even by name, are defined by what they are not rather than specifically as what they are. This study defines them by the Cotonou Agreement (2000) concept of "an array of actors in development outside governments." Specifically, Article 6 defines NSAs as "the private sector and all social and economic partners, including trade union organisations, the civil society of all ramifications, and its diversity according to national characteristics". Thus NSAs include actors such as community-based organisations (CBOs), women's groups, human rights associations, non-governmental organisations (NGOs), religious organisations, farmers' cooperatives, trade unions, and private sector (Oguyemi, Tella, and Venditto, 2005).

This study was conducted in five districts of Wassa: Tarkwa Nsuaem Municipality, Wassa Amenfi East, Wassa Amenfi Central, Wassa Amenfi West, and Wassa East. The Wassa enclave of the Western Region, with its Tarkwa Nsuaem at its centre, presents a wealth of opportunities to examine the subject of accountability of NSAs in SP for one main reason: the area is well-endowed with natural resources including gold, diamonds, bauxite, and forest products such as cocoa, timber, and oil palm, with the consequent presence of wealthy corporate, individual, and multi-lateral institutions. Yet it is also an area where poverty and vulnerability are endemic. The presence of extractive industries that use unskilled labour provides opportunities for all sorts of people to migrate there in search of jobs. It also presents a fertile area for labour exploitation. Given the limited reach of the state, there are many NSAs including mutual self-help organisations that provide diverse SP services to vulnerable households and community groups.

The study mapped the number of NSAs operating in the area at 635 in the five districts. Some 68 per cent of them operate at the community level, meaning their services do not go beyond the boundaries of the communities in which they operate. Their services can be grouped under livelihoods, child rights, environmental, health, education, and other welfare provisions. More than half the NSAs provide livelihood or "promotive" SP – mostly in agriculture, animal husbandry, and poultry farming. Welfare services or "protective" SPs are their second-highest priority. These services include social support systems during birth and death of a community member. This appears to be an inversion of the traditional "protective" first, "promotive" later.

The study sampled 66 mutual organisations relating to livelihoods and child protection for in-depth analysis (see Table 3.1).

Table 3.1 Breakdown of mutual organisations selected for the in-depth analysis

Non-state actors	Number sampled	%
Faith-based organisation (FBO)	10	15.2
Social club	22	33.3
Occupational welfare association	14	21.2
Farmer-based association	5	7.6
Development association	4	6.0
Non-governmental organisation	11	16.7
Total	**66**	**100**

Source: Field data 2013

The NSAs sampled are mutual aid organisations because their members recognise the need to support each other in times of need. They also reach out to other community members when they face difficulties. Since community-based mutual organisations operate largely at the micro-level, their governance structures, communication methods, and accountability mechanisms were examined through the lens of their members.

Governance structures of non-state actors

Eighty-three per cent of NSAs identified in the study have never been formally registered with the Registrar General's Department, Department of Social Welfare, or the District Assembly. More than three-quarters of NSAs were fairly young, having been formed between 2000 and 2012. Although Ghana experienced economic growth averaging more than 5 per cent per year over this period, the parallel growth of self-help mechanisms suggest the benefits of national growth have not been inclusive. Poverty levels are worse in rural areas than in urban. Rural livelihoods have not seen much economic or structural transformation (Olumuyiwa, Du, and Opoku-Afari, 2013).

Of the 12,000 NSAs that were registered with the Registrar General's Department as of November 2012, only 700 have renewed their status with the Department of Social Welfare. While this could mean that many have collapsed, the key explanation is that many NSAs do not bother to regularize their status with the state regulatory agency. A few NSAs have well-defined boards of directors, organisational structure, and membership regulations, but the substantial majority do not have well-defined systems of operation, management, minutes of meetings, reports, by-laws, or constitutions.

Patterns of reporting among community-based mutual aid associations

The study examined each group's internal structures and systems for reporting, record keeping, and feedback to members. Verbal reporting was twice as prevalent as written reporting (see Table 3.2)

The frequency of verbal reports to members ranges from weekly, monthly, and quarterly to sometimes yearly. These reports centre on income and expenditure, as well as key activities undertaken during the period. These periodic meetings also enable members to interact with the management and take major decisions concerning the association.

> The leadership of the association provides verbal reports to members regularly; we have never had written reports since we started the association. We all understand each other and there is nobody to write anything.
> (FGD Participant, Wassa East District, 7/5/2013)

> Oh, we just tell them what we have done over the period when we meet. Everybody believes what we say because there are visible actions and outputs on what we use the association's or members' contribution for.
> (FGD Participant, Wassa East District, 7/5/2013)

Predictably, formal written reporting was universal among NGOs, which are perforce registered and have formal hierarchies of leadership, management structures, and reporting systems that all include accountability.

Table 3.2 Forms of reporting

Type of NSA	Number	Formal written report (%)	Informal verbal report (%)
Faith-based organization	10	20	80
Social club	22	31.8	68.1
Occupational welfare association, excluding farming	14	28.6	71.4
Farmer-based association	5	0	100
Development association	4	25	75
Non-governmental organization	11	100	0
Total	**66**	**34.2%**	**65.8%**

Source: Field data, 2013

Perhaps more significant than their 100 per cent on written reporting was their 0 per cent on verbal briefing of (often illiterate) people for whom they exist to support.

Only one in three informal NSAs indicated, with evidence, that they kept financial records and had files for activities. The rest did not have readily retrievable records; some depend on leadership or collective membership memory. Limited educational capacity was a prime factor.

The study tried to examine financial reporting practices, but data was not readily available and sometimes the leadership was reluctant to divulge financial information. Where information was available, NGOs could show proper bookkeeping, financial statements, and even audited reports. The mutual aid organisations had membership cards in which contributions were recorded, but there was no indication of written financial reports. The leadership provides income and expenditure balances to members at regular meetings.

Drivers of reporting patterns among mutual aid organisations

The study sought to understand the underpinning factors that drive the persistence of both reporting formats, especially the oral type. The literature suggests that greater transparency and accountability in mutual organisations will improve sustainability and service delivery to members/beneficiaries (Edwards, 2002; Ackerman, 2004; Henke, Kelsey and Whately, 2011). Transparency in this sense also includes regular reporting of activities.

Affinity and solidarity

The members of mutual associations have close affinity to each other, which strengthens the trust they have for their leadership. In times of need, the entire group rallies behind the affected member to ensure that he/she is protected. A beneficiary noted during a focus group discussion that

> we came together to form this club and we make sure we support each other in times of need. I was supported financially and materially when I lost my father. My friend here was also supported when he was marrying. Several of our members have received various forms of support and we make sure that we meet regularly to promote the interest of the group.
>
> (FGD respondent, Tarkwa-Nsuaem Municipal)

This sense of affinity is even more intense among some FBOs, especially those linked to established churches in the communities. The desire to be "each other's keeper" is manifest. This tends to overshadow the seemingly weak informal reporting that is associated with community-based mutual aid groups. They are judged by the function they perform and not the structural or reporting format that they adopt. It is therefore not surprising from analysis of the data that in 60 per cent of cases, it is individuals who are either members of the organisation or non-members who apply for support and not the mutual organisations that identify the needy. An elderly woman who had benefitted from one of the mutual groups that her late husband used to subscribe to noted,

> When my husband passed away, I was in dire need of money so I called on the group for support. I know that the group has the tradition of supporting each other in times of crisis so I was confident that they would come to my aid. They provided financial support that helped me a lot.
>
> (FGD participant, Wassa East District)

Paperwork is not their priority

Literacy levels are a key factor in the rather loose reporting among informal NSAs. About 35 per cent of members had no formal education, or at best some primary education, and 45.8 per cent had not progressed beyond Ghana's equivalent of middle or junior high school. Education is relatively higher among male members. For example, 25.5 per cent of the females had no formal education compared to 10.2 per cent of their male counterparts; 53.7 per cent of males had attained middle/junior high education compared with 43.3 per cent of females. Some 7.4 per cent of males had university education compared with 2.8 per cent of females To some extent, the level of education of the members is consistent with their occupations. They are mainly in the informal sector such as farming, petty trading, and artisan.

It is not surprising that the majority of mutual aid groups accept oral reporting, even on matters relating to finance. Even those that provide written reports do so on an irregular basis. While the principles of affinity and solidarity built around mutuality and trust drive the nature of reporting, the low level of literacy should be recognised as a major contributory factor. Focus group members noted that paperwork was not their priority. One participant who seemed to be speaking for the consensus said,

> We are satisfied with the way things are done in the group; we discuss almost all issues, and whenever somebody needs to be supported, our

leaders call us together. We don't speak your big English (referring to the study team); we understand ourselves, and so we do what we can do to support ourselves.

(FGD participant, Tarkwa-Nsuaem Municipal)

Accountability is about meeting people's needs

Community-based mutual organisations are formed by a critical mass of members who live in the community and who have a common interest and goal. Thus members determine how they operate, their sources of funding, and their intended activities. It is therefore not surprising that an overwhelming majority (94 per cent) of respondents indicated that their organisations met their needs. Most highly rate the timeliness, appropriateness, and effectiveness of the services they receive.

Their modus operandi requires the active involvement of members, and this influences the pattern of reporting. Members have sufficient knowledge of what goes on in the group that they do not need to insist on written reports. They assume that such reports will only repeat what they already know. Activities and transactions are too few to cause confusion or challenge memory.

Penny wise: no need to spend money on writing down the obvious

Funding is a crucial governance and accountability issue among NSAs. Most are funded through membership contributions (60.7 per cent). Other sources include special offerings and fundraising events, funding from local partners, and rarely from government support. External funding from international partners or bank loans is negligible.

So self-help attitudes can generate self-funding to provide services. In the study area, funding levels were low but most organisations were able to meet the essential needs of members and other beneficiary groups. As members' contributions constitute the main source of funding and members are involved in the decision-making processes and have a common goal, they accept the nature of reporting. There appears to be no need to spend money hiring somebody to write reports on obvious issues that members are aware of and can readily remember.

Conclusion and policy implications

Community-based mutual aid associations' reporting systems are generally informal and verbal. This format thrives in organisations that operate on the principles of mutuality, trust, and reciprocity among common-goal members. Another important factor is the low level of literacy among members. The key finding of the in-depth analysis of 66 mutual aid organisations is that members participate in decision making and understand every element of the organisation. With limited funding from membership contributions, these organisations are prudent in the use of their resources, so they do not spend money to hire somebody to write up information their members already know.

The predominance of informal reporting has implications for accountability. The study shows that the use of trust as a measure of accountability is still valid among mutual aid organisations whose members mostly cannot read and write. If governance is defined as a means by which social coordination is achieved, then it is important that mutual trust is seen as "good-fit governance" because it enables informal groups to organise and meet their members' needs. Thus, irrespective of the nature and form of informal NSAs' accountability structures, their legitimacy is not questionable, at least in the eyes of their immediate beneficiaries. Nevertheless, trust must be upheld, and where structures for upholding trust fail, the group could be severely affected.

Bigger organisations that could give substantial support to small community groups invariably insist on formal accountability mechanisms with independent verification. So governments, external organisations, and formal development partners are reluctant to support mutual aid organisations that practice only oral reporting. External organisations keen to support community-based mutual aid groups may consider capacity building to enhance record keeping, but care should be taken to ensure that such support does not distract these organisations from their main goals and trust-based ethos.

References

Ackerman, John. (2004). *Social Accountability for the Public Sector: A Conceptual Discussion*. Draft paper prepared for the World Bank.

African Union. (2010). *Declaration on Social Policy Action Towards Social Inclusion*. Draft, 2nd Session of the AU Conference of Ministers for Social Development, 21–25 November, Khartoum, Sudan.

Bassett, Lucy; Giannozzi, Sara; Pop, Lucian; and Ringold, Dena. (2012). *Rules, Roles, and Controls: Governance in Social Protection with an Application to Social Assistance*. Background Paper for the World Bank 2012–2022 Social Protection and Labor Strategy March 2012. Retrieved from: www.worldbank.org

Edwards, Michael. (2002). *NGO Rights and Responsibilities: A New Deal for Global Governance*. London: The Foreign Policy Centre.

Ellis, F.; Devereux, S.; and White, P. (2009). *Social Protection in Africa*. Cheltenham: Edward Elgar Publishing.

Henke, N.; Kelsey, T.; and Whately, H. (2011). Transparency: The Most Powerful Driver of Health Care Improvement? *Health International*, Report No. 11, McKinsey Health Systems and Services Practice.

Holzmann, R., and Jorgensen, S. (2000). *Social Risk Management: A New Conceptual Framework for Social Protection*. Social Protection Discussion Paper No. 0006, The World Bank, Washington DC.

International Labour Organization (ILO). (2011). *Social Protection Floors for Social Justice and a Fair Globalisation*. Report IV (1), 101st Session of ILO, Geneva.

International Labour Organization (ILO). (2012). *Social Security for All Building Social Protection Floors and Comprehensive Social Security Systems: The Strategy of the International Labour Organization*. Geneva: ILO.

Kumado, K., and Gockel, A. (2003). *A Study on Social Security in Ghana*. Ghana: Accra, Trades Union Congress.

Mead, L. M. (1997). *The new paternalism: Supervisory approaches to poverty*. London: Jessica Kingsley Publishers.

Murray, Robin. (2012). *The New Wave of Mutuality: Social Innovation and Public Sector Reform*. Policy Network Paper. Retrieved from: www.policy-network.net

Norton, A.; Conway, T.; and Foster, M. (2001). *Social Protection Concepts and Approaches: Implications for Policy and Practice in International Development*. Centre for Aid and Public Expenditure, Working Paper No.143. London: Overseas Development Institute.

Oguyeni, B.; Tella, S.; and Venditto, B. (2005). *Non State Actors Under the Current ACP-EU Cooperation Agreement: A Sectoral Review of the Nigerian Context*. An ISSM Working Paper.

Olumuyiwa, S. Adedeji; Du, Huancheng; and Opoku-Afari, Maxwell. (2013). *Inclusive Growth: An Application of the Social Opportunity Functions to Selected Countries*. Working Paper 13/139, International Monetary Fund.

Osei-Boateng, C., and Ampratwum, E. (2011). *The Informal Sector in Ghana*. New Delhi: Friedrick Ebert Stiftung. Retrieved from: http://library.fes.de/pdf-files/bueros/ghana/10496.pdf

Ramia, G., and Carney, T. (2010). "The Rudd Government's Employment Services Agenda: Is it Post-NPM and Why is that Important?" *Australian Journal of Public Administration*, 69 (3): 263–273.

Risse, Thomas. (2011). "Governance in Areas of Limited Statehood: Introduction and Overview". In Thomas Risse (ed.), *Governance Without a State? Policies and Politics in Areas of Limited Statehood*. New York: Columbia University Press, pp. 1–35.

4 Social protection and citizenship rights of vulnerable children

A perspective on interventions by non-state actors in western Kenya

Auma Okwany and Elizabeth Ngutuku

Introduction

The Constitution of Kenya (Republic of Kenya, 2010) guarantees all citizens the right to social security and commits the state to make appropriate provision to those who are unable to support themselves and/or their dependents. The rights include social protection (SP), health care, decent working conditions, and justice. While these are citizen "entitlements", in practice they are either negotiated between the state and citizens or mediated by civil society organisations. In the governance of limited statehood (Risse, 2011), the state is unable to deliver all the rights because of inadequate resources or inadequate policy support. This creates an entitlement void in Kenya as in many African countries. Limited state provisioning of SP services means that non-state actors (NSAs), many based at the community level, are safety nets of first, or only, resort for the poor who are unable to get access to constitutionally guaranteed services. Most especially in the case of services to protect vulnerable children, these community-based NSA services need to go beyond being "preventive" and "protective" and become "transformative"; not only palliative but also addressing the structural roots of child vulnerability.

Citizenship is construed in its legal significance, symbolic meaning, claims, responsibilities, and practice (Cammett and Maclean, 2011). This chapter posits that SP that is responsive to children and their caregivers "as a right" will

- expand children's citizenship;
- anchor the status of their rights and entitlements;
- promote a broader transformative agenda (Devereux and Sabates-Wheeler, 2004).

Conversely, if the ethos underpinning SP is viewed and delivered as charity, then it will disempower vulnerable groups by denying them active voice and participation.

This would degrade the social contract between the state and its citizens. Kenya is grappling with general insecurity, weak economic structure and transformation, increasing conflict and terrorism, rapid urbanisation, and high prevalence of HIV/AIDS (KNCHR, 2014; Lieten, 2015; UNICEF, 2014; Oxfam, 2009). These adversities interact to intensify children's vulnerability. Drawing on empirical evidence from a yearlong study on child vulnerability in Western Kenya, this chapter examines the range of services that community-based NSAs provide and interrogates the governance and accountability structures of these organisations with regard to the citizenship rights of vulnerable children.

The study was carried out over a year in Kisumu, Siaya, and Kakamega counties (Okwany and Ngutuku, 2014), which were selected because they suffer high child vulnerability levels and a proliferation of NSAs that are compensating for limited state outreach. For instance, the HIV prevalence rate is about 29 per cent in Kakamega and 30–40 per cent in Siaya. The national average is 6.7 per cent.

The study identified 501 NSAs providing SP services in the three counties and carried out an in-depth study among purposively selected community-based interventions that provide child-focused[1] services. Of the total NSAs mapped, 195 provided SP services for children at the community level. Of these, 49 were selected for in-depth analysis that included interviews with selected beneficiaries on the impact of interventions.

Child rights, citizenship, and social protection

Demographically, Africa is the youngest continent with 44 per cent of the population below 15 years of age and 70 per cent under 30 years (Ensor, 2012). Yet there is a stark discrepancy between the rhetoric of young people's importance and the reality of their lives. Children are at a higher risk because they are not independent economic actors and rely on the distribution of resources within their households or communities. They are socially subordinate. As noted by Gittins (1998: 45), "children are born into webs of power relations and of discourse and narratives". This relational vulnerability is a factor of their life-cycle positioning. This is compounded by their lack of voice in households and intervention policy.

In 2008, the African Child Policy Forum (ACPF) ranked Kenya first among all African countries for its efforts to establish an appropriate legal and policy framework for children (ACPF, 2008: 1). Kenya is creating a unified policy framework, adopting crucial reforms, and growing investments in the SP sector (GoK, 2012: 2). The state has implemented programmes in agriculture, health, nutrition, and education with social assistance, social security, and health insurance. Child-specific programmes include targeted

Social protection and citizenship rights 57

cash transfer for orphaned and vulnerable children (CT-OVC) and school feeding programmes, and the state has expanded the Free Primary Education Policy of 2003 and a Free Secondary Education Policy since 2008. Other programmes include government-devolved funds, targeted health programmes, and fee waivers in public hospitals for children below five years of age. The Bill of Rights in the new Constitution 2010 enshrines the right to social security and the National Social Protection Policy articulates a vision for progressively delivering this entitlement.

Despite these advances, there are still major gaps and inherent weaknesses in multidimensional support of vulnerable children. The lack of a universal SP programme means current interventions are narrowly selective and incapable of dealing with the scale of challenges for vulnerable children. Non-state interventions are trying to fill the developmental space.

Kenya defines SP as "policies and actions aimed at enhancing the capacity and opportunities for the poor and vulnerable to improve their livelihoods and welfare" (GoK, 2011: 2). SP strengthens the contract between the state and citizens. However, acknowledging SP as a right is one thing, ensuring that it is delivered is another. This requires a transformative agenda which, according to Devereux and Sabates-Wheeler (2004), promotes social justice by ensuring equity and empowerment.

Childhood is not a singular "construct". It varies by gender, class, geographic location, over time, and, as noted by Montgomery (2008: 3), it must be "defined internally and in its own context". Childhood is also subject to politics at local, national, and international levels. Parents, society, state, and interventions influence the way in which children are provided for and engaged. Children are "beings" – already people in their own right – but there is a disproportionate policy emphasis framing them as "becomings" (adults in the making). This locates their citizenship in the future so their "now" voices are muted in policy and practice (Coady, 2008; Cheney, 2008; Okwany, 2009). Children's subordinate position means adults' ideas about childhood constrain their agency and voice, and, as noted by Lister (2003: 433), the significance of their current experiences of poverty is neglected. Adequate SP is thus not only a right but also a fundamental prerequisite for reducing child vulnerability and a means for enhancing citizenship.

According to Manning and Ryan (2004), citizenship can be viewed in two ways: in the legal and formal sense of rights and responsibilities, including SP rights, and in the broader and more substantive sense of participation, access, and involvement in political and socio-economic life. This study draws on the citizenship definition of Tilly (1995), which is useful for assessing young people's daily lives. He views citizenship on a continuum ranging from "thin" citizenship with limited rights, entitlements, and interactions to "thick" citizenship where rights and interactions between states and subjects are strong and well established. Children's subordinate relational status means they are a constrained agency and have thin citizenship. SP requires a focus on downward accountability so that beneficiaries – including children – can hold providers, including the state, accountable and can negotiate or even demand inclusion in SP programmes if they feel underserved or unjustly excluded. For children, vulnerability has social and subjective dimensions beyond material aspects. Social vulnerabilities are fertile ground for children's deliberate abuse and exclusion.

Social relations should be the starting point for any intervention, and young people's voices should be paramount. This is consistent with the notion of inclusive citizenship (Lister, 2007: 4), with its emphasis on the voice and action of marginalized groups such as young people. Ellis et al. (2008) point out the need to move beyond the "why'" and focus on the "how" of SP. This chapter highlights the importance of a child-focused analysis and intra-household dynamics.

Responding to the needs of vulnerable children: community-based non-state actor interventions

Community-based NSAs provide a range of intervention services that respond to child vulnerability. While some of the services are integrated – especially for children who are sponsored by a particular organisation or those in children's orphanages or rescue centres – the study reveals that in many cases the services are provided separately. Children reported receiving services from more than one organisation. Figure 4.1 shows the range of services provided by the interventions

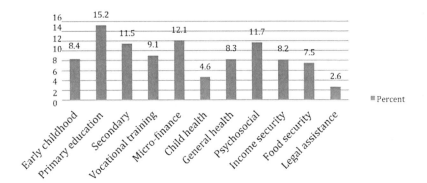

Figure 4.1 Range of services.

Education services

Despite government-supported free primary and universal secondary education in Kenya, non-government education support is one of the key services provided through self-help groups. Government's subsidies are for tuition fees only and do not cater for other direct costs including feeding programmes, purchase of uniforms, transport, levies, and scholastic materials, with dire implications for poor households. Some 45.7 per cent of caregivers noted that education support for their children was their greatest need.

One of the pivotal NSA services in the study sites was the school feeding programme, because hunger and undernourishment are key problems facing children from poor households. Indeed, 13.7 per cent of children and 25.7 per cent of caregivers noted that nutrition support was their greatest need. The feeding programme provides children with a hot meal once a day while at school and sometimes involves holding camps for children where they are provided with nutritious meals. School feeding is designed to enhance the well-being and performance of children in school in addition to improving their health, alertness, and concentration in class, thus reducing the rates of absenteeism.

Discussions with children indicate that this type of support has benefitted them and boosted their participation in school. As noted during interviews,

> Before . . ., my stomach was always rumbling and I could not concentrate in class.
> I wish all days were school days because I get food at school.

According to Devereux (2002), school feeding programmes aim to increase child enrolment and attendance as well as improve academic performance. The nutritional benefits for children are not guaranteed, as a child who is fed at school may forego a meal at home, where there might be children who do not go to school. Some children stated a preference to always attend school and said holidays and weekends were difficult because they did not get school food. This points to a need to combine school feeding with simultaneous household and general food security.

Children benefitting from the interventions are provided with a school uniform at the beginning of the year. Other materials provided include books, pens, and school bags. Some NSAs provide money for extra tuition for children lagging in performance. Some children receive school fees support from sponsoring organisations to supplement government partial subsidies for secondary education. Some organisations run their own fully fledged primary schools in which they offer learning services in line with the approved curriculum. Other self-help groups fully support early childhood development centres; they pay for teachers and feeding programmes as well as providing psychosocial support. Additionally, there are organisations supporting vocational training programmes.

In the study areas, training provided in vocational centres was gender stereotyped; the options available for girls included hairdressing and dressmaking, while boys chose from the more lucrative and marketable training in auto mechanics, carpentry, or masonry. Some 52 per cent of beneficiaries regarded educational support as a key benefit, and some reported that their academic performance had improved as a result of school-related support. The educational interventions are strengthening pathways to breaking the intergenerational cycle of poverty.

Education support is predicated on children's regular attendance and improved performance. Staff note that these conditions are open to abuse since some caregivers are colluding with head teachers to doctor academic results to attain or maintain eligibility. For children with disabilities, the prerequisites can be exclusionary. There is also a silent (and often false) assumption that education supply-side factors, such as availability of qualified teachers, facilities, and school amenities, are available to complement demand-side growth, but the larger study revealed that this is not the case. (Okwany and Ngutuku, 2014).

Health and psychosocial support

The study sites had high numbers of children affected by HIV/AIDS and very high dependency ratios. To address other child-health vulnerabilities, different organisations are providing insecticide-treated mosquito nets, vitamin A supplements, provision of UNIMIX (a nutritional supplement for underweight children), growth monitoring and promotion, water disinfection tablets, bar soap, and general medical care, including deworming and payment of medical bills.

These services are provided at home, at school, or at clinics, as well as in the communities. Some organisations help pay for children and their caregivers to travel to hospitals to obtain antiretroviral drugs for managing HIV/AIDS, and others support treatment of opportunistic infections. Other health-related services include training by community health workers on preventive health care. Children and caregivers reported positive benefits from community-based health support, but there was criticism of programmes which targeted only one child in a vulnerable household without parallel support for the rest of the household. There were cases where mosquito nets for children were repurposed to cover vegetable gardens. For the specific case of children affected by HIV/AIDS and their families, some organisations run post-test clubs where these families can share experiences and encourage one another as well as deal with the stigma that accompanies their status. In school, children are also involved in different clubs where they are given training in life skills and strategies for protecting themselves against HIV/AIDS.

Orphaned and vulnerable children face much trauma and stigma. Interventions are supporting them by providing counselling and psychosocial support services. Many orphaned and vulnerable children are seen as a burden by their caregivers, and in some cases, they are cared for by elderly people who may lack appropriate parenting skills. Community-based interventions target OVC caregivers and offer mentoring on childcare and psychosocial support for fostering and adoptive families. Children are also provided with resilience-building skills including guidance in starting and maintaining kitchen gardens and other small-scale, income-generating activities.

Micro-finance and livelihood enhancement activities to support children

Poverty levels in the study area (UN-Habitat, 2005, 2008; Moulidi, 2011), indicate 57 per cent prevalence in Siaya, 52 per cent in Kakamega, and 48 per cent in Kisumu. Unemployment levels are 5.2 per cent in Siaya, 6.3 per cent in Kakamega, and 8.2 per cent in Kisumu (KNBS and SID, 2013). In Kisumu, about 60 per cent of people live in informal settlements (UN-Habitat, 2005: 20). At the household level, about 33 per cent of the interviewees noted that economic insecurity was their greatest threat. To boost beneficiaries' incomes and strengthen the capacity of caregivers to support vulnerable children, intervention programmes are supporting income-generation activities (IGAs) including micro-finance and other livelihood strategies. Caregivers organise themselves into self-help groupings and pool resources in the form of village savings and loan schemes, rotational saving schemes ("merry-go-rounds"), and small-scale IGAs. Some of the self-help groups noted that in the past they received one-off funding from international or national NGOs as well as sporadic capacity-building support. In Kakamega, a self-help group called Ship of Sailors has supported more than 120 households since its inception and supports vulnerable children with school uniforms and school fees. Through payment of fines on members for late repayment of loans or penalties for late attendance at group meetings, the CBO has managed to get extra money to support the orphans in its care.

In Kisumu, the K'Okumu self-help group supports itself through enhancing its income and livelihood, and providing nutritional support and early education for vulnerable children. The Fathers Foundation group in the Lower Ambira Community Child Development Programme (LACCDP) in Siaya is challenging social stereotypes about gendered childcare by highlighting, reconfiguring, supporting, and stimulating the involvement of fathers in childcare and protection. The group is organised around social fatherhood, and older males are mentoring young fathers in childcare and support. They are also mobilising resources to provide food and scholastic materials from within their own resources.

In many cases, self-help groups are given an interest-free seed loan by an NGO or micro-finance organisation. All the informal groups have savings schemes where members pool money and share it rotationally among themselves each week. The groups also stipulate that each member has to save. The money can be loaned to members at preferential interest rates. Members use the money to generate income by engaging in small-scale business activities such as operating kiosks, selling vegetables in the market, or selling fish. Members exert peer pressure on one another to enhance repayment of loans and ensure the money is spent on IGAs. In a few cases, the NSA's have their own IGAs such as hiring out tents and chairs, providing mobile money transfer services, and hiring office space. A network of women's activities in Siaya – the Kind Women for Development Organisation – purchased tents and chairs and use the rental income to sustain their support of early childhood education centres (including teachers' salaries and a feeding programme). Other IGAs include sugar cane farming, horticulture, dairy farming, poultry keeping, piggeries, goat keeping, tree nurseries, water vending, and commodities trading. Beneficiaries and programme staff noted that members use earnings to provide for their families and for the needs of the children they are supporting. These organisations also conduct training to empower vulnerable youth on entrepreneurship and small business management skills.

NSA services help improve nutrition, especially when dealing with households and communities that are heavily affected by HIV/AIDS. However, increased food production does not always translate into improved food access, especially for the poorer sections of society. The food security objective is therefore often pursued in tandem with income security. Improved food production can be a means to boost household incomes through the sale of agricultural produce in local markets. It enables households to access better nutrition, especially in HIV/AIDS-affected households where patients are supposed to take ARVs while observing stringent dietary regimens. In Kakamega, an NSA was involved in the provision of social and financial education with the goal of inculcating a savings culture in children. Their activities aim to teach young people social and financial literacy skills as well as why and how to save for future use.

Support for income sustainability is therefore building the self-capability of caregivers. A number of secondary beneficiaries (caregivers) affirmed that support with income generation improved the well-being of their children.

A caregiver in Kisumu noted the positive effect of improved income and food security:

> I could not stand before the community before because I was like an outcast, I had nothing and I was shunned and marginalized but my participation in this project has enabled me to interact with other people.
>
> (Caregiver, Kisumu)

These changes can therefore be used as proxies for the improved bargaining power of caregivers, most of whom are women.

> We used to rely on money from our husbands but now we have a voice in the household; he brings money, I also bring money so we both have a voice.
>
> (FGD, caregivers Kisumu)

However, because of its small-scale nature, income support does not adequately meet the multidimensional needs of vulnerable households. A more comprehensive and holistic approach is needed. Indeed, about 31 per cent of beneficiaries noted that support from one organisation was not adequate to meet their needs, so they subscribe to more than one group.

Legal support

Vulnerable children are susceptible to physical, social, and psychological abuse as well as the risk of being disinherited by avaricious relatives. Discrimination is an idiosyncratic risk and therefore many interventions are engaged in advocacy to protect children. Some organisations provide legal aid against such abuse and exploitation and also link children with the department of children's services for support. The study findings reveal that a handful of community-based NSAs are involved in addressing the legal and human rights concerns of widows, orphans, and other vulnerable groups especially in relation to property inheritance and ownership. Only one NGO provided legal advice on health and HIV-related human rights issues. Widows, who are the majority of caregivers, face threats of dispossession and displacement by relatives after the death of their husbands. Organisations providing legal advice take up clients who directly seek their services or those referred by partner NSAs with a grassroots presence and networks.

Other support includes helping clients to use Alternative Dispute Resolution (ADR) mechanisms. Organisations use existing structures – including clan elders and other local leaders – to boost the right to access and to own and inherit property. In cases where displacement has already taken place, widows and vulnerable children are assisted with resettlement. Where such mechanisms fail, court action is pursued. Court action presents some risks of stigma from family and community members who may not take kindly to the prosecution of their kin.

Institutional care

About 15 per cent of child-focused NSAs provide orphanages and child rescue centres. Street children and others dislocated from their families were the most numerous beneficiaries. As a legal requirement, these children are placed in a children's home through a court order and through collaboration with the Department of Children's Services. Study findings revealed that a lack of rigorous oversight from state institutions means some centres recruit some children without proper commitment documents. Many institutions lacked transparency and were very wary of granting the research team access for fear that they were going to be evaluated. Many might contend that government involvement is less a way to avoid cheating and more a way to be cheated. The in-depth study revealed that because some institutions based in one community draw their clientele from dispersed communities, secondary beneficiaries such as caregivers may not be available to participate and provide community-level oversight.

Governance characteristics of community-based, child-focused interventions

The governance and accountability for most community-based interventions of any kind are informal, with unwritten rules and flexible leadership arrangements devoid of hierarchy but nevertheless able to define rules of engagement adhered to by trust. To control fraud and ensure proper management, all decisions about finances are made during group meetings, and consensus is obtained on how to spend funds. For groups operating savings and loan schemes, the fraud controls are more stringent with cash boxes having three padlocks and with keys kept by different group members, excluding the treasurer. This ensures that consent to draw savings has to be obtained from at least four members. For bank withdrawals, each group has two or three signatories, all required for any withdrawal. Monitoring and evaluation are organised around assigning responsibilities to different members. For example, the Fathers Foundation group in Siaya has different committees responsible for oversight to ensure that group activities such as IGAs, food security, and support to vulnerable children are carried out as agreed by the group. Similarly, the Kind Women for Development group in Siaya has different committees that supervise activities to ensure smooth operation. Activities include early childhood services (a daily nutritious meal, school uniform, adequate care in school, and supporting teachers' salaries and learning materials).

Beneficiaries' assessment of the impact of intervention programmes

Overall, the services provided by NSAs are helping to alleviate child vulnerability and support poor households providing childcare. The survey of 600 beneficiaries asked them to assess the impact that intervention programmes had on their lives and their children. Most beneficiaries felt they were better off, sometimes much better off. However, in-depth discussions revealed limits (see Figure 4.2).

The support beneficiaries receive is small scale, so the impact on poverty situations, however positive, is perforce limited. For example, 39.8 per cent of the caregivers live in households with four to six members and 31.8 per cent in households with seven to eight members. A majority of caregivers (73 per cent) were women, and 70.8 per cent were household heads. It is questionable if the support caregivers receive from better-resourced NSAs, such as NGOs, is making a significant contribution to lifting them out of poverty. Discussions with children indicate that their voices are largely absent in decisions about what is provided or how. About 31.5 per cent of the children noted that they wanted to complain about the services being provided to them but were afraid of repercussions.

> My sponsor sent my school uniform to the school but the headmaster kept on denying this and nothing was done about it, even after I complained three times.
>
> (Male, primary school beneficiary)

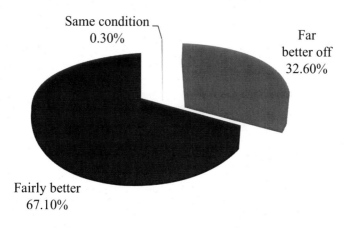

Figure 4.2 Impact of interventions.

Sometimes I am expecting to get particular support, but then I don't get it and nobody explains; I don't tell anybody but I just remain disappointed.

(Female, primary school beneficiary)

Interventions need to involve young people more actively, and adults should be aware there is space for young people to air their views and be key agents in programmes, not just passive recipients.

Many beneficiaries (45.6 per cent) said they typically welcome whoever comes to give them support. About a quarter of the beneficiaries receive support from more than one NSA, ranging from local to national or international NGOs.

Conclusions: social protection and securing citizenship rights

Community-based SP organisations and groups are promoting child well-being through "horizontal philanthropy", but they are clearly overstretching their resources without external support. Many community-group interventions depend on members' contributions in fees, fines, and penalties for not conforming to unwritten rules. That adds up to "small" funds to support their activities. Those who cannot meet or sustain the criteria for membership are forced to exit the group, and their households are rendered more vulnerable. Informal interventions can therefore be exclusionary for low-capacity or incapacitated households, including elderly caregivers or child-headed households – the very people SP is supposed to help most. As noted by Ezemenari et al. (2002: 30), informal transfers and networks, while rendering vital help to some, may also reinforce existing patterns of poverty by maintaining existing economic and social barriers along ethnic, gender, class, and generational lines.

Community-based interventions also have limited outreach and lack the structural accountability for large-scale support. So while their efforts are preventive and protective, they are largely palliative and cannot address the many interlinked causes and consequences of child vulnerability. As noted by Samoff (2007), it is only the state that has the institutional capacity to provide for all. In a limited state, augmented by limited NSAs, exiting poverty remains a dream, and many people's reality is no more than survival. NSA interventions are safety nets of first resort. They are not ruptured, but they remain safety nets "with holes", Baylies (2002: 622), and we add stretched holes, overextended and limited in outreach. In the long run, these efforts cannot transform the structural forces that underpin child vulnerability. Drawing on study evidence, the poor helping the poor cannot sustainably, or universally, relieve, much less cure, profound need. Many poor households and communities do not feel the impact of the state in their lives at all. This raises questions about the sort of social contract that exists between citizens and the state.

SP is a right for all citizens, including children, and the state has the ultimate authority – and responsibility – to assure that right. However, the study reveals that the dominant philosophy underpinning child-focused non-state SP is charity. Beneficiaries, including children, cannot demand their rights or accountability from providers.

The state has been unable to fulfil its obligations adequately and has in many contexts ceded this role to NSAs. The state can, therefore, be said to have entered into an informal "trustee" relationship with NSAs. In providing different services to vulnerable children and their caregivers, the NSA interventions can be said to be "surrogates" for the state's social contract with citizens.

In supporting vulnerable children, the traditional, local, and community-based bulwark is central, not peripheral. This suggests an interesting notion of citizenship itself: "communities" are de facto citizens of the state, and individuals are citizens of their local community. Indeed, membership in local community groups is where resources for SP come from and where people feel they belong.

That is not an impossible construct, but it means a state which cannot fulfil its obligation to every individual citizen is arguably obliged to honour the constitutional pledge to every community citizen by building the capacity of community-based interventions to enable them to offer effective support to individuals including vulnerable children.

The challenge then is who should build/enhance that community capacity in a context where NGOs provide most of the technical support. Delegating this responsibility to formal NSAs has the potential to deprive community organisations of their identity and distinctiveness – the very individuality and informality that helps them thrive. The state must therefore lead representation of its own "community citizens" and help them fix their collective weaknesses without impairing their unique individual strengths.

NSAs, both formal and informal, take what Tendler (2002: 119) terms a "projectised and micronized" approach to social development. While research reveals that – to at least a better-than-nothing extent – the support given to targeted children meets their SP needs, the project approach taken by these interventions means that support is piecemeal and provided at a very micro-level. This parcel provisioning (ibid) does not adequately address the multidimensionality of children's material, social, and relational vulnerability, and needs to be more integrated. The projectised approach is attributable to funding arrangements and suggests a need to focus on a systems approach instead. This, as noted by Nyamu-Musembi and Cornwall (2004), would embrace the multiple dimensions of child vulnerability by cushioning the impacts of shocks and stresses on households and reducing poverty. It would also ensure that specific localised risks are addressed. While individual NSAs might not accomplish this, NSAs working together might succeed. Linkages would enable the creation of a critical mass of resources that would be complementary to state services by reducing targeting errors, increasing coverage, and addressing child poverty more holistically

There is also need to ensure downward accountability, from initial conceptualisation of needs to implementation and monitoring. This means that the voices of the caregivers and children themselves, as well as their citizenship actions, should be given precedence over funding modalities. It is important to ensure that the support provided meets articulated and not assumed needs of beneficiaries and is of a desired quality. This can be achieved through several methods including signing up to of Codes of Conduct and accountability charters with beneficiary communities. According to Biekart and Fowler (2013), this would especially make formal NSAs cede some of their sovereignty in exchange for the collective value of compliance with negotiated standards. The MV Foundation, a local NGO in India, has succeeded in ensuring accountability by signing mutual commitments with communities in elimination of child labour and universalisation of education.

In the wake of the AIDS orphan crisis, some analysts argued that the informal social safety net of the extended family in Africa has ruptured and can no longer provide adequate support to vulnerable children. The efforts of community-based interventions witnessed in this study counter this simplistic assessment. According to Mathambo and Gibbs (2008), Okwany et al (2009) families and households, like other social institutions, are not static entities but are dynamic and do change and adapt when faced with a shock (Abebe and Aase, 2007). This study presents evidence of community-based NSAs, many of which receive no external support, providing a raft of SP services to vulnerable children. Wilkinson-Maphosa et al. (2005) highlight the multidimensionality of philanthropy by distinguishing between vertical resource transmission (external support and resources to communities, also called philanthropy *for* the poor) and horizontal transmission, or philanthropy *of* the poor as exhibited by these groups. These interventions in the form of self-help and kin-based groups, most of which are loosely organised, do have basic accountability and micro-governance rules that members adhere to based on mutuality, reciprocity, and trust. They provide risk and vulnerability coping mechanisms *ex ante* to avert risk or mitigate its possible effects *ex post* to cope with the effects.

Ultimately, enhancing citizenship of children through SP is a right, and beneficiaries, including children, should lay a claim to it.

A citizenship approach – rather than a client-based approach – to SP includes the progressive building of sustainable structures and capabilities of individuals and groups. The process starts by making them aware of their rights and entitlements, enabling them to claim those rights, and supporting the delivery (by duty bearers) of those rights. While it cannot be argued that the interventions have entirely succeeded in accomplishing this, their activities are a vital step in realising children's citizenship rights to SP.

Note

1 A child was conceptualised in this research in the age brackets 0–14 years.

References

Abebe, T., and Aase, A. (2007). Children, AIDS and the Politics of Orphan Care in Ethiopia: The Extended Family Revisited. *Social Science and Medicine*, 64: 2058–2069.

African Child Policy Forum. (2008). *The African Report on Child Wellbeing: How child-friendly are African Governments?* Addis Ababa: The African Child Policy Forum.

Biekart, K., and Fowler, A. (2013). *Relocating Civil Society in a Politics of Civic Driven Change*, manuscript submitted to Development Policy Review.

Cammett, M. Claire, and MacLean, Lauren M. (2011). Introduction: The Political Consequences of Non-state Social Welfare in the Global South. *Studies in Comparative International Development*, 46 (1): 1–21.

Cheney, K. (2008). *Pillars of the Nation: Child Citizens and Ugandan National Development*. Chicago: University of Chicago Press.

Coady, M. (2008). "Beings and Becomings: Historical and Philosophical Considerations of the Child as Citizen". In G. MacNaughton, P. Hughes, and K. Smith (eds.), *Young Children as Active Citizens: Principles, Policies and Pedagogies*. Newcastle: Cambridge Scholars Publishing, pp. 2–24.

Devereux, S. (2002). *Social Protection for the Poor: Lessons from Recent International Experience*, IDS Working Paper No.142. Institute of Development Studies, University of Sussex.

Devereux, S., and Sabates-Wheeler, R. (2004). *Social Transfers and Chronic Poverty: Emerging Evidence and the Challenge Ahead*, Transformative Social Protection, IDS Working Paper No.232. London: DFID.

Ellis, F.; White, P.; Lloyd-Sherlock, P.; Chhotray, V.; and Seeley, J. (2008). *Social protection research scoping study*. Norwich, UK: Governance and Social Development Resource Center, Overseas Development Group, University of East Anglia.

Ensor, M. (2012). *African Childhoods: Education, Development, Peacebuilding, and the Youngest Continent*. Basingstoke: Palgrave MacMillan.

Ezemenari, Kene; Chaudhury, Nazmul; and Owens, Janet. (2002). *Gender and Risk in the Design of Social Protection Interventions.* Washington, DC: The World Bank Institute.

Gittins, D. (1998). *The Child in Question.* New York: St. Martin's Press.

Government of Kenya (GoK). (2011). *Kenya National Social Protection Policy.* Nairobi: Ministry of Gender, Children and Social Development, Government of Kenya.

Government of Kenya (GoK). (2012). *Kenya Social Protection Sector Review.* Nairobi: Government Printer.

Kenya National Bureau of Statistics (KNBS) and Society for International Development (SID). (2013). *Exploring Kenya's Inequality: Pulling Apart or Pooling Together?* Nairobi: KNBS and SID.

Kenya National Commission on Human Rights. (2014). *'Are We Under Siege? The State of Insecurity in Kenya.* An Occasional Report 2010–2014, Nairobi: UNDP.

Lieten, G. (2015). *Victims of Obtrusive Violence: Children and Adolescents in Kenya.* Berlin: Springer.

Lister, R. (2003). *Citizenship: Feminist Perspectives.* 2nd Edition. Basingstoke: Palgrave MacMillan.

Lister, R. (2007). From Object to Subject: Including Marginalized Citizens in Policy Making. *Policy and Politics,* 35 (3): 437–455.

Manning, B., and Ryan, R. (2004). *Youth and Citizenship.* A Report for NYARS Canberra: Australia National Youth Affairs Research Scheme

Mathambo, V., and Gibbs, A. (2008). *Qualitative Accounts Of Family And Household Changes In Response To The Effects Of HIV and Aids: A Review With Pointers To Action. Joint Learning Initiative on Children and HIV/AIDS.* Retrieved from: www.jlica.org

Montgomery, H. (2008). *An Introduction to Childhood: Anthropological Perspectives on Children's Lives.* Oxford: Wiley-Blackwell.

Moulidi, M. (2011). *Health Needs Assessment for Kisumu Kenya MCI Social Sector.* Working Paper Series No.19/20.

Nyamu-Musembi, C., and Cornwall, A. (2004). *What Is the Rights Based Approach All About? Perspective from International Development Agencies.* Working Paper No.234.

Okwany, A. (2009). *Children and Poverty: Notions of Childhood in Development Discourses and Policies.* Distance Learning Unit for The Tanzania Diploma in Poverty Analysis. Module 3 unit 10, ESRF/REPOA, Tanzania.

Okwany, A., and Ngutuku, E. (2014). *Social Protection to Enhance the Citizenship Rights of Vulnerable Children in Western and Nyanza.* Report submitted to PASGR.

Oxfam. (2009). *Urban Poverty and Vulnerability in Kenya.* Background analysis for the preparation of an Oxfam GB Urban Programme focused on Nairobi.

Republic of Kenya. (2010). *The Constitution of the Republic of Kenya.* Nairobi: Government Printer.

Risse, Thomas. (2011). "Governance in Areas of Limited Statehood: Introduction and Overview". In Thomas Risse (ed.), *Governance Without a State? Policies and*

Politics in Areas of Limited Statehood. New York: Columbia University Press, pp. 1–35.

Samoff, J. (2007). "No Teacher Guide, No Textbooks, No Chairs. Contending with Crisis in African Education". In Robert F. Arnove and Carlos Alberto Torres (eds.), *Comparative Education: The Dialectic of the Global and the Local*. Boston: Rowman and Littlefield, pp. 409–443.

Tendler, J. (2002). "Why Social Policy Is Condemned to a Residual Category of Safety Nets and What to Do About It". In T. Mkandawire (ed.), *Social Policy in a Development Context*. Basingstoke: Palgrave Macmillan, pp. 119–142.

Tilly, Charles. (1995). Citizenship, Identity and Social History. *International Review of Social History*, 40 (Supplement S3): 1–17.

UN-HABITAT. (2005). *Situation Analysis of Informal Settlements in Kisumu*. Nairobi: United Nations Human Settlements Programme.

UN-HABITAT. (2008). *Kisumu Urban Sector Profile*. Nairobi: United Nations Human Settlements Programme.

UNICEF. (2014). *The United Nations Children's Fund (UNICEF) State of World Children 2015*. New York: UNICEF.

Wilkinson-Maposa, S.; Fowler, A.; Oliver-Evans, C.\ and Mulenga, C. (2005). *The Poor Philanthropist: How and Why the Poor Help Each Other*. Cape Town: Graduate School of Business, University of Cape Town.

5 Governance mechanisms of burial societies in western Uganda

Narathius Asingwire, Denis Muhangi, Rose B. Namara, and Margaret Kemigisa

Introduction

Uganda achieved economic growth rates of 8 per cent per year over the period of 2004 to 2008 (National Planning Authority, 2010), but some seven million of its citizens are still chronically poor. The state is obliged to respond to their social needs; the 1995 National Constitution (GoU, 1995) makes the state responsible for protecting and providing fundamental human rights and freedoms including protection of the aged, recognition of the dignity and rights of persons with disabilities, the right to education, the rights of women, the rights of children, etc. Article 5 is unequivocal:

> The State shall guarantee and respect institutions, which are charged with responsibility for protecting and promoting human rights by providing them with adequate resources to function effectively.
>
> (GoU, 1995: Article 5(1))

The need for social protection (SP) services in Uganda is extreme in the wake and midst of civil wars, HIV/AIDS, natural disasters, changing macro-economic contexts, large household size, and increased life expectancy (National Planning Authority, 2010). SP responses are deemed essential, as they seek to reduce individual vulnerability and improve people's well-being (Upreti et al., 2012: 37).

However, existing state SP services do not reach 95 per cent of the Ugandan population (Barya, 2009). Recognising the paradoxes of economic growth, poverty, and increasing vulnerability, in recent years, the government has piloted the Social Assistance Grant for Empowerment, which aims to directly improve poor people's welfare through cash transfers. Even this social support benefits only a fraction of the population of the chronically poor. The state is mandated but unable to provide sufficient SP – a condition known as "limited statehood". Non-state actors (NSAs) have to, and do, step in to honour at least part of the constitutional pledge to citizens (Risse, 2011).

Many Ugandans support each other through self-help groups in the form of community-based organisations (CBOs). The number and type of CBOs and other NSAs may not be known, but the number is necessarily large and there is no doubt that, in the state default, they play a crucial role in meeting the social welfare needs of the people.

Among the longest established and most universal types are burial societies. Elaborate funerals are culturally mandatory and a rite that is important to community cohesion. The extent to which individual burial groups help their members depends on a wide range of factors, not least being their governance structures. Formal SP schemes have written and registered rules and procedures for delivering public services. Informal groups such as burial societies often lack such standardised mechanisms. The literature shows that the quality of governance can go a long way in determining the outcomes of any service delivery intervention (Bassett et al., 2012), so a key question of this study was how burial societies are governed. CBOs evolve diverse forms of governance, which have not yet been sufficiently and systematically analysed.

Governance characteristics of self-help membership organisations

Governance is the means by which social coordination is achieved (Lowndes and Skelcher, 1998). It encompasses processes, policies, procedures, systems, and practices, how they are used, their results, and the nature of relationships among members/stakeholders (Centre for African Family Studies, 2001). All membership organisations are in some way governed by norms of exchange and reciprocity, mediated by rules and institutions. The distinction between "formal" and "informal" is a matter of style and structure, not principle. Much of the literature on self-help groups characterises them as patronage systems with "inadequate" supervisory systems, "poor" problem-solving approaches, "limited" internal democracy, "weak" human resource capacity, "limited" managerial skills, and "uncertain" funding (Centre for African Family Studies, 2001; Harvey et al., 2007, UNICEF, 2009; Foster et al., 2001). Critics argue that patronage culture is responsible for the poor always looking up to the benevolence of the better off to avert risk, while in reality they are being exploited (Harvey et al., 2007, UNICEF, 2009; Thomson and Posel, 2002; Kasente et al., 2004; Oduro, 2010; Ellis; Van Ginneken).

Self-help systems may be unconventional and sub-optimal, but of course they do have their own form of governance, and the poor depend on them. A study in India on the empowerment of women shows that self-help groups have emerged as an important link between the poor, especially women, and the formal/state systems (Gaonkar, 2004). Women have improved their quality of life, increased their income, savings, and consumption expenditure levels; they have gained self-confidence and created opportunities to improve their hidden talents by joining self-help groups (Gaonkar, 2004).

Burial societies

Death in the family is costly, and the poor at times have to sell scarce assets to meet those costs. In traditional African systems where respect and dignity are accorded to the dead, burials must be laborious and extended rites that can often throw households into destitution. Burial societies thus avert potential crises through the communal provision of burial and funeral support to their bereaved members. Burial societies typify the concept of mutual help groups consisting of a membership of community members from the same village or neighbourhood who come together to pool risks by collecting resources in order to support each other during times of risk, shock, or difficulty. Many burial societies may not perform any other functions; others do build other services on the same foundations. When a member household loses a loved one, members of the group bring food, dig the grave, contribute money to buy a coffin, and bring other essentials such as firewood and water for cooking. They also attend the vigil and the burial, thus providing psychosocial support to the affected family and reaffirming the community's identity and cohesion. Such groups have existed in many parts of Africa for many decades. They are usually informal and may not be registered with any authority. Their membership is usually open to any community adult as long he/she is willing to contribute the agreed resources and finances to others, whether by subscription or on an ad hoc basis, to be used to pay for funerals and other ceremonies at the time of death. Participation is a form of socio-economic insurance.

This chapter shows that, despite their unconventional governance approach, burial societies in Uganda have consistently provided support services to their members over a long period of time. More recently, some of these societies have started to diversify into savings and credit services and run income-generating activities (IAGs) in order to address general income vulnerability among members (Asingwire et al., 2013). These groups are managed by members and have their own rules, enforced in their own way – an indication that their unique governance characteristics may not be the problem; they may be the secret of their success and sustainability.

Study approach and major findings

This study mapped all NSAs in SP services in the districts of Bushenyi, Kole, and Rakai. A total of 536 NSAs were in operation and 191 of them (35.6 per cent) were burial societies. The researchers then conducted an in-depth study of 64 of those burial societies, using focus group discussions (FGDs) among members and leaders of the NSAs. The study especially asked members to assess the governance of their organisations and the quality of services they received using the report card survey method.

Burial societies

There are two types of burial societies:

i   those that provide inputs (food, labour, and condolences) required for a decent burial of a household member;
ii those that provide inputs for burials and also venture into other social support activities such as savings.

These groups are unregulated and unsupervised, but they have rules, regulations, and organisational structures that, while less formal, are no less specific and binding. They are based in communities, having been founded by the members themselves to provide mutual social insurance.

More than half the burial societies in the study area were formed before 1999, and a few were formed in the 1970s. The proliferation of burial societies started in the 1980s in response to increasing levels of poverty and vulnerability and alongside emergence at that time of many other NSAs such as CBOs and non-governmental organisations (NGOs) amid dysfunctional state services. Some literature refers to this trend as "gap filling" by NSAs in the face of deficient or limited statehood. Many writers (Dicklitch, 1998a, 1998b; Muzaale, 1996; De Coninck, 2004; Thue et al., 2002; Semboja and Therkildsen, 1995) attribute the wave of NSA growth to socio-economic and political conditions that came with the Idi Amin regime during the 1970s, the 1979 liberation war, and the subsequent instability and crisis during the 1980s, further exacerbated by the HIV/AIDS epidemic.

Almost all the burial societies (94.7 per cent) were secular. Uganda has many religious denominations, notably 42 per cent Roman Catholics, 36 per cent Anglican Protestants, 12 per cent Muslims, and 10 per cent others (UBOS, 2002). The secular nature of the burial societies points to their inclusive and non-discriminatory character. Subsistence agriculture was the dominant occupation or source of livelihood of 80 per cent of beneficiaries, while a few were petty traders.

76 *Narathius Asingwire et al.*

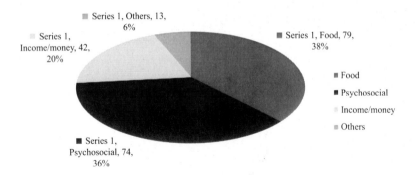

Figure 5.1 Type of services provided by burial societies (%).

Services provided by burial societies

All the burial societies in the study helped bereaved member families with cash, food, non-food items, and social comfort. These forms of support could be considered both preventive and protective. While all 191 burial societies provided assistance to bereaved households, 85 per cent of them delivered no other direct services. The balance of 15 per cent used their established grouping and resources to address members' other needs also. See Figure 5.1.

Governance features of burial societies

Bassett et al. (2012) conceptualises governance in three components – namely, (i) rules of the game, (ii) roles and responsibilities of actors, and (iii) control and accountability mechanisms.

Rules of the game

The Government of Uganda (GoU) requires all organisations to register with a relevant government office before starting a business. CBOs or other community groups are required to register with the sub-county local government and the district. Registration requires documents including a constitution, a list of members, and a set of recommendation letters from the village and parish council authorities. Yet about 79 per cent of the burial societies have not registered with any government authority. The groups that have registered are mainly those that have graduated from only burial assistance to promoting services such as IGAs.

Internal regulations, norms, and operating guidelines

Only one-third of the burial societies have a constitution; the rest rely on rules, mostly unwritten. Rules encompass membership, contributions, conduct, and attendance at meetings. Members know the rules, as evidenced in focus groups:

> There are some unwritten rules and norms that help us in management. Men's responsibilities and women's responsibilities are clearly known to all members though they are not written. For example, men have to dig the grave and women help in cooking. Also every member is required to visit the bereaved at home.
>
> (Interview, leader, Rwancunda Twezikye Group)

The rules were formulated by all members in a participatory manner and were binding on all. Members say the rules help their groups to remain united, regulate members' behaviour, protect the assets, and create predictability. This was deemed to make the work of leaders easier, as each member knew what was expected.

Criteria for membership

Membership is open to all adult residents of a village. A member is required to make financial or other specified contributions and to attend burials and meetings. In some groups, membership fees are based on the assets of the organisation used during funerals (such as chairs, tents, saucepans) and computed to arrive at the value of "shares" held by existing members. New entrants pay their share value. Because the cost of membership fees based on "shares" can be very high in groups that have a lot of assets, some groups have created two types of membership. The first has a nominal fee of about US$2 to be a group member with partial entitlements. These include food, local drinks, labour for digging the grave, a coffin, and a few other things. The second form of membership has a higher fee for more entitlements, including use of group assets.

Roles and responsibilities of members

The division of roles and responsibilities among members is clearly articulated and known by all, though not documented. Only 3.7 per cent of societies had traceable organisational charts. A further 15.3 per cent said they had charts but could not produce them; the remaining 81 per cent acknowledged they had no such document. All groups had an executive committee, with all members well aware of the leadership and management structure. All members participated in electing their executive committee to formulate by-laws and regulations, convene meetings, and handle financial issues. Although there were no written job descriptions or terms of reference for the executive committee, members generally knew the roles of their executive leaders.

The predominant expectation of members was attending meetings and burial ceremonies, contributing items and labour to a bereaved family, and offering general psychosocial support. Members commonly discussed any important issues in their meetings such as the challenges faced by the burial group as well as any complaints and grievances from beneficiaries. Gender differences feature in the nature of participation and operations. Men contribute money (for buying the coffin), dig the grave, and discuss the required budgets. Women bring food and participate in cooking it, wash utensils, fetch water, and collect firewood.

Mechanisms for control, accountability, and transparency

Control, accountability, and transparency were assessed in terms of how the leaders accounted to the members – primarily through written or verbal reports during meetings. There was no evidence that burial societies reported to any government office or other authority. Reporting to the sub-county local government authority does not happen in most societies. Rarely, burial societies take matters to the chairperson of the village council – usually in cases of conflicts or problems such as theft rather than routine reporting.

No system of external audit of the finances of burial societies was found. Reports (written or verbal) of incomes and expenditures are presented to members during meetings. In the same vein, no oversight from the state or another supervisory authority was found to regulate activities. Unlike other types of NSAs that have formed networks or alliances that have supportive and regulatory functions, this has not happened with burial societies. Transparency is ensured through doing things in the open and in the presence of other members. Compulsory attendance at meetings and funerals is not infrequent; the salient points to be remembered are not complex; everything is witnessed, personally and face-to-face.

> When a member is in need of, for example, food, money or labour, the services are delivered to their home. This helps ensure transparency since everything is done in the presence of all members.
> (Group leader, Orugondo Mwezikye)

Trust was found to be a key ingredient that smoothed operations and worked in place of written rules and sanctions. Members of burial societies chose leaders they trusted in order to minimise the possibility of dishonesty of any kind. Far from being deficient in accountability and transparency, informal CBOs are arguably models of both.

Box 1: Trust in a burial group as a foundation of institutional sustainability

"When we are electing leaders, we choose trustworthy members and we don't select people who we know will misuse our money. If we realize that someone has traits of embezzling money, we don't elect such a person to the post of the finance secretary. Any time accounts are rendered, there are people who memorise the figures. They will always remember. Hence in case we are called for another meeting and the finance secretary reads another figure different from what he had rendered in our previous meeting, one can easily say that 'for me I recall that when we sat at so-and-so's home you read 100,000; how come you are now presenting a different figure?' At this point, we assure the person that we abhor cheating. In case one tries to misuse our money, we stop him before he goes ahead. However, the people we elect are transparent, and we are also transparent" (FGD, group members, Orubingo Twezikye).

Leaders of burial societies affirmed that their members were working for their own benefit, hence they would not cheat themselves. After every burial, a meeting is held and all outstanding issues are discussed and a report given. All beneficiaries are in attendance. About 82 per cent of members indicated that they received information regularly about their associations. The information commonly relates to schedules of meetings and financial matters.

Another issue is how groups handle grievances and resolve conflicts. Interviews with leaders and members indicated that the executive committees and general meetings acted as mediators and arbitrators, and, in the last and rare resort, intractable cases were referred to the local council of the village.

Members' perceptions about the performance of their organisations

Performance was assessed in terms of the nature of services provided, the members' perceptions of and satisfaction with service quality, the level of

80 *Narathius Asingwire et al.*

benefits, and the issues of equity. In a report card, 93 per cent of respondents rated their executives' performance satisfactory or very satisfactory. Some 60 per cent rated the group services as either good or very good (see Figure 5.2 and Table 5.1).

Analyses of members' perceptions of governance characteristics show a score of satisfaction that would be the envy of any government or multinational corporation. In terms of services, there are divergent views. The reason is that members expect their organisations to undertake more than protective services. They want promotive services that can respond to their long-term income needs. Most groups had a standardised package of benefits that every bereaved family would receive, including a coffin, digging a grave, food, and social support of members. Beneficiaries interpreted this as a measure of equity; all members were treated in the same way without discrimination. Equal treatment was perceived not only in terms of what the group as a whole offers with regard to benefits but also how the individual members treat each other or respond to each other's needs. The only exceptions were a few groups which had differentiated between members getting the standard package of benefits and those who could use group assets. The balance between lower input and lower out-take did not appear to console the lower grade.

Group members and leaders were also asked how, overall, they had benefitted from their membership. The most outstanding benefit reported by all was the pooling of risk and being able to offset the cost of burials that would otherwise fall on the bereaved family alone. This was reported to have cushioned households against selling off their assets and property in order to meet burial costs as used to happen in the past.

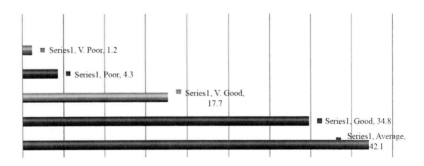

Figure 5.2 Beneficiary assessment of organisational performance in terms of quality of services received.

Table 5.1 Report card results of members' perceptions of their organisation and leaders

Perceptions	Agree %	Disagree %	Don't know %
The services from the organisation are addressing my priority needs.	45.5	54.5	0.0
The services provided are adequate for my needs.	31.1	68.9	0.0
The services provided are adequate for the needs of my family.	30.5	69.5	0.0
The quality of the services provided is of high standard.	47.9	50.9	1.2
The services are provided to me in the same way as other beneficiaries without any discrimination.	92.8	7.2	0.0
The group leaders do their work with commitment.	79.0	19.8	1.2
The group leaders treat me with respect and dignity.	91.0	8.4	0.6
The group provides beneficiaries opportunities to participate in its affairs.	95.8	4.2	0.0
The group leaders use group resources properly to help members/beneficiaries.	90.4	6.0	3.6
The organisation informs members/beneficiaries how resources have been used.	92.8	5.4	1.8
The services provided are suited to my cultural beliefs, values, and practices.	94.6	1.2	4.2
The services provided by the organisation have improved my living conditions.	44.9	53.9	1.2
The services provided by the organisation have improved the living conditions of my family members.	41.1	56.3	1.8

In the past, people used to sell their property to meet burial costs. In the past, bereaved families used to suffer to meet the burial expenses and could be plunged into poverty... People have realised how important it is to be in a group.
(FGD, group members, Rutooma Tweyombekye Group)

Transition to other forms of social protection

One criticism of burial societies is that the role they play remains at the protective level, which does not necessarily sustainably advance people's well-being. As the results of the perception survey show, members would prefer additional services to make their organisation more relevant to their needs. Some of the burial societies have transitioned to promotive and even (though rarely) transformative SP services. Promotive services include income-generating projects and savings and loan schemes. Other burial societies have attempted to expand into health insurance as illustrated in Case 1.

Case 1: Kyakabeizi Twimukye Association: The association started in 2000 as a burial support group and has 200 members. ("Twezikye" means, "Let's support our own burial"). Then the members heard about what was called "tweragurize" (meaning, "Let us seek medical care for ourselves when we are sick") and this challenged them to seek both burial and care support. In 2001, some members registered with Ishaka Health Plan, a hospital-based health insurance scheme. The office of the association now has a slogan pinned up which reads, "Tweragurize, kuturaafe, twezikye" (meaning, "Let us seek medical care, and if we die, we support our burial"). The association now also has a savings and credit cooperative with about 100 members. It has not been an easy ride, as some members of the health insurance plan fail to pay their premiums, while others who pay and do not get ill during that period feel that their premiums were wasted. Although about 50 families initially registered with Ishaka Health Plan, this number now fluctuates and sometimes goes as low as 13, depending on those who are able to pay quarterly premiums.

Implementing social protection services: lessons from burial societies

Burial societies in Western Uganda have some unique governance features and play key roles in providing promotive and preventive SP. The fact that more than 50 per cent have survived for more than 15 years suggests they have a higher survival rate than other types of voluntary organisations. The reason appears to be rooted in their resident-based, secular, purely member-supported initiatives (not driven by short donor-funding cycles). Clearly, SP initiatives are more likely to last longer if members themselves initiate them out of a shared localised need, if they are member owned in the true sense of the word, and they are member financed. It is interesting that in a country where 90 per cent of the people subscribe specifically to one religion or another; where NGO activities, education, and health services are commonly provided under religious affiliation; and for a rite whose protocols are religiously denominated, burial societies are wholly non-sectarian and include people of all religious backgrounds.

Informality and lack of documentation (or registration) stand out as a key feature of their operations. This implies that groups are not held together by some form of legal or bureaucratic requirement, but by shared norms and trust. This feature indicates the failure of the state to regulate NSAs in Uganda. It reflects the long-standing tension in the relationship between the state and NSAs in the regulatory landscape. Attempts by government to regulate NSAs through both legislation and practice have been interpreted as control rather than facilitation (Muhangi, 2009; Asiimwe-Mwesigye, 2003). The poor have little reason, and cannot afford, to give government the benefit of the doubt.

Burial societies are highly inclusive organisations and equitable distributors. They display innovation and creativity in sustaining affordability. One of the most unique features of burial societies is that they usually hold their meetings at funeral ceremonies, because this is both strategic and convenient. At a funeral, the agenda is self-evident, and attendance is automatically high. The piggybacking of meetings at funerals also ensures regularity – death is a frequent occurrence among the poor in Uganda. Burial societies are able to meet more regularly than most other organisations, where coordinating all for regular meetings can be a challenge.

Burial societies practise high levels of transparency and accountability. In particular, their accountability is almost entirely to the beneficiaries. Unlike bigger NSAs that are caught up in pressures to account to external donors, burial societies devote their primary allegiance to their members. They also have unique ways of ensuring transparency, such as "doing things together". This strategy is not unique to burial societies – it is a common practice among other types of CBOs such as women's groups (Asingwire et al., 2013).

Whereas mainstream conceptions of governance emphasise written constitutions, rules, and other formal mechanisms, these do not feature as key tools in the running of burial societies. Instead, trust emerges as a defining feature. It is also notable that big and formal NSAs that have elaborate rules are not protected from corruption and other accountability problems.

While burial societies may not have transformed their members and beneficiaries economically or pulled them out of poverty, they must be credited for cushioning them against one of their most prevalent and severe shocks and costs. In this respect, burial societies have continued to provide a form of protective and preventive SP that no other actor, whether government or non-government, is providing. They have therefore filled a gap in the needs of families in the face of life's only certainty: death.

Conclusions and policy implications

Burial societies are delivering essential preventive and protective services in Uganda that no one else is providing. Although their structures are unconventional and informal, and their very existence is often unregistered, they achieve exceptionally high levels of accountability and transparency to their constituents and are highly appropriate systems of governance. This calls into question the insistence on conventional governance models and ideals.

Burial societies have survived longer than most other types of NSAs and some state agencies, probably because they are member founded, member owned, member managed and operated, member supported, secular, built on trust, and respond to a phenomenon that is universal. Solidarity minimises their risks.

They are not alone in having failed, so far, to deliver a long-term cure for poverty itself. While there may be a need to build or strengthen governance structures and processes in small and informal NSAs *to enhance their performance*, such efforts should build on their norms and trust rather than displace them in the name of conventional governance principles.

It is highly unlikely that the limitations of the state to fulfil the Constitution in terms of SP will go away any time soon, even with consistently high economic growth. So NSAs and their governance mechanisms that have sustained the poor and vulnerable for so long without help will live on and not rupture.

There is a clarion need to look outside mainstream preconceptions about governance and good governance, and to consider what may be termed "good-fit" or "best-fit" governance (Booth, 2011; APP et al., 2012); a type that is appropriate for certain types of organisations and not others. The universal best practice approach to governance for development is not necessarily right, and there are no institutional templates that are valid everywhere and for all stages in a country's development. It is time to consider "best fit", not "best practice". This requires building on existing institutional arrangements that already have demonstrable benefits in particular contexts rather than importing new models altogether.

It is worth remembering that mainstream models of SP are often designed by societies where the poor are in the minority, and the rich majority can readily afford to support the poor few. Not by a very long way indeed is that the situation in Africa. The existence of very numerous small-scale and informal SP actors in Uganda reflects the fact that government is not the only – and in fact not even the biggest – responder to crises that the populace faces.

An issue of policy concern therefore is the lack of recognition of informal NSAs in national planning and budgeting. Informal CBOs and other NSAs render enormous and unconditional help to the state. The time has come for government to reciprocate.

References

APP (Africa Power and Politics Programme). (2012). *The Political Economy of Development in Africa*. A joint Statement from five research programmes. Retrieved from: http://differenttakeonafrica.files.wordpress.com/2012/04/jointstatement.pdf

Asiimwe-Mwesigye, J. (2003). "The Situation of Human Rights and Governance in Uganda Today: A Civil Society Perspective". In *Voices for the Public Good: Civil Society Input into the 2003 Consultative Group Meeting*. Kampala: Uganda National NGO Forum, pp. 11–17.

Asingwire, N.; Muhangi, D.; Namara, R.; and Kemigisa, M. (2013). *Governance, Performance and Sustainability of Social Protection Services in Uganda*. Final Report of study conducted under the auspices of PASGR.

Barya, J.J. (2009). *Interrogating the Right to Social Security and Social Protection in Uganda*. HURIPEC Working Paper No.23. Uganda: Makerere University.

Bassett, L.; Giannozzi, S.; Pop, L.; and Ringold, D. (2012). *Rules, Roles, and Controls: Governance in Social Protection with an Application to Social Assistance*. Background Paper for the World Bank 2012–2022 Social Protection and Labor Strategy, March 2012, Retrieved from: www.worldbank.org

Booth, D. (2011). *Governance for Development in Africa: Building on What Works*. Africa power and Politics (APP) Policy Brief 01, Overseas Development Institute, London.

Centre for African Family Studies. (2001). *A Situation Analysis of NGO Governance and Leadership in Eastern, Southern, Central and Western Africa, African Family Studies*. Nairobi, Kenya.

De Coninck, J. De. (2004). "The State, Civil Society and Development Policy in Uganda: Where Are We Coming From?" In K. Brock, R. McGee, and J. Gaventa (eds.), *Unpacking Policy; Knowledge, Actors and Spaces in Poverty Reduction in Uganda and Nigeria*. Kampala: Fountain Publishers, pp. 51–73.

Dicklitch, S. (1998a). "Indigenous NGOs and Political Participation". In H.B. Hansen and M. Twaddle (eds.), *Developing Uganda*. Kampala: Fountain Publishers, pp. 145–158.

Dicklitch, S. (1998b). *The Elusive Promise of NGOs in Africa*. London: Macmillan Press Ltd.

Foster, M.; Norton, A.; and Conway, T. (2001). *Social Protection Concepts and Approaches: Implications for Policy and Practice in International Development*. London: Centre for Aid and Public Expenditure.

Frank, Ellis. (1993). *Peasant Economics: Farm Households and Agrarian Development*. 2nd Edition. Cambridge: Cambridge University Press.

Gaonkar, R. (2004). *Role of Self-help Groups in Empowerment of Women*. Paper presented at the ISTR Sixth International Conference, Toronto, Canada, 11–14 July, 2004.

Government of Uganda. (1995). *Constitution of the Republic of Uganda*. Kampala: The State House.

Harvey, P.; Holmes R.; Slater R.; and Martin, E. (2007). *Social Protection in Fragile States*. London: Overseas Development Institute (ODI).

Kasente, D.; Asingwire, N.; Banugire, F.; and Kyomuhendo, S. (2004). Social Security Systems in Uganda. *African Journal of Social Work*, 22 (1/2): 27–42.

Lowndes, V., and Skelcher, C. (1998). The Dynamics of Multi-organizational Partnerships: An Analysis of Changing Modes of Governance. *Public Administration*, 76: 313–333.

Muhangi, D. (2009). *Local Government – Non-profit Sector Partnerships in HIV/ AIDS Response: Policy Narratives and Local Practices*. Ph.D. Thesis, Queens University Belfast.

Muzaale, J.P. (1996). *UNHCS/HABITAT's Community Development Programme*. A study of the evolution and application of the programme's concepts of community participation, community management and enabling government in Uganda. Draft.

National Planning Authority (2010). National Development Plan 2010/11 - 2014/15. Republic of Uganda, Kampala

Oduro, A.D. (2010). *Formal and Informal Social Protection in Sub-Saharan Africa*. Final report for ERD, Department of Economics, University of Ghana, Legon, Ghana.

Risse, Thomas. (2011). "Governance in Areas of Limited Statehood: Introduction and Overview". In Thomas Risse and Ursula Lehmkuhl (eds.), *Governance Without a State? Policies and Politics in Areas of Limited Statehood*. New York: Columbia University Press, pp. 1–35.

Semboja, J., and Therkildsen, O. (eds.). (1995). *Service Provision Under Stress in East Africa: The State, NGOs, and People's Organizations in Kenya, Tanzania and Uganda*. Portsmouth, NH: Heneman.

Thomson, R.J., and Posel, D.B. (2002). The Management of Risk by Burial Societies in South Africa. *South Africa Actuarial Journal*, 2: 83–128.

Thue, N.; Makubuya, A.N.; and Nakirunda, M. (2002). *Report of a Study on the Civil Society in Uganda*. Report for the Royal Norwegian Embassy in Uganda, NORAD- Norwegian Agency for Development Cooperation.

UBOS. (2002). *2002 Uganda Population and Housing Census: Main Report*. Kampala: Uganda Bureau of Statistics.

UNICEF. (2009). *Strengthening Social Protection for Children West and Central Africa*. London: ODI Report.

Upreti, B.R.; Sony, K.C.; Mallet, R.; Babajanian, B.; Pyakuryal, K.; Ghimire, S.; Ghimire, A.; and Sharma, S.R. (2012). *Livelihoods, Basic Services and Social Protection in Nepal*. Working Paper No.7. ODI, London: Secure Livelihoods Research Consortium.

Van Ginneken, W. (ed.). (1999). *Social Security for the Excluded Majority: Case Studies of Development Countries*. Geneva: ILO.

6 Hedging against vulnerability

Associational life as a social insurance strategy by the poor in the central region of Ghana

Akosua K. Darkwah, Mavis Dako-Gyeke, and Edward Nketiah-Amponsah

Introduction

Kwamena Andoh, a 43-year-old agricultural extension officer, is a resident of Asebu, a small town in the Central Region of Ghana. He recently obtained a tertiary degree after two decades working to save for university fees. Over 20 years, he joined five different types of associations. He pays

- $1 per month to the Pentecost Church welfare fund, which helps pay for funerals;
- $25 per month to the Teachers' Credit Union, which gives loans that help Kwamena stock his agro-chemicals shop;
- $2 per month to a workplace group, the Central Region Agro-Chemical Association;
- $1.50 a month to a district welfare fund, which gives funeral support;
- $5 per month to a regional welfare fund, which gives funeral support;
- $18.75 to Enterprise Life Assurance's funeral fund insurance;
- $20 per month to two child education policies for his daughter.

Kwamena is also a member of a local keep-fit club. Although he does not make any financial contributions to this group, members provide emotional support and other forms of assistance, particularly with funeral arrangements.

Kwamena's total monthly contribution to all the associations is about $75 – a significant sum in rural Ghana. He received a total of $912.50 from various sources on the recent death of his father – significantly less than he had paid in funeral support contributions over the years (financially, he would have done better by putting the money into a savings account), but there was a major bonus in community/social support.

He deems the cost worthwhile because he knows he can depend on the associations when the need arises, both financially and socially. His father's funeral was well attended with good hospitality for the guests – the two criteria for a "successful" funeral in Akan society (Arhin, 1994). He believes he can count on the educational policies to cover the costs of his daughter's secondary and tertiary education when she grows up.

Esi Arthur is a petty trader in her late twenties, born and raised in the slightly bigger town of Winneba in the Central Region. An active member of her church for the past 20 years, she belongs to six different church associations and plays a variety of roles including leadership. Indeed, most of her evenings are taken up with association activities. She goes to meetings four days a week, sometimes attending two meetings in a day. Her motive is to ensure church members know her well so that when she has a problem, be it financial or emotional, she has allies in the church who will work to ensure her needs are met. So far, active membership in church associations has paid off in both monetary and non-monetary terms. She has not lost any close family member yet, but when an uncle died, the choir performed at the funeral (a non-member would have had to pay $400 for that). Non-monetary benefits from association life include learning to become functionally literate, acquiring public speaking skills, and learning a range of cooking techniques, as well as networking.

Kwamena and Esi are both "hedging": risk-pooling (one membership) and risk-pool spreading (multiple memberships) to safeguard against vulnerabilities such as ill health or old age in a context of very limited financial resources and without overt assistance from the state despite its constitutional obligation to poor and vulnerable citizen's welfare.

As the social welfare contract between the state and citizens is de facto broken, people turn to non-state action and their own informal mechanisms. In the context of limited statehood (Risse, 2011), citizens' own informal social pooling and hedging schemes provide the only viable strategy. While there is a large body of literature on hedging through formal insurance (Iacoviello and Ortalo-Magne, 2003; Nance et al., 1993; Smith, Searle and Cook, 2009; Tufano, 1996), much less attention has been paid to the benefits of informal hedging. The one exception in Africa has been studies on burial groups ((de Weerdt, Dercon, Bold and Pankhurst 2007; Bahre, 2012; Dafulenya and Gondo, 2010; Ngwenya, 2003; Thomson and Posel, 2002).

This chapter extends analysis of informal social hedging, investigates the determinants of participation, and explores the extent to which risk-pool spreading provides additional protection. The chapter is presented in six parts: an investigation of the social insurance literature, a contextual understanding of the social protection (SP) measures available, the methods utilised to undertake the study, the factors that increase the likelihood of an individual choosing to participate in informal forms of social insurance, the benefits to be derived from such participation and from multiple memberships, and conclusions and recommendations.

Hedging in informal associations

Devereux and Sabates-Wheeler (2004: 10) categorise SP programmes in four types – preventive, promotive, protective, or transformative. Preventive programmes include health insurance and pension schemes (Oduro, 2010), as well as activities such as multiple cropping to diversify risk. Promotive mechanisms focus on income-creation through provision of micro-credit or subsidised inputs for artisans and small-scale entrepreneurs. According to Fiscian and Casely-Hayford (2006), promotive measures aim to make the lives of the vulnerable better through livelihood-improvement strategies.

Protective programmes give assistance to disadvantaged groups who cannot earn a living, such as orphans and abandoned children. Protective measures are directed at people who are incapable of participating in promotional and preventive forms of SP (Fiscian and Casely-Hayford, 2006). These interventions could be in the form of targeted cash transfers from state coffers, donor agencies, and/or through NGO activities. Transformative programmes focus on social justice through civic education and advocacy, which require national reach to achieve the necessary political leverage.

The costs of formal social insurance programmes are prohibitive for most citizens of developing countries (Mazzucato,, 2009), Ghana included. Affordable insurance needs reciprocal support arrangements which pool risk among members for times of shock and adversity, and ideally cut out middlemen and commercial margins, and enable barter where money is not available (Habtom and Ruys, 2007; Mazzucato,, 2009; Van Ginneken, 2002). These are factor-advantage qualities for homogenous groups such as communities with similar backgrounds in language, religion, and/or neighbourhood.

Many of these informal insurance programmes cover one-off individual shocks such as job loss, bereavement, or illness (Bhattamishra and Barrett, 2010; Porter, 2008; Vanderpuye-Orgle and Barrett, 2009) because informal insurance is usually inadequate to cover macro-shocks that affect all, such as civil unrest or drought (Alderman and Haque, 2007). In Northern Ghana, for example, insurance and coping strategies against job loss and crop failure are very poor (Dercon, 2004). The magnitude of a shock is measured by its severity, including scale) regularity, and the means by which it can be alleviated (Porter, 2008). In Ghana, health care and funerals are the major shocks for which insurance is sought (Mazzucato,, 2009).

Goldstein, de Janvry and Sadoulet (2004) recognise that informal social support systems smooth consumption and maximise utility over time (see also Morduch, 1999; Platteau, 1997). However, there is evidence that many people in low-income communities are left uninsured in risk-pooling arrangements. They are the "invisible", with low profiles and fragile connectedness in the community. These include the very poor and recent (less than one generation ago) migrants (Bhattamishra, 2008; Lyon, 2003, Vanderpuye-Orgle and Barrett, 2009).

Informal hedging is more effective in groups because risk is spread over a broader base, members act as a check on each other, and information is shared quickly and completely. Social networks are pivotal to hedging, which is why, per the case of Esi Arthur, active participation is as important as monetary contribution (Vanderpuye-Orgle and Barrett, 2009).

Work-based and religious associations are different from community-based, risk-pooling arrangements because they have more formal rules, regulations, and objectives when well-defined events occur. De Weerdt Dercon, Bold and Pankhurst (2007), in a study in Ethiopia and Tanzania, found that well-structured groups existed to provide insurance for members, particularly for funerals and medical costs. While Barnes and Peil (1977) found membership associations to be scarce in low-income areas, Essamuah and Tonah (2004) found the reverse to be true. Barnes and Peil (1977) also found that people with some formal education joined more associations than those with little or no formal education. Yet the elites were more careful in choosing associations and therefore joined fewer.

Hedging can be defined as a risk-management strategy, foregoing the possibility of maximum gains to reduce or offset the probability of losses. Owusu-Antwi (2010) affirms that non-state and informal SP have the ability to hedge members against crisis. Indeed, they can offset increases in vulnerability (Baker, 2002; Dorward Wheeler, MacAusian, Buckley, Kydd and Chirwa, 2006). The probability is high of people joining non-state social protection (NSSP) groups primarily as a form of hedging. Kimuyu (1999) revealed that the use of rotating savings and informal credit associations was crucial in meeting the cost of education and medical expenses among households in rural East Africa.

However, while the benefits from informal sources are essential and welcome, they are seldom adequate and often uncertain. Consequently, individuals are motivated to join multiple associations – to further spread risk and/or increase potential benefits. After all, a risk-pool is a "basket", and the axiom suggests you should not put all your eggs in just one of those. Financial convention would call the intensity of associational membership "an improvised hedging and portfolio diversification strategy" adopted to mitigate potential losses in household welfare. For instance, Grootaert Gi-Taik and Swamy (2002) opine that membership of local associations and networks is associated with higher per capita expenditure and better access to credit in rural households in Burkina Faso. Just like financial hedging, individuals join multiple associations with the expectation that at least one will be high yielding in monetary and/or non-monetary terms. This chapter investigates the extent to which such informal spreading practices are actually beneficial.

The Ghanaian context

A range of actors provides SP services in Ghana. The most long-standing of these is the family. Based on established customs of obligation and reciprocity, families provide support to household members, extended family, and neighbours. These include cultural practices such as land sharing, cooperative crop harvesting and storage, volunteerism, and other communal support activities (Patel Kaseke and Midgley, 2012). As many scholars (Kaseke and Dhemba, 2006; Moleni and Gallagher, 2006, Patel et al., 2012; Rankopo Osei-Hwedie and Modie-Moroka, 2006) have suggested, traditional values and religious beliefs underpinned these practices. This guaranteed that vulnerable families and individuals were assisted (protected).

Missionaries have also been key actors. Through the establishment of mission schools, especially in Southern Ghana (Miller, 1993), they introduced preventive kinds of SP. The colonial government also played its part. In the early 1900s, the colonial government extended health facilities to Ghanaians by establishing the Korle-Bu teaching hospital. The health system was urban biased, and by 1930, only about 10 per cent of Ghanaians had access to public health care (Senah, 2001). In the immediate post-independence era, the state sought to ensure equality for all, particularly in education and health. Both were free, and education was compulsory (Konadu-Agyemang, 2000). A pension programme was also introduced for formal sector workers.

During the 1970s and 1980s, however, Ghana experienced a serious economic crisis (Sandbrook and Oelbaum, 1997). As Tangri (1992) notes, to salvage its failing economy, Ghana adopted a Structural Adjustment Program (SAP) in the early 1980s. However, its implementation worsened the plight of the poor and widened the inequality gap. The government then introduced a SP scheme, the Programme of Action to Mitigate the Social Cost of Adjustment (PAMSCAD) in 1985 to alleviate the negative effects of SAP. This was unsuccessful (Gyasi, 1995). To make matters worse, social support from family began to wane as individual members found it more and more difficult to cater for themselves, let alone others (Abebrese, 2011; Baffoe and Dako-Gyeke, 2013). Urban migration also dislocated and distanced extended family linkages.

Since 2000, the government has introduced a series of SP programmes to cover all vulnerable persons in Ghana. These include government commitment to the Millennium Development Goals in 2000, the establishment of a National Health Insurance Scheme in 2003, the introduction in 2006 of a Growth and Poverty Reduction Strategy, and the Livelihood Empowerment Against Poverty (LEAP) programme, which was first piloted in 2008 to address child poverty and vulnerability. Even though the national SP strategies represent a vision of an all-inclusive society through the provision of sustainable protection of those in extreme poverty, they have not achieved much in that regard. Many of the programmes are poorly regulated, inconsistently implemented, and have actually worsened access to services for the poor (Blanchet Fink and Osei-Akoto 2012; Nyonator and Kutzin, 1999; Waddington and Enyimayew, 1990). The majority of Ghanaians rely on non-state actors (NSAs) for SP, yet there is little understanding of the extent to which they offer viable protection. As Patel et al. (2012) argue, although informal and indigenous NSAs have promoted the social well-being of Africans, their role and contributions have hardly been recognized. This chapter investigates the intensity and benefits of association membership and the extent to which Ghanaian citizens are hedging in the informal sector and whether that works. Grootaert et al. (2002) demonstrate in the case of Burkina Faso that households with higher levels of social capital have better access to credit, so this study asks whether monetary and non-monetary benefits rise in proportion to the number of associations an individual joins.

Research design and methods

A mixed-methods approach was used to explore the extent to which citizens in the Central Region joined NSAs and the extent to which doing so protected them from vulnerabilities. The study sites were four communities in Central Region, one of ten regions, located in the southern part of the country. While the southern regions are better off than the north, the Central Region ranks among the poorest. The most recent Ghana Living Standards Survey (GLSS V) shows the Central Region is the poorest region in Southern Ghana and has the highest infant mortality rate in the country (Ghana Statistical Services and Ghana Health Service, 2009). Yet, unlike the northern part of Ghana where both state and international development organisations concentrate on redressing the imbalances and ameliorating living conditions for the vulnerable, the Central Region receives far less attention.

This study aimed to assess the extent to which NSAs are filling the gaps in SP. Two urban communities (Cape Coast and Winneba) and two rural communities (Asebu and Biriwa) were selected. Cape Coast is the administrative capital and the biggest city in the region; it is home to many secondary institutions as well as a public university. Winneba is the second-largest city in the region and home to one of Ghana's six public universities. Asebu is a farming community that is well known for citrus production. Biriwa is a small fishing community. The two urban communities, as well as Biriwa, lie on the Atlantic Ocean, while Asebu is approximately 50 kilometres inland.

Random sampling identified respondents for the household vulnerability surveys. Each town was divided into quadrants and quota sampling recruited 101 persons in Asebu (48 males and 53 females), 115 people in

Biriwa (50 males and 65 females), 165 individuals in Winneba (79 males and 86 females), and 255 individuals in Cape Coast (133 males and 122 females). In total, 636 individuals comprising 310 males and 326 females were surveyed. In addition to the quantitative data, five in-depth interviews (IDIs) were conducted. Participants were purposively selected for the qualitative component of the study. Regression-analysis and cross-tabulation were used in analysis of the quantitative data and content analysis for the qualitative data.

Vulnerability of respondents and households

The sample was predictably youthful. Respondents ranged in age from 15 to 90 years, and the average was 40. Age-related illnesses that could affect earning ability were therefore not likely to be high. In terms of education, residents in the urban areas were more likely to have been provided with this preventive form of SP than rural dwellers. In the urban areas, 84 per cent of respondents had some level of formal education, while 16 per cent had never attended school. The comparable figures for the rural areas were 65 per cent and 35 per cent, respectively. In addition, the larger a household, the greater the likelihood that its members would be vulnerable. The mean household size was 5.2 (SD = 1.7) with a minimum of one and a maximum of ten. Concerning financial dependency, a household head takes care of an average of 3.6 persons (SD = 2.2), implying that approximately 22 per cent of household members are financially dependent on the respondents for their livelihood. A final measure of individual vulnerability focused on employment. Being employed, and particularly in the formal sector, provides individuals with access to some formal SP such as workplace health insurance and pension schemes. Three-quarters of the sample had engaged in an economic activity over the previous 12 months. The rural dwellers were less likely to work in the formal sector and therefore have less access to formal SP. While 69 per cent of the urban dwellers received remittances from (primarily family) members, the same could be said for only a third of rural dwellers (31 per cent).

There are a number of indicators that predispose households to vulnerability, particularly anything that would reduce the household's earning power or increase its care costs – such as chronic/terminal illness, old age, disability, and orphaned children. The study showed a terminal illness split of 65 urban and 35 per cent rural. This is consistent with de-Graft Aikins et al. (2012), which acknowledges the gradual urbanization of certain disease conditions owing to changes in lifestyle, especially limited exercise, urban pollution, and consumption of fatty foods. It is also consistent with locational distribution of the terminal illness burden with Cape Coast respondents experiencing the highest at 40 per cent followed by Winneba at 25 per cent and Asebu at 16 per cent.

Of all those aged 70 years and above, 69 per cent were urban and 31 per cent rural. This imbalance is partly attributable to the relative abundance of health facilities and health workers in urban areas. The trend was echoed, in almost identical proportions, by people with disabilities (hearing and visually impaired). A greater proportion was resident in urban households (63 per cent), and again this was reflected in localized distribution: Cape Coast and Winneba 31 per cent each, Asebu 13 per cent, and Biriwa 21 per cent. The number of orphaned children in households was almost evenly split between rural (48 per cent) and urban (52 per cent) areas. However, proportions by location bucked the trend. Biriwa (30 per cent) had the largest proportion, while Asebu had the least (19 per cent).

Findings of the study

Determinants of non-state associational membership and the effect of membership intensity on benefits

Budget allocations have been inadequate to achieve Ghana's growth and poverty reduction strategies to reduce vulnerability and strengthen basic social services and SP. Citizens rely largely on informal SP. In this study, 80 per cent of respondents were members of one association, 16 per cent were members of two, and 4 per cent were subscribers to three or more.

Analysis of the socio-economic and demographic factors that influence membership and the effect of membership intensity on benefits is necessary to appreciate the rationale for joining one or more associations. Using the study's field data, binary logistic regression was applied to identify correlations. The dependent variable is coded 1 for individuals belonging to at least one association, while those not belonging to any associations are assigned 0. The decision to join an association or otherwise is a function of individual demographic and socio-economic characteristics. It is assumed that the decision to join an association is based on perceived benefit.

The estimates in the full model (see Table 6.1) show that only three of the predictor variables are significant – age, being a Christian, and presence of a household member aged over 70 years.

An increase in a person's age by one year increases the chances of joining an association by 2.4 times (OR = 2.4). Orthodox and Pentecostal Christians have a greater likelihood of joining an association (OR = 3.0) compared with other Christian denominations (Latter-Day Saint, Jehovah's Witness, and Seventh-Day Adventist). Being a Muslim is positively correlated with membership, but the effect is not statistically significant. In his study on the

Table 6.1 Determinants of associational membership (full sample)

Membership in any association (yes =1)	Coef.	Std. Err.	p-value
Age (in continuous years)	0.85**	0.433	0.048
Christian (Ref: other religions)	1.086***	0.395	0.006
Moslem	0.844	0.551	0.126
Never married (Ref: others-singles, divorced, etc.)	0.051	0.310	0.871
Married	−0.119	0.272	0.663
Number of economic activities	−0.491	0.325	0.131
Household receives remittance	−0.145	0.225	0.521
Household has more than an income earner	0.164	0.214	0.444
Household has a member with terminal illness	−0.145	0.225	0.521
Household has an orphaned child	0.545	0.384	0.471
Household has a member aged over 70 years	0.796**	0.338	0.019
Household has a member with disability	0.046	0.593	0.939
Constant	−2.334**	1.028	0.023
−2 Log likelihood = 584.507			
Cox and Snell R Square = 0.061			
Nagelkerke R Square = 0.081			
Number of observations = 636			

OR = Odds Ratio

role of Ghanaian immigrant associations in Toronto, Owusu (2000) concluded from empirical investigation that level of education, income, and residential location were among key determinants of membership in associations for Ghanaians. This study controlled for education, income, and location, but none of them was found to be statistically significant. This variance is probably due to differences in demographic and socio-economic attributes between the Ghanaian immigrant population in Canada and the Central Region sample. This study's finding on the importance of age in inducing membership is consistent with Katungi et al. (2007), who worked in Central Uganda and identified age, wealth, and social status as dominant influencers.

To verify probable gender differences, the sample was further divided into male and female sub-samples and a separate logistic regression was performed. There were significant gender differences in the determinants of associational life (see Table 6.2). For males, the most important correlates were being a Christian (consistent with the full sample) and being a member of a household with more than one income earner.

With the female sub-sample, the number of economic activities and households receiving remittances were found to be the most important

Table 6.2 Determinants of associational membership (by gender)

Membership of any association (yes =1)	Male		Female	
Independent variables	Coeff.	p-value	Coeff.	p-value
Age (in continuous years)	0.860	0.218	0.621	0.314
Christian	0.967** (OR = 2.6)	0.049	1.123	0.160
Moslem	1.086	0.115	0.138	0.896
Never married	−0.127	0.794	0.640	0.16
Married	−0.585	0.204	0.401	0.284
Number of economic activities (1= yes)	0.444	0.351	−1.638*** (OR = 0.2)	0.005
Household receives remittance	0.210	0.580	−0.602** (OR = 0.5)	0.05
Household has more than one income earner	0.771** (OR = 2.2)	0.019	−0.307	0.322
Household has a member with terminal illness	−0.600	0.370	−0.099	0.843
Household has an orphaned child	0.054	0.939	0.872* (OR = 2.3)	0.085
Household has a member aged over 70 years	0.819	0.119	0.659	0.171
Household has a member with disability	0.046	0.939	−0.602	0.650
Constant	−2.334**	0.023	0.121	0.914
−2 Log likelihood = 292.843				
Cox and Snell R Square = 0.11				
Nagelkerke R Square = 0.15				
Number of observations = 636				

OR = Odds Ratio

predictors, though the stronger those factors were, the lower the probability of such households joining an association.

This study controlled for household vulnerability by using four proxies: household has a member with terminal illness, household has an orphaned child, household has a member aged over 70 years, and household has a member with disability. While the presence of an orphaned child and a person with disability were correctly signed and showed a positive link to membership in an association, it was only the presence of a member aged over 70 which was statistically significant. Considering that a typical funeral in Ghana can cost as much as $14,000 (Mazzuccato, Kabki and Smith, 2006), this makes sense. Participating in associations will help defray the costs associated with funerals, which could otherwise impoverish households.

Intensity of associational membership and comparative benefits

It is incontrovertible that individuals and households join both formal and informal associations due to the monetary, cultural, and social benefits inter alia that they expect to derive (Owusu, 2000). Nevertheless, the literature is grey on whether joining more associations, referred to as associational intensity, is significantly correlated with benefits. Empirical evidence emerges via a simple econometric model using the Ordinary Least Square (OLS) method of estimation. Table 6.3 shows the results.

Prior to the estimation, all the predictor variables were tested for accuracy using mean Variance Inflation Factors (VIFs) and were well within the no-problem threshold. The treatment variable – the intensity of association – is measured by the number of associations to which the respondent currently

Table 6.3 Effect of associational intensity on monetary benefits

Monetary value of benefits	Coef.	Robust std. Err.	t-statistic
Number of associations joined (= 2)	1.0261**	0.4098	2.5
Number of associations joined (= 3)	1.0096	0.8545	1.18
Number of associations*gender	−0.3402	0.4930	−0.69
Number of times attended meeting	0.494**	0.1623	3.05
Residence (Rural = 1)	−0.8323**	0.3253	−2.56
Gender (Female = 1)	0.7157	0.7269	0.98
Household has a person with term. illness (No = 1)	0.1054	0.4300	−0.25
Household has an orphaned child (No = 1)	−0.5378	0.4088	−1.32
Household has a person aged 70 + (No = 1)	0.778*	0.4138	1.88
Household has a member with disability (No = 1)	0.0660	0.6040	0.11
Income earner has lost earnings (No = 1)	0.3146	0.3185	0.99
Age of respondent	−0.014*	0.008	−1.82
Religion is Christianity (Yes = 1)	0.0274	0.4599	0.06
Respondent is married (Yes = 1)	0.3361	0.2931	1.15
Household size	−0.0692	0.0857	−0.81
Wealth (Poor)	−0.1325	0.3008	0.99
Wealth (Middle)	0.3665	0.4438	0.83
_cons	3.2011**	1.1763	2.72

Number of obs = 78
F (17, 60) 3.5
Prob > F = 0.0004
R-squared = 0.4
Root MSE = 1.11
VIF = 2.25

belongs and are categorized into those who were members of just one, two, and, finally, three associations.

Though membership of three associations was positive it was not significant at the conventional 5 per cent level. Therefore, it is probable that membership of two associations delivers optimum monetary benefits. Analysis showed the number of times a member attends meetings has a positive relationship with the value of both monetary and non-monetary benefits, so the frequency with which a member attends meetings is "doubly" important.

There are no significant gender differences in these respects. In particular, being a woman is associated with about 0.72 per cent more benefits than men, and living in a rural area decreases respondents' benefit by approximately 0.83 per cent. Urban residents are usually more financially secured than their rural counterparts and hence better able to pay their membership dues. FGDs found that most benefit failures were caused by inability to pay dues, and this problem is more pronounced in rural areas. As one respondent said,

> Not all the members are able to pay every month because we have many challenges with our work. It has become very difficult to get wood so our earnings are small. The 2 Ghana Cedis is a small amount but our work is not rewarding so we cannot ask for more . . . we have many people who are members of this association, but the committed ones who pay dues are few.

Although the study controlled for households' socio-economic attributes – such as education and wealth – these variables were not statistically significant. Other control variables such as household size, age, religion, were not significant in explaining the variation in monetary benefits.

Informal social protection helps the poor to survive, improves their livelihoods, and reduces vulnerability by allowing costs and resources, opportunities and shocks to be shared and redistributed (du Toit and Neves, 2009). The empirical estimation included four variables that could render households vulnerable and thus potentially engender poverty at the household level – namely, the presence of a household member with a terminal illness, whether there is an orphaned child living in the household, the household has a member aged 70 years and above, or, lastly, the household has lost an income earner in the last year.

The presence of a household member with an illness (especially terminal or chronic) constitutes an idiosyncratic shock and a recipe for potentially catastrophic health expenditures. It is envisaged that membership of an association will ensure access to some monetary benefits to reduce the financial burden on such households.

Interestingly, none of the vulnerability indicators was statistically significant, with only the presence of an orphaned child in the household, in statistical terms, correctly signed. This implies that informal SP is more responsive to orphaned children relative to other vulnerable groups. To verify further whether membership intensity reduces vulnerability of households, a cross tab between the number of associations (intensity) that an individual joins and the food security situation at the household level was done. Occasional food shortage decreases as people join more associations. Of those who are members of three or more associations, only 5 per cent suffer occasional food shortage compared with 81 per cent (!) of members of only one association. This pattern resonates with the other vulnerability indicators.

It is important to note that all the respondents who belonged to three or more associations had all children and adults in the household eating protein every day. Membership intensity is highly correlated with the use of antenatal care services and the use of treated bed nets by pregnant women. So even without recourse to the monetary benefits received from such associations, membership in more associations significantly reduces household vulnerability.

Conclusions

The reasons for joining NSAs are basically social and economic protection in times of crises. Members make strategic decisions to join one or more non-state organisations knowing that the state cannot be relied on as a safety net. Three major characteristics set apart members who join solidarity groups from those who do not. Members are older, Christian, and much more likely to have a family member aged above 70 years living with them. Stark differences emerge in membership of these organisations when analysed by gender. Men who are Christian and live in households with more than one income earner are more likely to join associations, while women who engage in more than one economic activity or receive remittances are less likely to join.

The threshold for receiving more benefits from joining many associations is two memberships (that is the practice of 20 per cent of citizens), and regular attendance at meetings is also positive. Non-monetary benefits peaked at membership in three associations. This prioritises awareness creation about the threshold for monetary and non-monetary benefits and the importance of attending meetings.

It is important for those who have joined only one association to recognise that they would derive fuller benefits of associational life if they joined more than one. Similarly, those who have joined only two associations should know that while joining a third association would have no impact on their monetary benefits, it would increase non-monetary benefits. Joining more than three enters the realms of diminishing returns.

Finally, this study documents the huge role that non-state associations are playing in reducing the vulnerability of citizens in the Central Region of Ghana. It is imperative, then, that these associations are recognised as key stakeholders in policy discussions on SP and that they are enabled and supported accordingly.

References

Abebrese, J. (2011). *Social Protection in Ghana: An Overview of Existing Programmes and Their Prospects and Challenges*. New Delhi: Friedrich Ebert Stiftung.

Alderman, H.G., and Haque, T. (2007). *Insurance Against Covariate Shocks: The Role of Index-Based Insurance in Social Protection in Low-Income Countries of Africa*. World Bank Working Paper No.95. Washington, DC: Africa Region Human Development Department, The World Bank.

Arhin, K. (1994). The Economic Implications of Transformations in Akan Funeral Rites. *Africa*, 64 (3): 307–322.

Baffoe, M., and Dako-Gyeke, M. (2013). Social Problems and Social Work in Ghana: Implications for Sustainable Development. *International Journal of Development and Sustainability*, 2 (1): 1–17.

Bahre, E. (2012). The Janus Face of Insurance in South Africa: From Costs to Risk, from Networks to Bureaucracies. *Africa*, 82 (1): 150–167.

Baker, B. (2002). Associational Life in African Cities. *Forum for Development Studies*, 29 (2): 414–422.

Barnes, S.T., and Peil, M. (1977). Voluntary Association Membership in Five West African Cities. *Urban Anthropology*, 6 (1): 83–106.

Bhattamishra, R., and Barrett, C.B. (2008). *Community-based Risk Management Arrangements: An Overview and Implications for Social Fund Programs*. SP Discussion Paper No. 830, World Bank.

Bhattamishra, R., and Barrett, C.B. (2010). Community-Based Risk Management Arrangements: A Review. *World Development*, 38 (7): 923–932.

Blanchet, N.J.; Fink, G.; and Osei-Akoto, I. (2012). The Effect of Ghana's National Health Insurance Scheme on Health Care Utilization. *Ghana Medical Journal*, 46 (2): 76–84.

Dafuleya, G., and Gondo, T. (2010). Deficits of Microfinance Institutions and Informal Responses Under Rapid Urban Growth: A Funeral Insurance Perspective. *American Journal of Entrepreneurship*, 1: 52–65.

De-Graft Aikins, A., Addo, J., Bosu, W.K., Ofei, F., and Agyemang, C. (2012). Ghana's Burden of Chronic Non-communciable Diseases: Prospects and Challenges for Research, Practice and Policy. *Ghana Medical Journal*, 46 (2): 1–4.

Dercon, S. (2004). "Risk, Insurance, and Poverty: A Review". In S. Dercon (ed.), *Insurance Against Poverty*. Oxford: Oxford University Press, pp. 9–37.

Devereux, S., and Sabates-Wheeler, R. (2004). *Transformative Social Protection*. IDS Working Paper No.232. Brighton: IDS.

Dorward, A.; Wheeler, R.; MacAuslan, I.; Buckley, C.P.; Kydd, J.; and Chirwa, E. (2006). *Promoting Agriculture for Social Protection or Protection for Agriculture: Strategic Policy and Research Issues*. Future Agricultures Discussion Paper, Brighton: University of Sussex.

duToit, A., and Neves, D. (2009). *Informal Social Protection in Post-Apartheid Migrant Networks: Vulnerability, Social Networks and Reciprocal Exchange in the Eastern and Western Cape, South Africa*. BWPI Working Paper 74. Brookings World Poverty Institute, University of Manchester, Manchester.

Essamuah, M., and Tonah, S. (2004). Coping with Urban Poverty in Ghana: An Analysis of Household and Individual Livelihood Strategies in Nima, Accra. *Legon Journal of Sociology*, 1 (2): 79–96.

Fiscian, V.S., and Casely-Hayford, L. (2006). *A Study into Existing Social Protection Policies and Mechanisms for Children in Ghana*. Associates for Social Change, Annual Report.

Ghana Statistical Services and Ghana Health Service. (2009). *Ghana Living Standard Survey: Report of the Fifth Round (GLSS V)*. Accra: Statistical Service.

Goldstein, M.; Janvry, A. de; and Sadoulet, E. (2004). "Is a Friend in Need a Friend Indeed? Inclusion and Exclusion in Mutual Insurance Networks in Southern Ghana". In S. Dercon (ed.), *Insurance Against Poverty*. Oxford: Oxford University Press, pp. 217–246.

Grootaert, C.; Gi-Taik, O.; and Swamy, A. (2002). Social Capital, Household Welfare and Poverty in Burkina Faso. *Journal of African Economies*, 11 (1): 4–38.

Gyasi, S.K. (1995). *Adjusting to the Social Cost of Adjustment in Ghana: Problems and Prospects*. Kumasi, Ghana: University of Science and Technology.

Habtom, G.K., and Ruys, P. (2007). Traditional Risk-sharing Arrangements and Informal Social Insurance in Eritrea. *Health Policy*, 80: 218–235.

Iacoviello, M., and Ortalo-Magne, F. (2003). Hedging Housing Risk in London. *The Journal of Real Estate Finance and Economics*, 27 (2): 191–209.

Kaseke, E., and Dhemba, J. (2006). *Five – Country Study on Service and Volunteering in Southern Africa: Zimbabwe Country Report*. Johannesburg, South Africa: VOSESA; Centre for Social Development in Africa. Retrieved from: www.vosesa.org.za/cross-country.pdf

Katungi, E.; Machethe, C.; and Smale, M. (2007). Determinants of Social Capital Formation in Rural Uganda: Implications for Group-based Agricultural Extension Approaches. *African Journal of Agricultural and Resource Economics*, 2: 167–190.

Kimuyu, P.K. (1999). Rotating Saving and Credit Associations in Rural East Africa. *World Development*, 27 (7): 1299–1308.

Konadu-Agyemang, K. (2000). The Best of Times and the Worst of Times: Structural Adjustment Programs and Uneven Development in Africa: The Case of Ghana. *Professional Geographer*, 52 (3): 469–483.

Lyon, F. (2003). Traders Associations and Urban Food Systems in Ghana: Institutionalist Approaches to Understanding Urban Collective Action. *International Journal of Urban and Regional Research*, 27 (1): 11–23.

Mazuccato, V. (2009). Informal Insurance Arrangements in Ghanaian Migrants' Transnational Networks: The Role of Reverse Remittances and Geographic Proximity. *World Development*, 37 (6): 1105–1115.

Mazuccato, V.; Kabki, M.; and Smith, L. (2006). Locating a Ghanaian Funeral: Remittances and Practices in a Transnational Context. *Development and Change*, 37 (5): 1047–1072.

Miller, J. (1993). Missions, Social Change, and Resistance to Authority: Notes toward an Understanding of the Relative Autonomy of Religion. *Journal for the Scientific Study of Religion*, 32 (1): 29–50.

Moleni, G.M., and Gallagher, B.M. (2006). *Five Country Study on Service and Volunteering in Southern Africa*: Malawi Country Report. Johannesburg, South Africa: VOSESA, Centre for Social Development in Africa. Retrieved from: www.vosesa.org.za/cross-country.pdf

Morduch, J. (1999). Between the State and the Market: Can Informal Insurance Patch the Safety Net? *World Bank Research Observer*, 14 (2): 187–207.

Nance, D.R.; Smith, C.W.; and Smithson, C.W. (1993). On the Determinants of Corporate Hedging. *The Journal of Finance*, 48 (1): 267–284.

Ngwenya, B.N. (2003). Redefining Kin and Family Social Relations: Burial Societies and Emergency Relief in Botswana. *Journal of Social Development in Africa*, 18 (1): 85–110.

Nyonator, F., and Kutzin, J. (1999). Health for Some? The Effects of User Fees in the Volta Region of Ghana. *Health Policy and Plan*, 14 (4): 329–341.

Oduro, A.D. (2010). *Formal and Informal Social Protection in Sub-Saharan Africa*. Paper prepared for the Workshop 'Promoting Resilience through Social Protection in Sub-Saharan Africa' organised by the European Report on Development in Dakar 28–30 June 2010.

Owusu, T.Y. (2000). The Role of Ghanaian Immigrant Associations in Toronto, Canada. *International Migration Research*, 34 (4): 1155–1181.

Owusu-Antwi, G. (2010). The Analysis of the Rural Credit Market in Ghana. *International Business and Economics Research Journal*, 9 (8): 45–56.

Patel, L.; Kaseke, E.; and Midgley, J. (2012). Indigenous Welfare and Community-Based Social Development: Lessons from African Innovations. *Journal of Community Practice*, 20 (1/2): 12–31.

Platteau, J.P. (1997). Mutual Insurance as an Elusive Concept in Traditional Rural Communities. *The Journal of Development Studies*, 23 (6): 764–796.

Porter, C. (2008). *Examining the Impact of Idiosyncratic and Covariate Shocks on Ethiopian Households' Consumption and Income Sources, Mimeo.* Oxford: Department of Economics, Oxford University.

Rankopo, M.J.; Osei-Hwedie, K.; and Modie-Moroka, T.M. (2006). *Five Country Study on Service and Volunteering in Southern Africa: Botswana Country Report.* Johannesburg, South Africa: VOSESA, Centre for Social Development in Africa. Retrieved from: www.vosesa.org.za/cross-country.pdf

Risse, Thomas. (2011). "Governance in Areas of Limited Statehood: Introduction and Overview". In Thomas Risse (ed.), *Governance Without a State? Policies and Politics in Areas of Limited Statehood*. New York: Columbia University Press, pp. 1–35.

Sandbrook, R., and Oelbaum, J. (1997). Reforming Dysfunctional Institutions Through Democratisation? Reflections on Ghana. *The Journal of Modern African Studies*, 35 (4): 603–646.

Senah, K. (2001). In Sickness and in Health: Globalization and Health Care Delivery in Ghana. *Research Review*, 17 (1): 83–89.

Smith, S.; Searle, B.A.; and Cook, N. (2009). Rethinking the Risks of Home Ownership. *Journal of Social Policy*, 38 (1): 83–102.

Tangri, R. (1992). The Politics of Government-Business Relations in Ghana. *The Journal of Modern African Studies*, 30 (1): 97–111.

Thomson, R.J., and Posel, D.B. (2002). The Management of Risk by Burial Societies in South Africa. *South African Actuarial Journal*, 2: 83–128.

Tufano, P. (1996). Who Manages Risk? An Empirical Examination of Risk Management Practices in the Gold Mining Industry. *The Journal of Finance*, 51 (4): 1097–1137.

Vanderpuye-Orgle, J., and Barrett, C.B. (2009). *Risk Management and Social Visibility in Ghana: African Development Bank*. Oxford: Blackwell Publishing Ltd.

Van Ginneken, W. (2002). Social Security for the Informal Sector: A New Challenge for the Developing Countries. *International Social Security Review*, 52 (1): 49–69.

Waddington, C., and Enyimayew, K. (1990). A Price to Pay, Part 2: The Impact of User Charges in the Volta Region of Ghana. *International Journal of Health Planning and Management*, 5 (4): 287–312.

Weerdt, J. de, and Dercon, S. (2006). Risk-Sharing Networks and Insurance Against Illness. *Journal of Development Economics*, 81 (2): 337–356.

Weerdt, J. de; Dercon, S.; Bold, T.; and Pankhurst, A. (2007). "Membership Based Indigenous Insurance Associations in Ethiopia and Tanzania". In M. Chen, R. Jhabvala, R. Kanbur, and C. Richards (eds.), *Membership Based Organizations of the Poor*. London: Routledge, pp. 157–176.

7 Women's economic empowerment in Kenya

Lessons from non-state social protection actors and services in the Nyanza region

Akinyi Nzioki and Winnie Mwasiaji

Introduction

The Constitution of Kenya requires the state to provide social security to persons who are unable to maintain themselves and their dependants (Republic of Kenya, 2010. The Constitution Article 2: 5–6). Kenya has a long history of informal social protection (SP) services, but for the first time, the national SP policy is backed by legislation. The policy mandates the state to provide relief to the poor and vulnerable (Republic of Kenya, 2012a) and establishes a basis for individuals, groups, and communities to hold the government to account.

This constitutional support, coupled with recent economic growth, has enabled Kenya to attain a middle-income status and might give the impression that there is sufficient capacity to ensure all citizens' welfare. The reality is that the state has the capacity to reach out to many thousands, but those needing support to just survive, let alone move out of poverty, are numbered in the millions. Kenya thus has "limited statehood," which lacks the capacity to fully implement its own policy (Risse, 2011). It is non-state actors (NSAs) such as community-based organisations (CBOs) and non-governmental organisations (NGOs) that have stepped in to deliver SP services to the majority of vulnerable groups. In Kenya, as in many countries in Africa, poverty has a female face (IEA, 2008; Seguino and Were, 2014).

This chapter draws from a study in Kenya's Nyanza region, which assessed whether and how NSA SP services are empowering women at both the household and community levels, and expanding their ability to make strategic life choices – a status traditionally denied to them. The vulnerability to poverty of female-headed households is about 14 per cent compared with 5 per cent for male-headed households (Republic of Kenya, 2012b: 12). Gender disparity in access to resources, power, and division of household responsibilities contributes largely to this imbalance. Women are the primary producers of food, caregivers, and significantly contribute to the

Table 7.1 Registered women's groups by membership and contribution

Year	No. of women's groups	Membership	Group contribution (Ksh.million)
2007	138,753	5,417,850	544.6
2008	140,482	5,584,275	547.3
2009	141,560	5,516,396	548.4
2010	142,783	5,579,639	551.2
2011	143,792	5,618,064	553.8

Source: Kenya National Economic Survey 2012. Ksh85 is equivalent to US$1

household economy. Yet they are largely excluded from decision making at the household level; they have limited access to and control over resources such as land, capital, and technology; they work on farms as free family labourers, and their work is both undervalued and underpaid. Predictably, then, poverty has become a gendered phenomenon (Sweetman, 2011). Because of women's high vulnerability to economic and social shocks, many community programmes – especially those that target economic empowerment – are often aligned to women (Nzioki and Mwasiaji, 2013). Nationally, the number of women's groups and the resources they command is growing steadily (see Table 7.1).

However, gender analysis is rarely used as a differentiating lens through which to understand exposure to poverty, risk, and vulnerability, and how SP programmes are designed. While the government is the largest source of financing for formal SP programmes, these either do not reach or actively exclude the majority of the population; NSAs are widespread and numerous in both urban and rural communities, and they need to be. The government's own estimate suggests that there are more than 300,000 NSA groups operating countrywide (Republic of Kenya, 2009). This underscores the need for a more systematic look at NSAs, their associated SP activities, and especially their impact in responding to women's practical and strategic needs.

Social protection services – why empower women?

Women and men face different limits to their opportunities for well-being. These constraints are sometimes "gender specific" (societal norms and practices that are based on gender), or "gender intensified" (inequalities between household members reflecting norms and customs on the distribution of food, access to and ownership of resources such as land), or "gender imposed" (forms of gender disadvantage – discrimination – in the wider public and policy domain). SP has generally been presented in terms of categories of poor, excluded, and vulnerable social groups, differentiated according to age, health status, and relationship to formal labour markets. This leaves out women as a specific category warranting analysis (Sebates-Wheeler and Roelen 2004: 179–193; Patel et al., 2011: 231; Holms et al., 2011: 255–269).

Transformative approaches to SP have much in common with gender and development as a field of research, as well as activism, because they are fundamentally a political way of thinking about poverty, its causes, and its potential solutions. A transformative view of SP starts by analysing the causes of poverty, which acknowledges the political and social factors which shape poverty and deprivation. Policies and programmes informed by this analysis understand the relationship between resources, choice, and empowerment (Kabeer, 1999: 92).

Many SP programmes are designed to have multiple objectives, including attention to different gender-related risks and vulnerabilities. This study adopts "The Promotive and Transformative Framework" to articulate the role of SP in facilitating social transformation – by addressing economic, social, and cultural rights, as well as discrimination and exclusion. Promotive and transformative concepts are especially powerful, as they can be inherently protective and preventive as well (Kabeer, 1997: 4). As confirmed by Molyneux and Thomson (2011: 199), programmes of any kind with any target group are more effective if they strengthen awareness of rights and deliver relevant information, skills, and knowledge that enhance social and economic empowerment. At the same time, gender-sensitive programmes address socio-cultural norms and roles, and address the anomalies within them to nurture gender equality within communities and reduce poverty and vulnerabilities.

The literature describes empowerment as "having options, choice, control and power." According to Keller, women's empowerment is "a process whereby women become able to organise themselves... to increase their own self-reliance, to assert their independent right to make choices and to control resources which will assist them in challenging and eliminating their subordination" (Keller and Shuler, 1991). So empowerment is the process of removing the factors which cause powerlessness (Haque et al., 2011: 17). Women's ability to make decisions and affect outcomes of importance to themselves and their families, and to control their own lives and resources, is often stressed (Kabeer, 2001: 52). Services being provided by NSAs are expanding women's ability to make strategic life choices, for the first time (Kabeer, 200), (Kabeer, 2007).

Of particular importance is women's ability to decide on financial matters with their husbands or with other male family members. This improves their self-determination, self-esteem, status, and power relations within the household. Enhanced networking among neighbours as well as the decision to join groups and attend group meetings is necessary to improve their social networks and to reduce their level of poverty (Parveen et al., 2004). Women need skills and resources to sustain their lives, as well as fair and equal access to economic institutions. Women have the ability to succeed and advance economically and warrant the power to make and act on economic decisions (Golla, Malhorta, Nanda and Mehra, 2011). Having self-determination, making meaningful choices, and having equal decision-making power makes a person an "agent of change". Enabling women to have "agency" literally doubles the change-for-the-better human resource.

Material resources are essential elements of empowering women (their traditionally subordinate status is based on and perpetuated by the notion that those who have nothing can do nothing). SP programmes need to support women to work together to further their shared interest and collectively challenge the structural factors which discriminate against them. This can only be achieved by understanding the gaps and different challenges women and men face through the inequalities created by cultural and statutory systems over the years. By making all SP gender sensitive, every programme becomes a programme for women, and men (Kukrety and Mohanty, 2011).

In 2005/2006, the poverty incidence in Kenya was estimated at 47 per cent. About 16.3 million Kenyans were food poor, with poverty rates markedly higher in rural areas (50 per cent) than in urban areas (34 per cent). Poverty varied from a high of 74 per cent in north-eastern regions to a low of 22 per cent in Nairobi. It was also higher for households with orphans and vulnerable children (OVC; 54 per cent), older people (53 per cent), and people with disabilities (63 per cent for children with disabilities and 53 per cent for adults) than for the general population (Republic of Kenya, 2012a).

Women's economic empowerment programme in the Nyanza region

This chapter draws its analysis from both secondary and empirical data collected for a period of one year. Secondary data was collected from the national NGO registry, NGOs and faith-based organisations (FBOs), government ministries at the district level, especially the Ministry of Gender, Children and Social Services, which is also the agency responsible for the coordination of SP services in general. Mapping of NSAs in SP services was conducted in four counties in Nyanza – Bondo, Siaya, Kisumu, and Kisii. Some 376 NSAs were identified overall (see Figure 7.1).

Bondo County is one of the poorest with 25 per cent of its population experiencing absolute poverty. It has an HIV/AIDS prevalence of 23 per cent. An estimated 10,738 children have been orphaned, and there are a significant number of child-headed households. Considerable SP resources

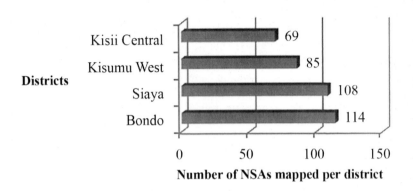

Figure 7.1 Number of non-state actors mapped by district (county).

and interventions, especially by NSAs, are being channelled into the county to mitigate the socio-economic impacts.

Siaya County's overall poverty is 40 per cent, and the incidence of HIV/AIDS is estimated at 24 per cent. The population is also largely a rural settlement with women forming almost 70 per cent of the population. The county is one of the nine Millennium Counties in Kenya and one of the two that have the Millennium Village Project initiatives.

Kisumu West County is the home of Kisumu City – the capital of the Nyanza Region – and hosts three main informal settlements: Manyatta, Nyalenda, and Obunga. Together they house more than 40 per cent of the county population. This has exerted pressure on social amenities such as housing, public health services, water, and sewage systems. There is also a large and increasing number of unemployed adults and street children.

Kisii Central County is one of the most densely populated areas in the country, with 758 people per square kilometre. Incomes are unevenly distributed, and many of the county's population live below the absolute poverty level. Some 46.8 per cent experience food poverty. Health facilities are inadequate, unevenly distributed, and lacking in essential medicines. A high percentage of children are stunted due to poor nutrition. Female genital mutilation (FGM) is still carried out on more than 80 per cent of girls, and this has led to a high school dropout rate, early marriage, and consequent poverty among girls and women.

Overall, 376 organisations were mapped and interviewed. They included local NGOs, CBOs, FBOs, and international agencies. The mapping identified

Women's economic empowerment in Kenya 109

NSAs providing active social protection (SP) services and discerning their funding sources, as well as how they governed themselves, the types and scale of services they provided, their targeted beneficiaries, their respective targets (e.g. support to women, youth, orphans), and the extent to which their programmes were specifically empowering women.

Three types of SP services were selected: cash transfer, women's enterprise fund (WEF), and youth development enterprise fund (YDEF). A sample of 35 NSAs and ten state agencies providing services were selected for in-depth analysis. Finally, 15 beneficiaries per NSA and individuals supported by state agencies were identified, giving a total of 695 beneficiaries who were asked to assess the quality of services they received. In the selection of beneficiaries, care was taken to ensure a mix of women, men, and other special groups. Three main assumptions were tested: (i) that NSA services address women's empowerment and assist in the cause of gender equality, (ii) that NSAs are more responsive to gender and women's empowerment than the selected state services, and (iii) that gender-focused and participatory programme design and implementation empower women.

Social protection services provided by non-state actors in the Nyanza region

Promotive services are the most common SP organised and delivered by NSAs in the Nyanza region. These include income-generating activities (IGAs), micro-credit, livelihood skills training, and capacity building.

Income-generating activities

NSAs provide start-up materials or equipment to women's groups, self-help groups, and people with disabilities to establish viable and sustainable projects/enterprises such as poultry keeping, weaving, beekeeping, and market-stall trading in cereals and vegetables. The total market value or capital for such IGAs could range from US$20 to US$50 per month compared to the poverty line of US$2.

Micro-credit, table banking, and merry-go-rounds

These systems provide very small loans to people who lack the collateral or steady employment (or literacy) required to secure formal advances. Most NSAs' micro-credit services are intended to support entrepreneurship and to alleviate poverty, and also to empower women and, by extension, support entire communities. Table banking typically involves a group of women (not more than 25 members) who literally "put money on the table" (circa

$3 each). This pool is then loaned to one or more of the members to start or grow a business. The group determines the amount of the loan and sets the repayment terms. The table money and net profit generated by interest on the loans (less an administration fee) is distributed to members on a rotating schedule and therefore named "merry-go-round." The continuous contribution by members ensures (and can build up) a revolving fund for short- or long-term loans at interest rates that are very low relative to independent "loan sharks" for whom 10 per cent per month – in advance – would be normal.

Livelihood/skills training and community capacity building

Training programmes are open to all and tailored to participants' chosen activities, such as new farming methods to improve crop yields, ways to improve the quality of a product or value addition, basic business practices such as balancing accounts, and how to be competitive in the marketplace. In parallel with any kind of skills training, they also receive community capacity building (CCB) lessons – a kind of civic education that focuses on understanding the obstacles to their development goals and creates an enabling environment for the beneficiaries to participate in political processes and community leadership.

Cash transfers (food and other resources) to vulnerable groups

Cash transfers (CT) – from the state – are increasingly provided to families living with OVC, persons with severe disability, and older citizens. Food and clothing can also be provided alongside non-state CT programmes, especially, but not only, by big-scale NSAs such as UNICEF and OXFAM. The CT is the Kenya government's flagship SP programme, reaching circa 100,000 households and 230,000 OVC across the country. Households considered "ultra-poor" are eligible and may have OVC. Beneficiaries receive a flat monthly transfer of US$21

Assessing women's empowerment in the provision of social protection services

To assess whether women's participation in promotive SP services provided by NSAs has improved their economic empowerment, there are four indicators: (i) participation, (ii) enhanced networking, (iii) decision making at the household level, and (iv) ownership of assets.

Women's participation in promotive social protection activities as empowerment

To transform gender relations, women must be directly involved in the planning processes of programmes. Participation in itself is empowering. The SP services address education, health, water, clothing, and food subsidies. These protective and preventive services are supplemented with promotive activities such as income generation, table banking/merry-go-round, compulsory savings and micro-credit support, business management training, community health, and leadership skills.

In CBOs in the study area, women were involved in the organisation of meetings, identification of group needs, accounting for money, and training programmes. In NGOs, women were generally seen as beneficiaries, not as co-planners. Typically, NGOs write proposals in line with the policies of development agencies so that they can get funding, and rarely do they consult the target beneficiaries or directly involve them at the planning stage. However, in-depth interviews with the NGOs that support women in the study area suggested beneficiaries were consulted about their priority needs and were involved in executive action and thereby also exerted peer pressure.

But how helpful to women's real empowerment is that? Do SP programmes that enable women to form groups and receive civic education build their confidence to participate in the public arena of community mobilisation and even political leadership? Compared with similar promotive services that the state supports – for instance WEF and the Youth Entrepreneurship Development Fund (YEDF) – non-state programmes appear to provide more opportunity for women's groups to participate in community governance. Indeed, twice (!) as many women in NSAs were involved in leadership, governance, and civic activities in their communities than women who received state SP such as CTs. Non-state programmes are generally small scale and at the community level, where monitoring and action is closer and more face-to-face. With devolved government creating power centres closer to communities, there are new opportunities for women's solidarity groups to have a voice and impact at an official level.

Enhanced networking for women

More than 90 per cent of the women interviewed reported that their social networks had improved with the SP programmes as they regularly attended group meetings and training. This meant new information and knowledge, and the freedom to talk to and network with other women and service providers. Mobility and interaction – long denied to many women – are empowerment tools, even though they compete for time with domestic chores. Husbands and extended family members are becoming more receptive to the empowerment group trend and better at recognising that they are no longer dealing with a personal "chattel", but with the solidarity of all women in the community. The opposition to practices that subordinate women is now formidable – locally, nationally, and globally.

Women's ability to make decisions at the household level

The study asked whether SP programmes implemented by NSAs had enhanced women's decision-making at the household level – decisions over family incomes and the use of family resources. Can and do women make independent choices and put them into action without consulting their spouses or any other members of the family? Have their skills improved, and have the decisions they make helped transform the welfare of the household?

Beneficiaries reported that before joining the women's groups, they did not have much to contribute in material assets or decisions over their use. Some endured domestic violence at the hands of their spouses or male relatives without recourse. However, after becoming members of women's groups, almost all (95.6 per cent) reported contributing to the family income, making decisions about family assets, and having more of a voice and even final say on daily purchases and on how household income is spent. They said domestic violence had reduced and that their spouses were showing more respect to them as equal partners in their marriages (see Table 7.2).

Table 7.2 Women's ability to make decisions as a result of non-state actors social protection programmes

	Responses of women		
	Yes	No	Somewhat
Ability to contribute in decision making over family income?	368 95.6%	10 2.3%	7 1.8%
Ability to contribute in making decisions over the use of family resources?	368 95.6%	10 2.3%	7 1.8%
Ability to make independent choices and put them into action?	290 75.3%	83 21.6%	12 3.1%
Improved skills as a result of SP?	380 98.7%	3 0.8%	2 0.5%

Source: Field data, 2013

Ownership of assets

The study assessed whether the creation of employable skills, micro-enterprise support, and other income support programmes supported by the NSAs had enabled women to acquire and own assets that they could convert in times of economic and social crises. Women beneficiaries reported having bought household assets such as utensils, furniture, and livestock (chickens, goats, sheep, and cows) using money from merry-go-rounds and savings and loans schemes. Some used their income to renovate their houses, build water tanks, etc. Nevertheless, none of the women had acquired land – probably the most valued productive asset in rural Kenya. Commonly, in many parts of Kenya, on the death of a patriarch, his land is substantively divided between all his sons; the more liberal legacies might set aside a small portion for the widow and/or all daughters combined. "Transforming" this culture is not a small matter; it has been a global tradition since the advent of land ownership, and even the "enlightened" First World has changed only recently and still not completely.

Innovative social protection mechanisms of non-state sectors

Initiatives implemented by CBO women's groups and their supporting NGOs arguably rank as "best practice" in SP, and they are creating their own innovative mechanisms to foster economic growth and prosperity. Women are taking over leadership roles to improve their lives and livelihoods and to build social safety nets. The in-depth study found grassroots women's groups had been leading and organising livelihood initiatives for the benefit of their members and wider communities, both because of and despite of high levels of poverty, weak infrastructure, frequent drought, and high HIV prevalence. They help members' access basic services such as water, energy, health, and education, as well as to ensure food security. Most of these groups aim at immediate poverty relief for the poorest and most vulnerable, strengthening livelihoods to reduce long-term chronic poverty, increasing resilience to shocks, and creating an enabling environment through awareness of rights and entitlement for the effective participation of all those they help.

Merry-go-rounds are pivotal. One day is set aside where the groups meet to collect and lend each other money, using these informal networks to support each other in times of need. Here are some of their testimonies:

Jane Awour, a woman who has spent about 20 years in a women's group: "I owe what I have to the merry-go-round. I have built a house, taken my children to school land up to university, and even boosted my business."

Paskalia Owaka sells groundnuts in Kisumu town: "Each day, we give one member 100 shillings (US$1) for stocking up goods, and by the end of the day, the money has become a substantial amount."

"We do not meet only to collect money but also to make sure that whenever we visit a house we would like to see some development in terms of new furniture, new utensils, or tablecloths, among others," explains Truphena, who is the chair of a women's group in Siaya County.

The women's group initiatives in SP were found to be unique in that poor and vulnerable women plan, implement, and manage their activities in their own communities based on the principles of collective action, self-discipline, and peer-group accountability. While the group members and activities are diverse, these common features stood out as sustainers of women's empowerment, built of both quite large and very small bricks.

Collective organising is a vital first step. Groups start by addressing collective problems, choosing their leaders through democratic consensus, and meeting regularly (usually weekly or monthly) to network, disseminate information, and respond to challenges and opportunities as they arise. Next is the combination of livelihood activities with protective and promotive services. To many women, economic promotion is the foundation of empowerment; it offers a degree of security that builds confidence to take further action on other issues, both macro and micro.

Peer pressure and consensus building is the basis of the groups' accountability. Their financial management dictates that money is collected, allocated, and disbursed openly. Group pressure ensures each member conforms to good governance behaviour, and legal redress is rare. The groups demonstrate that the benefits of informal SP programmes can go beyond offering immediate and practical benefits for individual households, to promotion of sustainable resilience to poverty.

Conclusions and policy recommendations

Women's groups are effectively pursuing activities that not only influence their livelihood chances but also transform their positions in society. The approach, which combines training with income generation and access, has given women confidence – at all levels – and a platform and network to occupy higher socio-political and economic ground.

The CT programmes do not deliver these transformative strategies. Perhaps the state's minimalist and one-dimensional CT programme could learn lessons from NSAs' (especially women's CBOs) multi-prong approach. The SP programmes must support both practical *and* broader strategic and transformative needs, preferably simultaneously. A clue to priorities is that SP (welfare) begins and ends with itself. Promotive and transformative SPs are open-ended and often inherently provide protective and preventive SP as they proceed.

Women's groups must be recast from "beneficiaries" to "active agents" of change. NSAs – local, national, and international – are essential to the transformative approach that community-based women's groups have taken to solve their practical and strategic needs. NGOs have better resources and more formal leverage than community organisations to promote high-level and national-scale public action to challenge existing laws and policies that constrain women. The SP programmes have a political role to fulfil as well as a practical one, enabling marginalised and excluded groups living in extreme poverty to challenge the status quo: poverty and economic insecurity are not freak accidents; they are a reflection of structural inequality of income, wealth, power, and status.

A practical approach for women's groups is to develop an umbrella organisation – a kind of federation that will coordinate the numerous women groups into a network with the critical mass to be unignorable. Collective action by women has enabled many to take up leadership positions in their communities. Kenya's current decentralisation policy offers opportunity for grassroots mobilisation.

References

Golla, A.; Malhortra, A.; Nanda, P.; and Mehra, R. (2011). *Understanding and Measuring Women's Economic Empowerment: Definition, Framework and Indicators.* Wasahington, DC: International Center for Research on Women (ICRW). Retrieved from: www.icrw.org/files/publications/Understanding-measuring-womens-economic-empowerment.pdf

Haque, M.; Islam, T.M.; Tareque, I.; and Mostofa, G. (2011). Women Empowerment or Autonomy: A Comparative View in Bangladesh Context. *Bangladesh e-Journal of Sociology*, 8 (2) July: 17–30.

Holmes, R.; Jones, J.; Mannan, F.; Vargas, R.; Tefere, Y.; and Woldehanna, T. (2011). Addressing Gendered Risks and Vulnerability Through Social Protection: Examples of Good Practice from Bangladesh, Ethiopia and Peru. *Oxfam GB: Gender and Development*, 19 (July): 255–269.

Institute of Economic Affairs. (2008). *Profiles of Women's Socio-Economic Status in Kenya*. Nairobi: IEA.

Kabeer, N. (1997). Editorial: Tactics and Trade-off: Revisiting the Links Between Gender and Poverty. *IDS Bulletin*, 28 (3): 1–13.

Kabeer, N. (1999). Resources, Agency, Achievements: Reflections on the Measurement of Women's Empowerment. *Development and Change*, 30 (3): 435–464.

Kabeer, N. (2001). *Reflections on the Measurement of Women's Empowerment in Discussing Women's Empowerment: Theory and Practice*. SIDA Studies no. 3 Stockholm, Swedish International Development Cooperation Agency.

Keller, B., and Shuler, S. (1991). Policy and Planning for the Empowerment of Zambia's Women Farmers. *Canadian Journal of Development Studies*, 12 (1): 75–88.

Molyneux, M., and Thomson, M. (2011). Cash Transfers, Gender Equity and Women's Empowerment in Peru, Equador and Bolivia. *Oxfam GB: Gender and Development*, 19 (July): 195–211.

Nzioki, A., and Mwasiaji, W. (2013). *Provision of Social Protection Services by NSA: A Gender Assessment in Nyanza Region, Kenya*. A project report submitted by the Centre for Land, Economy and Rights of Women. Nairobi: PASGR.

Parveen, S., and Leohauser, I.U. (2004). *Empowerment in Rural Women Bangladesh: A Household Level Analysis*. Paper presented at Conference on Rural Poverty Reduction through Research for Development and Transformation, Berlin, Germany 5–7 October.

Patel, L., and Hotchfeld, T. (2011). It Buys Food but Does Not Change Gender Relations? Child Support Grants in Seweto, South Africa. *Oxfam G: Gender and Development*, 19 (July): 229–239.

Republic of Kenya. (2009). *Kenya National Social Protection Strategy*. Nairobi: Government Printer.

Republic of Kenya. (2012). *Economic Survey*. Nairobi: Kenya National Bureau of Statistics.

Risse, T. 2011. "Governance in Areas of Limited Statehood: Introduction and Overview". In T. Risse (ed.), *Governance Without a State? Policies and Politics in Areas of Limited Statehood*. New York: Columbia University Press, pp. 1–35.

Seguino, S., and Were, M. (2014). Gender, Development and Economic Growth in Sub-Saharan Africa. *Journal of African Economies*, 23 (suppl1): i18-i61.

Sweetman, C. (2011). Introduction. *Social Protection: Gender and Development*, 19 (July): 171–177.

8 Governance of non-state social protection initiatives for addressing gendered poverty in Uganda
Beyond counting of women on governance committees?

Florence Kyoheirwe Muhanguzi

Introduction

In many countries, state responsibility for vulnerable citizens' welfare is specified in the Constitution or legislation. However, in cases of "limited statehood" – where government is unable to deliver adequate social protection (SP; Risse, 2011) – non-state actors (NSAs) have come to the people's rescue. Until recently, state SP in Uganda, through health insurance and unemployment benefits, reached only formal sector workers. In the wake of state failure to expand the scope or reach of such services, NSAs have become increasingly active in market, non-market, and informal support systems for individuals, groups, communities, and social networks. These arrangements are absolutely important and remarkably effective for both urban and rural households (De Coninck and Drani, 2009; Devereux and Getu, 2013; Luttrell and Moser, 2004; Norton, Conway and Foster, 2001).

There has been a rapid proliferation of NSAs in Uganda since 1986, with roles beyond the traditional charity-driven functions of relief and humanitarian service. They have increasingly been involved in developmental projects. Available records[1] indicate that there are currently nearly 13,000 NSAs that provide SP services countrywide. However, despite this trend and long-standing national commitment to gender equality and women's empowerment, gendered vulnerability to poverty remains a major social malaise.

Literature shows that gender-sensitive governance of SP has high potential to reduce some gendered poverty and vulnerability (Corner, 2005; Holmes and Jones, 2010a, 201b, 2010c), but the extent of this potential has not been thoroughly studied – how formal and informal policies, laws, and regulations, as well as participation in decision making in NSA operations might influence effective attention to women's or men's vulnerability to poverty. There is almost no information on how governance mechanisms and processes, in particular, facilitate transformative social and economic change.

While a number of studies in Uganda (Barya, 2009, 2011; Bukuluki and Watson, 2012; Kasente et al., 2002) have assessed the status of SP, they have generally not unbundled gender-specific issues. Calder and Nakafeero (2012) offer a gender-situational analysis of SP in Uganda but do not cover governance of NSAs. So this chapter draws on the broader study that investigated the "Governance of non-state social protection initiatives: implications for addressing gendered vulnerability to poverty in Uganda" (Muhanguzi et al., 2013).

Socio-economic and political contexts of vulnerability and poverty in Uganda

Since Uganda became independent from British rule in 1962, it has undergone a number of regime changes, which have had significantly negative socio-economic effects (Kanyeihamba, 2002). However, since 1986, with the arrival of President Museveni, there has been political stability and economic growth. Increase in Gross Domestic Product (GDP) has averaged about 6.7 per cent from 1986 to 2010 and 5.5 per cent between 2010 to 2014, thus enabling poverty reduction from 56.4 per cent in 1992/1993, 24.5 per cent in 2009/2010, to 19.7% in 2013 (The Republic of Uganda, 2015; Ministry of Finance, Planning and Economic Development, 2014). Nevertheless, about 43.3 per cent of all households that live above the poverty line are classified as vulnerable, meaning they can easily fall back into poverty.

The majority of poor people are women and children, especially orphans – whether living within households or roaming as street children. This is reflected in the Gender Inequality Index (GII) of 0.517, giving Uganda a rank of 110 out of 148 countries in the 2012 global listing (UNDP, 2013). Other vulnerable categories include people with disabilities, female-headed households (divorced, separated, widowed), elderly people, refugees and internally displaced people (IDPs), HIV/AIDS-affected households, and isolated communities (DRT and CPRC, 2013). Studies by Development Research Training (DRT) and Chronic Poverty Research Centre (CPRC) indicate that 93.2 per cent of the chronically poor are women; 37.1 per cent are female-headed households, and 20 per cent are widows.

Women in Uganda experience multiple constraints that increase their vulnerability. These are associated with low levels of education and multiple roles and responsibilities that subject them to "time poverty" and limit their mobility and engagement in productive activities outside the home (Blackden, 2004; Devereux et al., 2002; Nordic Consulting Group [NCG], 2008; Otiso, 2006).

Governance of non-state social protection 119

They also lack domestic voice and decision-making status, which limits their access to and control over productive resources/assets including land, credit, or inputs and earnings/income from the proceeds of their labour. There are biases in labour markets and exclusion from a variety of economic, social, and political institutions (Blackden, 2004; Devereux et al., 2002; DRT and CPRC, 2013; Kyalisiima, 2007; Ministry of Lands, Housing and Urban Development, 2008; NCG, 2008; UNFPA and Ministry of Gender, Labour and Social Development, 2009), as well as limited sexual and reproductive rights.

Blackden (2004) and other scholars argue that the economic dependency of women – their lack of control over productive resources and assets – intersect with cultural attitudes and beliefs (such as bride wealth, early/forced marriages, polygamy, widow inheritance) to increase their vulnerability and exclusion. Cultural factors further limit women's control over their physical bodies and safe spaces, manifested in sexual and gender-based violence[2] that has become common for the majority of women in Uganda (Forum for Women in Democracy, 2010; International Federation for Human Rights FIDH and FHRI, 2012; NCG, 2008; Otiso, 2006; United Nations Fund for Population Activities and MoGLSD, 2009). Such practices undermine girls' and young women's dignity, freedom of choice, and agency; lowers their status in society; and increases their vulnerability to poverty throughout and across life cycles.

Legal and policy context for social protection in Uganda

Uganda's 1995 Constitution provides for protection and promotion of fundamental and other human rights of vulnerable groups: children, elderly persons, persons with disabilities, women, and all other marginalized groups (Objective V; VII; XIV; XVI)[3] The Constitution guarantees rights to social justice and economic development, in particular rights and opportunities to access education, food security, clean and safe water, work, decent shelter, clothing, and pension and retirement benefits (Objectives XIV; XVI; XX; XXI; XXII). The Constitution's fourth chapter outlaws discrimination and obliges the state to take affirmative action in favour of groups marginalised on the basis of gender, age, disability, or any other reason created by history, tradition, or custom in order to redress the imbalances which exist against them. These constitutional provisions have been translated into specific laws, including the Children Act, CAP 59; the Equal Opportunities Commission Act, 2007; the Persons with Disabilities Act, 2006; the Domestic Violence Act, 2010; the National Social Security Act, Cap 222; the Education Act, 2008; and the Land Act, 1998, and amendment of 2004 (Republic of Uganda, 1997a; 2007; 2006; 2010a; 1997b; 1998 2004) among others.

Commitment to address risk and vulnerability to poverty through SP is articulated in the National Development Plan I (NDP) 2010/2011–2014/2015 and NDP II (2015/2016–2019/2020) under the social development sector (The Republic of Uganda, 2010, 2015). This is operationalised in the Social Development Investment Plan II (SDIP), which provides a planning framework to address risk and vulnerability among the poor, marginalized, and socially excluded groups such as older persons, persons with disabilities, orphans and other vulnerable children, women, nonliterate adults, and ethnic minorities for the five years to 2016 (MoGLSD, 2011). The plan provides interventions and strategies to transform the lives of the poor and vulnerable under the theme "Accelerating social transformation through promoting employment and the rights of the vulnerable and marginalized". Other policies guiding the SP sector include the National Orphans and Vulnerable Children Policy, National Policy on Disability, National Policy for Older Persons, the National Equal Opportunities Policy (2006), National Gender Policy (2007), Universal Primary Education and Universal Secondary Education policies. The National Social Protection Policy (2015) is in place and indicates government commitment to address vulnerability and inequities in the country (The Republic of Uganda, 2015). The integration of gender in all these initiatives is a central government objective, as guided by the National Gender Policy (MoGLSD, 2007). Reducing vulnerability and poverty are key concerns of the gender policy.

In sum, there is a paper mountain of legislative and policy frameworks.

NSAs made up of formal NGOs and mostly informal community-based organisations (CBOs) are providing SP services that support the poor in skills and knowledge, economic empowerment, relief and humanitarian service, adult literacy, education, and peacebuilding with neighbouring communities, among others (Lwanga-Ntale, Namuddu, and Onapa, 2008). A few are adopting advocacy roles to promote the human rights and social inclusion of minority groups. The CIVICUS, World Alliance for Citizen Participation study group, notes that CBOs (with no paper promises) are significantly more effective than the state in meeting the needs of the marginalised and providing better services to vulnerable groups (CPRC, 2009).

Gendered vulnerability to poverty and governance mechanisms of non-state social protection initiatives: reflections on existing literature

In most developing countries, SP initiatives are seen as significant in addressing the different vulnerabilities of men and women. There is an increasing body of knowledge on the current debates and work on SP by state and NSAs both internationally and country specific. This literature provides insights into the link between governance and gendered vulnerability to poverty.

Gender and vulnerability to poverty

Risk and vulnerability to poverty is complex. The CPRC (2008) identifies five dimensions:

- insecurity (environmental, conflict/war, violence, and lack of assets or entitlements)
- lack of political voice and representation/powerlessness (limited citizenship)
- spatial disadvantage (exclusion from politics, markets, and resources because of geographical remoteness)
- social discrimination (characterised by exploitative relationships of power and patronage)
- poor work opportunities (work does not allow asset accumulation and children's education)

Most SP programmes have focused on the economic risks and assumed the effects of these risks are homogenous across the gender divide (Holmes and Jones, 2009). But the economic impacts of environmental, natural, and social risks are influenced by gender dynamics (Holmes and Jones, 2011). For example, in times of economic crisis, women are often the first to lose jobs in the formal sector (Luttrell and Moser, 2004). Cuts in public expenditure are also likely to affect women more because they typically have greater responsibility for household health and education (Quisumbing, Meinzen-Dick and Bassett, 2008). The effects of economic malaise on men's self-image and status are increasingly recognised. Silberschmidt (2001) for instance, highlights the way in which rising unemployment and low incomes are undermining the male breadwinner role, resulting in negative coping strategies, such as sexually aggressive behaviour and gender-based violence, in a bid to reassert traditional masculine identities.

Kabeer and Subrahmanian (1996) identify three sources of risk for women and men that cause differences in vulnerability: gender-intensified, gender-specific, and gender-imposed constraints.

- Gender-intensified constraints arise from inequalities in opportunities and resource access, which reflect community or customary norms (quoted in Luttrell and Moser, 2004).

- Gender-specific constraints relate to the biological roles of reproduction and the socially ascribed role of caring, restrictions on women's behaviour in the social-norms domain, and taboos against women using certain technology and men doing certain tasks.
- Gender-imposed constraints result from discrimination by those who allocate resources outside the household or community such as informal cultural beliefs in institutions rather than formalised rules; for example, defining membership in such a way as to exclude women, recruitment in stereotypical gender roles, and so on.

These constraints translate into differential gender needs and interests – both practical and strategic.

The literature attests to higher risks of vulnerability to poverty among women than men, largely attributed to cultural perceptions of their position, role, and potential contribution to society (CPRC, 2008; Holmes and Jones, 2010a; Luttrell and Moser, 2004). Women are disadvantaged in intra-household distribution of resources and power; they contribute less to household income and flows, thus limiting their capacity to claim an equitable and appropriate share of scant resources (Luttrell and Moser, 2004). The gendered vulnerability to poverty characterised by social discrimination and unequal distribution of resources and power within the household keeps households poor (DRT and CPRC, 2013). Consequently, commitment to gender equality, social inclusion, and increased "agency" constitute "transformative" social change and should be vital goals in the quest to end chronic poverty. The OECD (2009) indicates that SP helps reduce gender disparities by helping men and women manage trade-offs between immediate needs and future livelihoods. Vreymans and Verhulst (2004), Pfeiffer and Anderson (2004), and Bergh (2006) suggest that high levels of SP provide a good basis for anchoring socio-economic growth at the household, community, and national levels.

Good governance as an effective strategy for tackling gendered vulnerability to poverty

Citizens' influence and oversight, responsive and responsible leadership, rule of law, and inter-group relations are the characteristics of effective governance. Effective governance is seen as a means for reducing poverty and ensuring more equal, democratic, and corruption-free societies, as well as a means of promoting social justice and gender equality, and furthering the rights of all citizens (Hyden, 1992; Brody, 2009). Brody argues that governance that is sensitive to both genders leads to more equal opportunities for women in terms of choices and rights; governance needs to engage both women and men meaningfully to ensure that programmes

- meet the separate and mutual needs;
- respond to the differing needs and priorities in spending, policies, and legislation;
- enable the rights of both genders to participate in decisions that affect their lives (Brody, 2009).

Equalising the status of both genders axiomatically benefits women (Holmes and Slater, 2012).

Governance style and structure are major determinants of performance and effectiveness. They shape policy, programme design and execution, and accountability (Boone, 2003). Certainly, formal non-state SP actors have institutional arrangements, rules, regulations, and accountability mechanisms (Amdissa, 2013). But so do informal NSAs. In a different style, they are also governed by a set of rules and regulations on disciplined behaviour, often backed by a well-developed system of penalties (Norton et al., 2001). Boone (2003) argues that non-state and non-profit organisations enjoy considerable autonomy in defining their missions, setting their own goals, and crafting their own strategies. The mission is at the heart of why the non-profit organisation exists and an important indicator of effectiveness in responding to the needs of beneficiaries – men and women. Boone notes that institutional choices are controlled by pre-existing structures such as political-economic relations and social hierarchy. According to Tsai (2007), results are better when organisations elicit moral commitment and bestow moral standing. Thus it is probable that CBOs, which have a bigger moral stake in members and communities, are more likely to be effective in the delivery of SP services than international or national NSAs.

Interventions work by protecting, preventing, promoting, or transforming to address the causes of vulnerabilities faced by individuals or communities. They address both the strategic and practical needs of men and women. Addressing gendered forms of vulnerability leads to significant gains in gender equity, poverty reduction, and human development, and these are key in unlocking economic potential and pro-poor growth (Thakur et al., 2009).

Effective gender protection – of any kind – requires gender sensitivity. In turn, gender sensitivity requires good governance. So the starting point is self-evidently governance mechanisms (policies, laws, and regulations) and processes (policy and programme design, implementation, monitoring, and evaluation) (Corner, 2005; Holmes and Jones, 2010c; Kabeer, 2008). The realisation of women's rights must be recognised as not just one component of, but as central to, the goals and practices of governance and whatever it is governing.

Studying non-state social protection initiatives in Katakwi and Kyegegwa districts

Data for this study was collected between December 2012 and May 2013 in Uganda's Katakwi and Kyegegwa districts. They were purposively selected to represent the two broad tribal/cultural groupings – the Nilo-Hamites (Katakwi) and Bantu (Kyegegwa) – in the north-eastern and western regions of Uganda, respectively. Criteria for selection of specific districts included their people's poverty and vulnerability status, as well as the presence of both state and non-state SP actors. The team conducted a mapping exercise of all non-state SP actors at sub-county level. Then two sub-counties with urban and rural communities portraying different characteristics and experiences with regard to gender and vulnerability to poverty were selected. In the Kyegegwa district, the Town Council and Mpara sub-county were selected for in-depth study based on high levels of vulnerability among three demographic types – long-established residents, internal migrants, and refugees – and on the high-tension population dynamics in the area. In Katakwi district, Omodoi and Katakwi sub-counties were selected because of their high concentration of NSA activity and high levels of vulnerability to poverty. Study participants were drawn from both urban and rural areas.

A total of 64 of the mapped NSAs were selected for in-depth study of their internal governance processes and mechanisms, and how these influenced effective tackling of vulnerability to poverty. Using the snowball method, and in liaison with local leaders and heads of NSAs, a total of 160 (95 females and 65 males) beneficiaries were purposively selected for interviews. Four focus group discussions (FGDs) (two for women and two for men) with an average of ten people each were conducted in each study area.

Study findings and analysis

The study focused on two main governance parameters: the laws and policies of groups, and the participation of their members in decision making (representation and voice).

Gender analysis of the laws, policies, and guidelines of non-state actors and targeting of social protection services

All the NSAs, whether formal or informal, have some form of governing policies and regulations, written and unwritten. In the Kyegegwa district, all registered NSAs said their members adhered to their constitutions, policies, and regulations. However, only 11 per cent were able to present written documents to the research team – despite the fact that ready-made templates and training for development of written constitutions were available to them through Patience Pays Professional Organisation (PAPRO). In the Katakwi district, 95 per cent of the selected NSAs said they had a constitution (only 26 per cent of those were able to present a copy to the research team) while 5 per cent had by-laws.

Constitutions provided vision, mission, name, and location; geographical coverage; aims and objectives; and activities to be implemented. They articulated the organisational structure, membership recruitment, composition and termination; election of leaders on committees; duties of office bearers in management of the organisation and programme implementation; membership fees and payment terms; fines and penalties for particular breaches; and sharing of benefits and guidelines for seeking assistance in case of bereavement or major illness. The constitutions specify the frequency of meetings to review progress and to make operational decisions, guidelines for the general meeting/assembly, reporting and feedback mechanisms, financial accountability, standing orders and by-laws, language of communication, and procedures in the event of dissolution. CBOs which did not have written constitutions had (usually unwritten) rules agreed in plenary to guide their operations. These typically included respect for each other and payment of fines for lateness, irregular attendance, misconduct during a meeting, or failure to repay loans. Respect for each other was the watchword of most CBOs. Other rules and regulations prohibited drunkenness and set requirements for borrowing by non-members (such as securing three members as guarantors).

Most of the documents were gender blind (or neutral), suggesting a lack of awareness (or cultural stagnation) of gender issues for men, women, girls, and boys in the community. The major objectives of most NSAs were provision of skills in income generation, prevention and treatment of HIV/AIDS, improved access to health facilities, sensitisation and awareness around issues of peace and reconciliation, and advocacy for the rights of vulnerable groups.[4]

A few organisations[5] had policies informed by gender-specific "objectives" such as promotion of education of both boys and girls, promotion of gender and human rights through community sensitisation on gender-based violence, promotion of modern farming practices among women to ensure improved livelihoods and food security, and promotion of credit and savings schemes that included women. Their gender-specific "action" addressed women's poverty, hunger, and maternal health; social discrimination against women and children; sexual harassment; male and female representation and voice; and gender-based violence. Also "acknowledged" were gender and human rights awareness, involving both women and men in elections, representation of males and females in the membership and on the executive board, equal opportunities in recruitment, provision for maternity and paternity leave for full- or part-time paid staff, training women and men in modern agricultural methods, and peacebuilding and conflict resolution. Most of the informal village group associations had a savings and credit component that emphasised equality of access to credit for members and non-members.

Nevertheless, the officials could not articulate how gender was integrated into programming and implementation, implying that the declared provisions were more random or incidental than purposefully driven principles. Interviews revealed that there is either a lack of or limited capacity and skills to conduct gender analysis and to use it to inform design and delivery of SP interventions.

A few organisations,[6] mainly the formal international, national, and larger district operations either conducted or arranged gender training for their staff, or they had specific gender policies. Human resource capacity for gender planning is a major challenge for NSAs if they are to integrate gender in their operations adequately.

About 33 per cent of the NSAs were involved in savings and credit initiatives where most of the women participated – for income support towards school fees and other basic needs such as payment of medical bills, food, mattresses, and blankets, as well as other household items to improve the family's welfare and at times of bereavement. In counterpoint, most women noted that although their local NSAs were small, they had helped them address their immediate needs to improve their household's welfare. A typical respondent comment was

> People have benefitted in getting mattresses; we agreed that every Sunday a member contributes (USD$0.8) towards purchase of a mattress for another member. The group contributes for a member who is in need, for example, to buy beddings, household utensils; some borrow money when they have problems and pay back with no interest. When we save we also buy cows, goats and whatever else we decide.
>
> (FGD women, Katakwi)

Most NSA services are protective and promotive, addressing "practical" (symptomatic) rather than "strategic" (transformative) needs. Although CBOs provide livelihood support programmes that enable women to earn income towards their children's education, health care, and household welfare, this very focus is as likely to reinforce as to remedy the gender trap of women's roles and responsibilities. Activities that focus on transformation of gender power relations (for example, gender-based violence and human rights) are rarely captured by CBOs because they operate in a socio-cultural setting led by men. International and national NGOs do drive transformative programmes but lack adequate coverage.

Representation and voice

In any organisation, women must be represented where policy decisions are made and programmes are designed to ensure their interests are included. Virtually all NSAs have a general assembly of some kind, where members elect an executive committee to "run" the organisation. Committee officials – conventionally a chairperson and deputy, a treasurer, a secretary, etc. – constitute the organisation's "leadership". It follows that the gender balance of the leadership will be an indicator (even a predictor) of the organisation's likely policy and programme design.

All the NSAs in the study districts had some form of decision-making governance structure composed of a general assembly of all members of the organisation/association and an elected executive board or committee headed by a chairperson with a vice chairperson, a treasurer, a secretary, and a mobiliser, as well as a few committee members. This study compared gender balance across overall membership, in leadership, and in seniority of leadership positions. Overall, females (71.5%) dominate the general membership of community-based, NSAs providing SP services. On the sex composition of the members in governance of the organisation (Table 8.1), the data shows that in both districts, there are more males than females in decision-making positions.

Table 8.1 Sex composition of members in senior decision-making positions in non-state actors in the study districts

Position on the committee	*Per cent sex composition*	
Formal (NSAs/CBOs)	*Male*	*Female*
Chairperson	77.8	22.2
Vice chairperson	40.0	60.0
Treasurer	30.2	69.8
Secretary	20.0	80.0
Committee members	47.1	52.9
Informal NSAs		
Chairperson	65.5	34.5
Vice chairperson	43.5	56.5
Treasurer	35.5	64.5
Secretary	20.8	79.2
Committee members	45.7	54.3
Membership to CBOs	28.5%	71.5%

Source: Field findings

The male members dominate the chairperson position, while females dominated the secretary and treasurer positions, because women are reported to be trustworthy; hence, they are entrusted with organisations/associations funds.

Data on gender difference in representation between CBOs and larger NSAs shows a similar pattern with males dominating the senior decision-making positions and females in the more subordinate and clerical positions (vice chairperson, treasurer, and secretary in the two categories of NSAs).

In both districts, the available group members make decisions during their meetings for implementation by either executive committee or selected members. Findings indicate that the local level NSAs involved women and men in decision making more than the international, national, and district NSAs, where consensus building was emphasised as one of the women noted:

> Decisions are made by consensus during monthly meetings – both men and women raise issues freely and reach consensus on the way forward. However, in case of an emergency, the board can meet at any time to decide on a course of action.
> (Female beneficiary, Kyegegwa district)

The importance of consensus building in CBOs was emphasised by one of the key informants:

> If you look at the way the village Savings and Cooperative Credit Schemes (SACCOs) are operating, they are composed of both men and women, and also in some cases the youth are given a special consideration. In such a case, you find that the group members are working together as a team and getting results. The same approach has been applied to revolving fund schemes ("aipoono") in the villages.
> (Male key informant, Katakwi district)

Women and men are not only encouraged but also specifically required to participate in the meetings; for some groups, a fine is charged for either irregular or non-participation. However, it was more difficult for women to attend regularly because they were busy with farming and domestic chores.

During interviews, the majority of formal NSAs said they involved both women and men in planning and implementation decisions. However, their beneficiaries in communities said decisions were always made at the sub-county and district levels by "representatives" of communities – usually local leaders and their relatives. Formal NSAs had field staff who called beneficiaries to consultative community meetings, but these were often organised at the sub-county level (and venues) and hence not accessible to all, especially women. In sum, this represents a theoretically inclusive system, but in practice, it is a non-participatory approach within formal NSAs. This led to poor design and targeting, and inadequate services that do not meet the expectations of community members, as illustrated by participants during interviews:

> Let them (meaning the NGOs) come and ask us what we want, and not them to determine for us. For instance, we may need a water borehole more urgently than a primary school where teachers don't teach our children. Our women have difficulty in getting treatment from the government hospitals because of the distance, no drugs and no doctors at the health unit, so in this case, we need support towards health care services.
>
> (Male beneficiary, Katakwi district)

In both study districts, more women than men were dissatisfied with the services of international and national NSAs. In the Omodoi sub-county, women in the FGD noted that leaders and their relatives benefited more than the poor from programme initiatives, that vulnerable groups (the non-active poor, youth, elderly people, Persons with Disabilities (PWDs) were sometimes excluded, that technical skills (especially gender analysis and mainstreaming) were lacking, and that capacity for report writing and provision of feedback was limited. Such shortcomings have significant implications for addressing gendered vulnerability to poverty.

Conclusion

The findings indicate that most NSA policies, laws, and regulations do not reflect clear and participatory identification of gendered economic and social vulnerabilities, needs, interests, and priorities. Hence their SP services are not informed by the gender situation, but based on broad national and district assumptions of vulnerabilities. The finding is similar to others by Holmes et al. (2011) in Bangladesh, Ethiopia, and Peru.

Gender-aware policies translate to gender-sensitive design features within all SP services. Most SP in the study sites targeted short-term practical needs, but gave little or no strategic attention to chronic problems of gender discrimination and oppression. Transformative gender strategies are not the end game; they are the starting point to ensure SP initiatives have built-in gender awareness and balance at the individual, intra-household, and community levels. Only if and where that is achieved will gendered vulnerability to poverty be addressed effectively.

The findings reveal that where women are not involved in decision making, their priorities and needs are less addressed. Formal NSAs were rated less effective by communities, largely on the grounds that they limited local community voice in their decision making, leading to inadequate and inappropriate responses to individual and group needs.

Only where there is clear recognition and appreciation of gendered vulnerabilities do the policies translate to effective objectives, interventions, and services. Participation in governance and design of programmes was more pronounced at the CBO level, and it is no coincidence that CBOs are seen to be more focused and effective in resolving specific community vulnerabilities.

Implications for policy and practice

NSAs should be encouraged to ensure that gender is integral to all they do. This requires gender-focused assessment and gender training for their staff. The policy framework for NSAs needs to embody these principles and encourage even large NGOs to prioritise grassroots engagement with communities through their local CBOs. The empowerment and inclusion approach encourages design of SP services that prioritise the transformation of gender relations – to the benefit of all.

Acknowledgements

I would like to thank Fred Kakongoro Muhumuza and Julius Okello for their valuable input to the research and report from which this chapter is drawn. Gratitude is also expressed to all those women and men who agreed to participate in the study.

Notes

1 From the NGO Board and NGO Forum membership directory 2012, National Association of Women's Organisations in Uganda (NAWOU) 2003, and Development Network of Indigenous Voluntary Associations (DENIVA). However, the total of NSAs must be taken with caution given that some of the organisations are neither registered at district nor national level and hence the records do not reflect a complete picture.
2 Including physical violence (battering); sexual violence in form of rape, defilement, and sexual harassment; abduction, trafficking, forced prostitution; and other harmful practices such as early forced marriage and female genital mutilation.
3 Under the National Objectives and Directive principles of state policy.
4 Help the needy, support disabled children, and address disasters that affect the clan.

5 These organisations include OTUKO People Living with HIV/AIDS, Omodoi Parents Association (OPA), Family Life Survival (FALISU) and Katakwi District Development Actors Network (KaDDAN), Musomba Farmers Association, Action Aid Uganda, and Lutheran World Federation, among others.

6 Action Aid Uganda, KaDDAN, Child Fund, SOCADIDO, and Lutheran World Federation.

References

Amdissa, T. (2013). "Informal and Formal Social Protection in Ethiopia". In S. Devereux and M. Getu (eds.), *Informal and Formal Social Protection Systems in Sub-Saharan Africa*. Addis Abba: OSSREA and Fountain Publishers, pp. 95–120.

Barya, J.J. (2009). *Interrogating the Right to Social Security and Social Protection in Uganda*. Kampala: Human Rights and Peace Centre.

Barya, J.J. (2011). *Social Security and Social Protection in the Eastern African Community*. Kampala: Fountain Publishers.

Bergh, A. (2006). Work Incentives and Employment Are the Wrong Explanation of Sweden's Success. *Economic Journal Watch*, 3 (3): 452–460.

Blackden, C.M. (2004). *Out of Control: Gender and Poverty in Uganda: A Strategic Country Gender Assessment*. World Bank. Unpublished Report.

Boone, C. (2003). *Political Topographies of the African State: Territorial Authority and Institutional Choice*. New York: Cambridge University Press.

Brody, A. (2009). *Gender and Governance: Overview Report*. Brighton: Institute of Development Studies.

Bukuluki, P., and Watson, C. (2012). *Transforming Cash Transfers: Beneficiary and Community Perspectives on the Senior Citizen Grant (SCG) in Uganda*. London: Overseas Development Institute.

Calder, R., and Nakafeero, A. (2012). *Uganda's Expanding Social Protection Programme: Gender Situational Analysis*. Development Pathways. Unpublished Report.

Chronic Poverty Research Centre (CPRC). (2008). *The Chronic Poverty Report 2008–2009: Escaping Poverty Traps*. Northampton: Belmont Press Ltd.

Chronic Poverty Research Center (CPRC). (2009). *Culture and Social Protection for the Very Poor in Uganda: Evidence and Policy Implication*. Unpublished Report.

Coninck, J. De, and Drani, E. (2009). *Social Protection Is Centuries Old! Culture and Social Protection for the Very Poor in Uganda: Evidence and Policy Implications*. Working Paper No.140. Manchester: Chronic Poverty Research Centre.

Corner, L. (2005). *Gender-sensitive and Pro-poor Indicators of Good Governance*. New York: UNDP.

Devereux, S., and Getu, M. (2013). "The Conceptualization and Status of Informal and Formal Social Protection in Sub-Saharan Africa". In S. Devereux and M. Getu (eds.), *Informal and Formal Social Protection Systems in Sub-Saharan Africa*. Addis Abba: OSSREA and Fountain Publishers, pp.1–8.

Devereux, S.; Lwanga-Ntale, C.; and Sabates-Wheeler, R. (2002). *Social Protection in Uganda: Vulnerability Assessment and Review of Initiatives*. Kampala. Unpublished Report.

DRT (Development Research and Training) and CPRC (The Chronic Poverty Research Centre). (2013). *The Second Chronic Poverty Report – Uganda: Is Anybody Listening?* Unpublished Report.

FOWODE (Forum for Women in Democracy). (2010). *Equal by Right: The Uganda Women's Agenda 2010–2016.* Kampala: FOWODE.

Holmes, R., and Jones, N. (2009). *Putting the Social Back into Social Protection: A Framework for Understanding the Linkages Between Economic and Social Risks for Poverty Reduction a Background Note.* London: Overseas Development Institute.

Holmes, R., and Jones, N. (2010a). *Rethinking Social Protection Using a Gender Lens.* ODI Working Paper No.320. London: Overseas Development Institute.

Holmes, R., and Jones, N. (2010b). *Gender Sensitive Social Protection and MDGs.* London: Overseas Development Institute.

Holmes, R., and Jones, N. (2011). *Gender Inequality, Risk and Vulnerability in the Rural Economy: Refocusing the Public Works Agenda to take Account of Economic and Social Risks.* London: Overseas Development Institute.

Holmes, R.; Jones, N.; Mannan, F.; Vargas, R.; Tafere, Y.; and Woldehanna, T. (2011). Addressing Gendered Risks and Vulnerabilities Through Social Protection: Examples of Good Practice from Bangladesh, Ethiopia, and Peru. *Gender and Development*, 19 (2): 255–269.

Holmes, R., and Slater, R. (2012). *Social Protection Series: Poverty, Vulnerability and Social Protection in the Pacific.* Canberra: Australian Agency for International Development (AusAID).

Hyden, G. (1992). "Governance and the Study of Politics". In G. Hyden and M. Dratton (eds.), *Governance and Politics in Africa.* London: Lynne Rienner Publishers, pp. 1–26.

International Federation for Human Rights(FIDH) and FHRI. (2012). *Women's Rights in Uganda: Gaps Between Policy and Practice.* Paris: Unpublished.

Kabeer, N. (2008). *Mainstreaming Gender in Social Protection for the Informal Economy.* London: Commonwealth Secretariat.

Kabeer, N., and Subrahmanian, R. (1996) *Institutions, Relations and Outcome: Framework and Tools for gender-aware planning.* Sussex: IDS. Retrieved from: www.ids.ac.uk/files/Dp357.pdf

Kanyeihamba, W. (2002). *Constitutionalism in Uganda.* Kampala: Fountain Publishers.

Kasente, D., Asingwire, N., Banugire, F., and Kyomuhendo, S. (2002). Social Security Systems in Uganda. *Journal of Social Development in Africa*: 157–183.

Kyalisiima, Z. (2007). *Factors Affecting Women and Men's Benefits from the Utilisation of Microfinance Services: A Case of Rubaga Division, Kampala District, Uganda.* Unpublished document.

Luttrell, C., and Moser, C. (2004). *Gender and Social Protection.* London: Overseas Development Institute.

Lwanga-Ntale, C.; Namuddu, J.; and Onapa, P. (2008). *Social Protection in Uganda: A Call for Action.* Discussion Paper No.1/2008, Kampala. Unpublished.

MOFPED (Ministry of Finance, Planning and Economic Development). (2014). *Poverty Status Report 2014.* Kampala: MOFPED.

MoGLSD (Ministry of Gender, Labour and Social Development). (2004). *The National Orphans and Vulnerable Children Policy*. Kampala: Republic of Uganda

MoGLSD (Ministry of Gender, Labour and Social Development). (2006a). *The National Equal Opportunities Policy*. Kampala: Republic of Uganda

MoGLSD (Ministry of Gender, Labour and Social Development). (2006b). *National Policy on Disability*. Kampala: Republic of Uganda

MoGLSD (Ministry of Gender Labour and Social Development). (2007). *National Gender Policy*. Kampala: Republic of Uganda

MoGLSD (Ministry of Gender Labour and Social Development). (2011). *The Social Development Investment Plan II (SDIP (2011/2012 to 2015/2016)*. Kampala: The Republic of Uganda.

MoGLSD (Ministry of Gender Labour and Social Development). (2015). *National Social Protection Policy*. Kampala: Republic of Uganda.

MoLHUD (Ministry of Lands, Housing and Urban Development). (2008). *Mainstreaming Gender and HIV/AIDS Issues into the Draft National Land Policy*. Kampala: MOLHUD.

Muhanguzi, F.K.; Muhumuza, F.K.; and Okello, J. (2013). *Governance of Non-state Social Protection Initiatives: Implications for Addressing Gendered Vulnerability to Poverty in Uganda*. Research Report, PASGR.

NCG (Nordic Consulting Group). (2008). *Evaluation of Gender Outcomes in Poverty Eradication Action Plan*. Kampala: Nordic Consulting Group.

Norton, A.; Conway, T.; and Foster, M. (2001). *Social Protection Concepts and Approaches: Implications for Policy and Practice in International Development*. Working Paper No.143. London: Overseas Development Institute.

OECD (Organization for Economic Co-Operation and Development). (2009). *Promoting Pro-Poor Growth: Social Protection*. Paris: OECD.

Otiso, K.M. (2006). *Culture and Customs of Uganda*. Westport, CT: Greenwood Press.

Pfeiffer, E., and Anderson, D. (2004). *Taxation and GDP Growth in the Nordic Welfare State Model*. Retrieved from: www.sandiego.edu

Quisumbing, A.; Meinzen-Dick, R.; and Bassett, L. (2008). *Helping Women Respond to the Global Food Price Crisis*. Policy Brief 7. Washington, DC: IFRPI.

Risse, T. (2011) "Governance in Areas of Limited Statehood: Introduction and Overview". In Thomas Risse (ed.), *Governance without a State? Policies and Politics in Areas of Limited Statehood*. New York: Columbia University Press, pp. 1–35.

Silberschmidt, M. (2001). Disempowerment of Men in Rural and Urban East Africa: Implications for Male Identity and Sexual Behaviour. *World Development*, 29 (4): 657–671.

Sweetman, C. (2011). Introduction: Special Issue on Social Protection. *Gender and Development*, 19 (2): 169–177.

Thakur, S.G.; Arnold, C.; and Johnson, T. (2009). "Gender and Social Protection". In OECD (ed.), *Promoting Pro-Poor Growth: Social Protection*. Paris: OECD, pp. 167–182.

The Republic of Uganda. (1985). *The National Social Security Act, Cap 222*. Kampala: Republic of Uganda.

The Republic of Uganda. (1989). *Non Governmental Organizations Registration Act Cap 113*. Kampala: Republic of Uganda.
The Republic of Uganda. (1995). *Constitution of the Republic of Uganda*. Kampala: Republic of Uganda.
The Republic of Uganda. (1997). *The Children Act: CAP 59*. Kampala: Republic of Uganda.
The Republic of Uganda. (1998). *The Land Act CAP 227*. Kampala: Republic of Uganda.
The Republic of Uganda. (2004). *The Land (Amendment) Act: Acts Supplement No.1*. Kampala: Republic of Uganda.
The Republic of Uganda. (2006). *The Persons with Disabilities Act*. Kampala: Republic of Uganda.
The Republic of Uganda. (2007). The Equal Opportunities Commission Act: Acts Supplement No. 23, *The Uganda Gazette*, No. 2 Vol. C.
The Republic of Uganda. (2008). The Education Act 13 (Pre-Primary, Primary and Post-primary) Act: Acts Supplement No. 8, *The Uganda Gazette*, No. 44 Vol CI.
The Republic of Uganda. (2010a). *Domestic Violence Act 2010 and its Regulations*. Supplement No 3. Kampala: Republic of Uganda.
The Republic of Uganda. (2010b). *The National Development Plan 2010/11–2014/15*. Kampala: National Planning Authority.
The Republic of Uganda. (2015). *The National Development Plan 2015/16–2019/20*. Kampala: National Planning Authority.
Tsai, L.L. (2007). *Accountability Without Democracy: Solidary Groups and Public Goods Provision in Rural China*. Cambridge: Cambridge University Press.
UNDP. (2013). *Human Development Report 2013*. Explanatory note on 2013 HDR composite indices, New York: UNDP.
UNFPA and MoGLSD. (2009). *Situational Analysis of Gender Based Violence (GBV) in Karamoja Region*. Kampala: UNFPA and MGLSD.
Vreymans, P., and Verhulst, E. (2004). *Growth Differentials in Europe: An Investigation into the Causes: Growth Stimulating Policies*. Retrieved from: www.workforall.org

9 Governance dynamics in the provision of community-based social protection services in Tanzania

Adalbertus Kamanzi, Emmanuel Nyankweli, and Auma Okwany

The poor "trickle up" to remedy State default.

Introduction

Since independence in 1961, Tanzania has transitioned from a single-party socialist system to a multi-party and market-based economy. That has brought political stability, but it has also removed a major social institution and, economically, there have been fluctuations. Widespread poverty and vulnerability characterise the general socio-economic conditions. The most severe poverty is among rural populations where subsistence production still dominates. Agriculture employs between 75 and 80 per cent of the rural population. It also accounts for about 28 per cent of GDP and 66 per cent of exports. While urban incomes are unsteady and poverty is pervasive, there is glaring inequality of income and social amenities compared with rural areas. Wuyts contends that it is best to define the socio-economic situation in Tanzania as one of "generalized insecurity" because vulnerability to impoverishment is so extensive (2006: 3).

According to the Tanzania Decent Work Country Profile (ILO, 2010), the informal sector employs more than 80 per cent of the labour force. This includes smallholder farmers as well as the self-employed and unpaid family workers. These people do not have access to state social protection (SP) because state mechanisms serve the formal sector only. Even the formal contributory systems offer limited benefit packages and are available to only 5 per cent of the population (URT, 2011). The other 95 per cent – who are highly vulnerable to socio-economic risks and uncertainties – rely on non-state SP provided by local and international non-governmental organisations (INGOs) and a plethora of traditional social security groups built on family and/or community support. Even people who may not be considered poor because they work in the formal sector are also members of the reciprocal community-based organisations (CBOs).

In recent times, the Tanzanian economy has experienced consistent growth with GDP up by about 7 per cent annually, but this has had little effect on the extension of state SP against vulnerability, deprivation, and other life exigencies. Trickle down simply has not happened. The establishment and steady growth of CBOs has been the only respite for most. People pooling resources to help each other is ingrained in culture, which is a tradition that the state has been only too pleased to promote – and depend on.

The ideology of the state since independence was based on the principle of *ujamaa* (familyhood), discussed in the next section. In the context of limited statehood, non-state actors (NSAs) respond to the failure of the state to fulfil its responsibilities (Risse, 2011), and the Tanzanian government has no problem with that, nor with recognising its own limitations – especially while grappling with structural adjustment (Geier, 1995; Bienefeld, 1995; Raikes and Gibbon, 1996). So the traditional culture of people seeing themselves as each other's keeper has been both a necessary and natural recourse. For many small, informal businesses and people aspiring to start micro-enterprises, community-based credit associations are the only sources of credit and loans (Kessy, 2014). In Zanzibar[1] alone, Anyango et al. (2006) found that membership in these groups rose from 1,172 in 2002 to 4,552 in 2006 – an annual growth rate of 64 per cent.

CBOs were increasingly institutionalised after independence, and especially after the *ujamaa* declaration in 1967. The economic constraints of the structural adjustment period strengthened the communitarian approach. Small organisations, groups, and associations provide all sorts of services, ranging from burial support to collective farming, micro-credit for small businesses, health-care and education support, health insurance, and women's and youth groups with a savings and loan model referred to in Kiswahili as *kupeana*, meaning mutuality and reciprocal "exchange". Despite the importance and ubiquity of these self-help systems, not much has been written about their governance and how these mechanisms translate to the performance of services they render to citizens.

Literature seems to suggest that globalisation and so-called modernisation of economies and society, alongside state attempts to expand formal SP, would crowd out informal SP operations. So far, that anticipation could hardly be more wrong. This chapter presents an analysis of the governance dynamics of CBOs. It draws on data from a larger study conducted in two rural districts of Bukoba and the urban context of the Dodoma municipality. It provides a window on the key roles played by CBOs in addressing risk and vulnerability among the impoverished. It examines accountability and other governance characteristics to determine their effect on performance. The next section examines the concepts of SP and community-based action, with a focus on the *ujamaa* philosophy. The methodology of the study is presented, followed by the research findings, and the public policy implications.

Understanding social protection from the principles of Ujamaa

Framing SP as a public concern and a formal state-regulated obligation does not mean that individual or private initiatives are disregarded. Indeed, Devereux and Sabates-Wheeler (2004: 9) provide a concept that includes both formal and informal delivery mechanisms. For the majority of vulnerable groups, community-based schemes are the first, and, often, only safety nets. In Tanzania, the role of CBOs is grounded in the state's definition of SP:

> Traditional, family and community support structures and interventions by the State and non-state actors that support individuals, households and communities to prevent, manage and overcome the risks threatening their present and future security and well-being, and to embrace opportunities for their development and for social and economic progress.

(URT, 2008: 1)

That is the communitarian approach institutionalised in the *ujamaa* policy crafted and propagated by the Nyerere-led government in the immediate post-independent period. Geared towards national development, *ujamaa* (literally "kinshipness'" or "familyhood") was a socialist ideology drawn from the indigenous principle of collective togetherness and harnessed as a new institutional arrangement for rural development. *Ujamaa* "villages" were conceived as rural communities in which people would live together on the basis of collective ownership of productive assets, cooperative production, and equitable sharing of what is produced. The goal was both to address the problem of chronic socio-economic insecurity and to seek to end social inequality (Kaijage, 2009).

Etymologically, the word *ujamaa* has two meanings significant for this study. Beyond the literal meaning of kinshipness or familyhood, the second meaning has to do with jamii, which literally means "society". The two combined highlight aspects of both the micro-context of local networks as well as the macro-context of larger society (national family) within which it is nested. The embodiment of *ujamaa* in African socialism is based endogeneity in which people develop using what they have – their own cultural, social, physical, and financial resources. There is space for borrowing what they do not have, so *ujamaa* is a viable framework for self-reliance (Kanyandago, 1998). The principles of collective reciprocity are important in understanding CBOs, which are guided by the same ethos.

CBOs based on networks of solidarity and reciprocity continue to serve the vast majority of Tanzania's people who do not have access to formal SP. While some literature suggests a relative decline in the mutuality and solidarity networks, many of these values and systems remain resilient and have not been lost or supplanted (Abebe and Aase, 2007; Hebo, 2013; Okwany et al., 2011). Their growth has been a function of both necessity and opportunity. The abandonment of a centrally planned economy in favour of market-based mechanisms in Tanzania, under international pressure, led to state withdrawal from a variety of activities, shifting the onus of service provisioning even further to the local level. This has increased the need for – and numbers of – NSAs.

There is popular participation in the development process and a predilection for associational life and self-help (Dill, 2010). The key element in group cooperation is cooperation. In their study examining family businesses, Eddleston and Kellermanns (2007) found that cooperation significantly reduces conflict and enhances participative strategy. This is in line with Corbetta and Salvato (2004) who contend that when a family is altruistic, it is likely to have an involvement-orientated organisational culture, which is collectivistic. It is this culture that leads to cooperation in decision-making processes.

Although the state is "absent" in the provision of social security to most Tanzanians, it expects all actors who provide services to the poor to be registered (aka regulated) (URT, 2011) to ensure that informal organisations conform to state rules. This shows the power of the state to maintain administrative control and sovereignty without giving reciprocal support. It is officially touted as a kind of oversight mechanism to prevent spurious organisations abusing the vulnerable.

Governance elements relevant to community organisations

Governance mechanisms in any organisation must have three key elements: accountability (including space for complaint and grievance), legitimacy, and performance. Accountability describes how an organisation can be held responsible for its use of funds and knock-on impacts of its activity. Legitimacy is largely related to the legality of its existence and its responsiveness to the needs of its members and society as a whole. In other words, the values and goals of an organisation are aligned to the values of their stakeholders. So even though CBOs may be registered to fulfil state conditions, their legitimacy must be analysed through the lenses of their members and beneficiaries too. According to Suchman, legitimacy "is a generalised assumption that the actions of an entity are desirable, proper and appropriate within some socially constructed system of norms, values, beliefs and definitions"(1995: 574). The basic tenets of legitimacy are that the values of the organisation correspond to both members' and societal values. Legitimacy provides the assurance that an organisation is endorsed, and its existence is justified by the value it renders to its stakeholders. As such, some level of formality of entity, leadership, and funding, as well as how the entity interacts with its environment, becomes an important determinant of legitimacy.

The performance of a mutual organisation is how well, effectively, and efficiently its functions are carried out. Performance is an important factor for people who cooperate; it is the currency in which "altruists" are paid. Performance, therefore, depends not only on levels of input-output accountability but also on outcomes, so real and positive impact on beneficiaries is a pivotal issue.

Armed with those understandings and definitions, the questions are how CBOs' governance fares, whether the mechanisms or styles have changed over time, and how, why, and with what result for vulnerable citizens? What are the perceptions of their members on the services they receive? Do CBOs need to be taught better practices, and/or could others (including the state) learn from them? These were the questions the study asked.

Studying community-based social protection mechanisms in Bukoba and Dodoma

Bukoba rural and Dodoma municipality were purposively selected to represent both urban and rural areas with high vulnerability levels and a burgeoning abundance of NSAs providing SP services. The first phase of study was quantitative mapping of all the non-state actors (NSAs) providing SP in the areas. This identified 426 CBOs. For in-depth analysis, the study drew two samples totalling 152 CBOs, limited to those that had at least 50 per cent of their budget financed by internally generated funds (either member contributions and/or profits ploughed back from income-generating activities (IGAs)). This condition identified CBOs that were owned and controlled by their own members. Qualitative data was obtained through in-depth interviews and focus group discussions (FGDs), and secondary data was used to complement the field data. Content analysis was used to explore the dynamics of accountability.

Study findings

Community-based social protection services and organisations

Literature is replete with terms for these informal or small-scale organisations and their functions. In Tanzania, they are community-based membership associations focused on the welfare needs of their members and local community as a whole. They support asset accumulation and make financial transfers to their members in times of socio-economic shock. Collectivity allows risk and resource pooling for readiness/response to crises and emergencies. For example, burial societies place high premiums on providing decent burials to members and their relatives. Many groups focus on livelihood improvement through IGA; community welfare for better housing, water, and other social services such as development of local schools; and supporting those at risk of marginalisation among them – widows, orphans, elder persons, or HIV-positive members needing at-home care.

CBOs are voluntary groupings of members who share one or more common denominator of interest and identity (and usually neighbourhood proximity). They generally have between 15 and 25 members, are initiated by local residents, and located within the communities they serve. Some also collaborate with larger and more formal organisations (Amelina et al., 2012; Develtere and Fonteneau, 2001; Oduro, 2010; duToit and Neves, 2006; Teshome, 2013; Yachkaschi, 2010: 196). Their solidarity, resource, and knowledge exchange is what du Toit and Neves refer to as "generalised reciprocity" (2009: 1). Despite the assumed homogeneity of the CBOs, some studies indicate these organisations may have issues concerning membership eligibility, equity, and exclusivity. As duToit and Neves (2006: vi) contend, "social capital" does not benefit everyone in the same way. Some of the forms of exchange on which it relies or enables are thoroughly unequal, and there are net winners and losers. Dill (2010) notes that many CBOs in Tanzania – for various social, logistic, and resource reasons – place limits on who can join. While no literature refutes this possibility, the numerous majority of studies find exceptional levels of cohesion within groups (which are, after all, self-generated and defined "communities"), and open-hearted/open-handed willingness to extend "neighbourhood" help beyond their immediate membership.

Some 97 per cent of the organisations in the two study areas were community-based SP organisations grouped predominantly on the basis of people residing in the same locality. Some others coalesce around religion, gender, or livelihood (carpentry, fishing, farming, etc.). Some are wholly independent; others work closely with local and/or international organisations (to tap skills, material resources, or policy leverage).

The other 3 per cent of the organisations identified in the two study areas were NGOs involved in SP services. They include World Vision and the Kolping Society of Tanzania, among others, and operate at national and international levels. About 48 per cent of the CBOs in SP were registered before 2009, while 32 per cent were registered between 2009 and 2011, the remaining 20 per cent more recently. Two-thirds operate mutual-assistance programmes on a not-for-profit basis, and even those that do target profits share the gains among all members.

Dynamics of community-based organisation governance mechanisms

Registration

Registration is done at different village, ward, and district levels for local initiatives. If an organisation operates beyond the district, then registration is expected to be at the national level. Almost all (95 per cent) of CBOs in the study areas were registered, at least at the ward level. To register, a group should have a bank account, opened after a general meeting where members agree on the signatories – invariably the chairperson, the treasurer, and/or the secretary. The group must have a constitution with at least the following content: name of the group, address, membership conditions, objectives, leadership issues including a list of officials, rules; regulations governing members; disciplinary measures to be taken; and finance regulations. Those registered must have fulfilled these state requirements to whatever (unofficially variable) extent is demanded by local level authorities.

While there is compliance with state conditions, CBOs' actual governance is based on norms and values set and operated from within, with the knowledge and consent of the entire membership and based on trust. Official titles bestow administrative roles rather than singular authority. The administrative efficiency of community organisations is a crucial aspect of their governance. They often face problems of illiteracy among members and poor accounting practices, yet accountability (for example in the micro-finance associations) is exceptionally high. Deposits, withdrawals, loans, and loan repayments are conducted at meetings with all members present. Everybody knows what is in the communal safe, and for avoidance of doubt, it has three locks requiring three keys held separately by three different members.

Funding of social protection services

Clearly, funding determines the extent to which CBOs are able to meet the needs of members. During the research, it was difficult to establish the

Table 9.1 Sources of funds for non-state social protection services

Sources of funds	N	Per cent
Solely from group/contribution	150	35.2
Generated solely from donors	26	6.1
Multiple sources of funds (government, group contribution, and donors)	250	58.7
Total	**426**	**100.0**

Source: Field data 2013

financial position of most of the organisations since this was seen as internally confidential. Only a small percentage of all the mapped organisations indicated that they rely solely on donor funding, as shown in Table 9.1. Most small-scale organisations generate all of their own funds.

One key informant from a CBO that provides food, clothing, and school items for orphans in Ibwera community stated,

> It is difficult to get sufficient funds to run our group activities. Yes, we have contributions, but we also have friends who help us. Some of these friends are here in Tanzania, but others are outside. Some people appreciate what we do, and they send us money, which we use to assist orphans with the cost of schooling.
>
> (Tubelege Community Care Coalition, Ibwera)

Organisations do rely on the philanthropic support of "friends", highlighting the importance of networks inside and outside their geographical boundaries. Importantly, philanthropic support is generally not conditional and does not interfere with what the group does or how it does it. These donors are "friends" (who support what the group wants to do) not "principals" (who impose the will of a paymaster). This is in stark contrast with NGOs, which are often puppets on (remote) donor purse strings, to the extent that programme choice and design can give precedence to funding potential over beneficiaries' most pressing needs.

Most CBOs are almost self-sufficient in funding, especially those that run IGAs. A FGD with *Jitegemee: Kilimona* na *Ufugaji* (Be Self-Reliant: Agriculture and Animal Husbandry) revealed that the group is able to meet 100 percent of its budgetary needs.

> We produce a lot more than we consume, so we sell the surplus and generate money, which is added to our group savings; members can then borrow money from the group at a very low interest rate to start

their own enterprises. We are also able to support our activities, and we can use the surplus to assist vulnerable people including the elderly and some children in need.

CBOs which offer social services without any IGAs risk failing to meet their financial needs. As one key informant noted,

> We have to take care of the orphans, widows. and the elderly; we depend a lot on people's assistance from within and outside Tanzania; the church and the government assist us, but also some members of this community give us money and material support. There is no way we can manage to finance our budget; we need additional assistance for sure. We are hoping things will change in the future because we intend to initiate some income-generating activities to supplement what we get from friends.

CBO efforts not only fill existing gaps but also enable the state to renege further on its duty of care. In addition, the NGO-based approach supported by international donors can fragment previously cohesive communities by unilaterally elevating and privileging a sub-category. Most importantly, this remote-control approach ignores the structural causes of the material deprivation they seek to mitigate, thus merely treating the symptoms and never curing the disease.

Leadership: election and succession

The study examined how CBO leaders were selected and how long they stayed in office. The results are shown in Table 9.2.

Leaders serve for between one and three years. A significant number of organisations do not have leadership term limits. Voting tends to ensure clear and smooth succession. The democratic nature, with an aspect of

Table 9.2 Selection of leaders

Means of selecting leaders	N	Per cent
Volunteering	90	21.1
Self-appointment	35	8.2
Appointment by higher authorities	11	2.6
Mutual agreement	29	6.8
Voting	261	61.3
Total	**426**	**100.0**

volunteering, shows a high level of commitment in the type of leadership CBOs use. One FGD participant noted,

> There is no way that one can become a leader without our consent; this is our group; we know what we want; we know where we came from. Each one should have a chance to become a leader; we should all carry the cross, not only one person. . . . and the best way to get the leader is to vote for him/her. Sometimes, people want much to become leaders and you wonder why; it could be because they want to exploit our resources. That is why the best way is to make sure you vote, and you are very strict with the tenure in leadership. We do not want people to turn our group into a kraal of cows.
>
> (Bethania Livestock Keeping, Kemondo)

Some selective preference is given to those with some level of formal education, or those who can write reports and file documents with appropriate authorities, though such skills can be sourced from any part of the membership.

Dynamics of organisational and management associated with community-based social protection

Organisations that largely self-fund also choose and deliver services themselves. In governance terms, they are thus the *"principals"* and the *"agents"* and the *"stewards"* of their own programmes. This type of CBO operates on the principles of group solidarity, shared goals, obligatory participation, peer influence, and internal dispute settlement mechanisms. The peer influence enhances cooperation among members, and their common interests and shared aspirations automatically nurture homogeneity.

CBO members are required to demonstrate commitment and actively contribute towards the effective function of the group. They must attend meetings regularly and contribute human, physical, and financial resources and ideas. Peer pressure as well as other forms of social sanction/censure ensures high levels of compliance, mutual accountability, and service energy. In some cases, hefty fines are imposed or services are withdrawn from members in breach of their obligations to the organisation. Community elders usually mediate or settle internally disputes within the group. There are provisions for warnings, penalties, and, if necessary, expulsion.

Organisations that generate their funds from external donors are "agents" who manage other people's money. They are contracted by donors (the "principals") to provide SP programmes to the donor's choice of clients. The majority of the organisations operating on the basis of "principal-agent" relations are NGOs. These formal organisations use written agreements and/or memoranda of understanding to ensure the accountability of services they deliver. These agreements are formally documented and stipulate agreed upon services to be offered, responsibilities and rights of partners, dates of the agreement, and time period for the contract. Some stipulate protocols for conflict resolution.

Such organisations also use a series of monitoring mechanisms, including regular visits to the people rendering services on their behalf, and implement a system of upward reporting from the field (for their own evaluations) and then upwards again to donors, with use of funds attracting the closest scrutiny.

One of the coordinators of a CBO that takes care of orphans in Bukoba district noted,

> I have been in this position for three years. I took over the coordinating role from another member who worked for six years. We do not get paid for this work. We are retirees from government work. We are voted in, and we work almost every day because the members trust us. If such an organization collapses, the vulnerability of needy children would be worse, and our society would have problems later. So I have to make sure that the organisation works to help vulnerable children, as they are the ones to take over from us, and they will be there when we are not.
>
> (Tubelege Community Care Coalition, Ibwera)

NGOs that operate principal-agent relationships are characterized by goal conflicts, information asymmetry, and polarised interests. Formal mechanisms of accountability are essential controls against opportunistic behaviour. Effectively, agent behaviour is forced into alignment with the principal's objectives through controls or inducements: audits, performance evaluations, or threat of withdrawal of funding. An interview with a director of an NGO in Bukoba is illustrative:

> We have many donors from within this country and outside. I account to them frequently on our finances. There is no way they can give you money if you have not accounted for the amount that is disbursed. I think that they are right to do this because so many NGOs have run away with donors' money.
>
> (Director NGO, Bukoba)

There is clearly a significant difference in the spirit and character of governance between informal CBOs (which raise the money, spend the money, and deliver the service themselves) and NGOs which receive the money from donors and sub-contract service delivery to others. The fact that the informal and unwritten systems are intrinsically more accountable than the most dogmatic paperwork may seem ironic, but it is nonetheless true.

Quality of services provided by different management mechanisms

The relative performance of large formal and small informal organisations was measured by beneficiaries' judgment of service quality in terms of affordability, availability, and proximity.

Affordability of services

Bearing in mind that groups are mostly self-funded by members' regular subscriptions, Table 9.3 shows the report card of the beneficiaries:

Generally, services are perceived as expensive (a term that needs to be qualified when used by people with almost no money) irrespective of the organisational type and management style. One participant in Bukoba stated,

> Well, the (NGO) school that takes care of orphans started as very affordable but is now one of the most expensive. Many children now have to look for sponsors.

Availability of services

The reach of individual CBOs is limited, but collectively they deliver by far the most comprehensive cover. They are embedded in communities rather than just "visiting" or "bolting onto" localities (see Table 9.4).

Beneficiaries perceive NGO services to be unavailable when they need them, although those who do have access are grateful. A beneficiary noted,

> I do not know what I shall ever do to repay this NGO. I received a small loan from them, and I now have my own small house. I am doing well with my business; I am able to pay my children's school fees. I am able to gradually repay the loan.

Table 9.3 Service affordability

Management type	No. of respondents	Affordable	Expensive
CBOs (Stewardship)	50	13 (26%)	37 (74%)
NGOs (P-A relations)	32	10 (31%)	22 (69%)

Table 9.4 Service availability

	Respondents	Available	Unavailable
CBOs (Stewardship)	50	100.0%	0.0%
NGOs (P-A relationship)	80	27.5%	72.5%

Proximity of services

For the very poor and immobile, and especially for services that demand the physical presence of support personnel, services that are not "on site" are de facto "not available". The greater proximity of a larger number of CBOs is therefore not a matter of perception but a matter of fact.

A community development officer illustrated the point:

> Most of these groups are composed of people who come from the same place and have certain common problems. For example, you see the old people who organise themselves, and they have some income generating activity like growing trees from which they divide their earnings. If they want certain services, then they should have them and within reach.
>
> These people come to my house and assist in cleaning; they fetch water and firewood for me; when I cannot cook, someone is sent here to cook for me.
>
> (Old woman beneficiary)

Networking for synergies

CBOs are inherently "networks" of individuals, harnessing collective and cooperative efforts. Members recognised the major role of reciprocal support, knowledge exchange, fundraising, and collective problem solving; they readily translated the internal principle to external (inter-group) networking. One group member noted,

> A Swahili proverb says, 'Kidole kimoja hakivunji chaw'! (You cannot kill a louse with one finger). Though we are a small organisation, our strength lies in our coming together to assist each other when one of us is dealing with ill health of a family member and has to bear the costs of caring for them at home or in hospital. Networking with other groups helps to get new ideas and access to information, resources, and additional support systems.

Study participants also acknowledged barriers to networking, including inability to confidently use "donor language'.' One member noted,

> We have a problem of language, so we cannot always network with other organisations. English is not easy, and we do not have people who can communicate in English. Again, who knows us out there? Our educational support programme for vulnerable children is a very localised activity that most donors would think should be handled locally. That is why I do not think many donors would be interested. . . . after all, the parents of these children are there, and they are the ones to take care of the children at the nursery. But it would be nice if donors would give us funds to improve the quality of the nursery school.

Conclusion

CBOs are available, affordable, and closest to the people at the community level. In many African countries (as shown in this book), most CBOs providing SP services are not registered, but in Tanzania, the majority are registered at the local level as providing social assistance that the state does not. While non-state intervention is traditional and necessary, such efforts unintentionally allow the state to perpetuate its default. The poor-to-poor funding of CBOs shows the spirit of collective action, but service resources are axiomatically limited, potentially fragile, and they do not institutionalise SP as a right that should be assured by a tax-collecting state.

The government needs to enable community mechanisms materially and financially to expand their services. While the government is trying to regulate activities of CBOs and to extend formal social security to informal workers, the whole state social security system covers less than 10 per cent of the population, and even prodigious growth will not remedy the shortfall quickly or completely enough. CBOs will need to operate – separately, or side-by-side, or as an integral part of formal social security mechanisms – to enable any chance of comprehensive and responsive SP for the vulnerable on a national scale.

Any support should not be geared to changing CBOs through knowledge transfer or regulation, but to enhancing their existing modus operandi, which is essentially tailored to their individual contexts. Capacity building should provide external resources but allow CBOs to focus on issues that matter to them, and that can only be decided on a case-by-case basis by their communities.

Note

1 Zanzibar, which comprises Unguja and Pemba islands, became part of Tanzania on 26 April 1964 when mainland Tanganyika and Zanzibar united to form the United Republic of Tanzania.

References

Abebe, T., and Aase, A. (2007). Children, AIDS and the Politics of Orphan Care in Ethiopia: The Extended Family Revisited. *Social Science and Medicine*, 64: 2058–2069.

Amelina, A.; Bilecen, B.; Barglowski, B.; and Faist, T. (2012). *Ties That Protect? The Significance of Transnationality for the Distribution of Informal Social Protection in Migrant Networks*. SFB 882 Working Paper No.6. Bielefeld: DFG Research Center.

Anyango, E.; Esipisu, E.; Opoku, L.; Johnson, S.; Malkamaki, M.; and Musoke, C. (2006). *VSLA Experience from Zanzibar*. Nairobi: Decentralized Financial Services/DFID.

Bienefeld, M. (1995). "Structural Adjustment and Tanzania's Peasantry: Assessing the Likely Long-term Impact". In V. Jamal (ed.), *Structural Adjustment and Rural Labour Markets in Africa*. London: The Macmillan Series of ILO Studies, Macmillan Press, pp. 88–130.

Corbetta, G., and Salvato, C. (2004). Self-serving or Self-actualizing? Models of Man and Agency Costs in Different Types of Family Firms: A Commentary on "Comparing the Agency Costs of Family and Non-family Firms: Conceptual Issues and Exploratory Evidence". *Entrepreneurship Theory and Practice*, 28 (4): 355–362.

Develtere, P., and Fonteneaum, B. (2001). *Member-based Organizations for Social Protection in Health in Developing Countries*. 2nd draft Paper prepared for ILO/STEP (Strategies and Tools Against Social Exclusion and Poverty, Social Security), Katholieke Universiteit Leuven.

Devereux, Stephen, and Sabates-Wheeler, Rachel. (2004). *Transformative Social Protection*. IDS Working Paper 232, Brighton: IDS

Dill, B. (2010). Community-Based Organizations (CBOs) and Norms of Participation in Tanzania: Working Against the Grain. *African Studies Review*, 53: 23–48.

duToit, A., and Neves, D. (2009). *Trading on a Grant: Integrating Formal and Informal Social Protection in Post-Apartheid Migrant Networks*. Working Paper No.75, Brookes World Poverty Institute. Manchester: University of Manchester.

Eddleston, K.A., and Kellermanns, F.W. (2007). Destructive and Productive Family Relationships: A Stewardship Theory Perspective. *Journal of Business Venturing*, 22 (4): 545–565.

Geier, G. (1995). *Food Security Policy in Africa Between Disaster Relief and Structural Adjustment: Reflections on the Conception and Effectiveness of Policies: The Case of Tanzania*. London: GDI Book Series No. 5.

Hebo, M. (2013). "Giving Is Saving: The Essence of Reciprocity as an Informal Social Protection System Among the Arsii Oromo, Southern Ethiopia". In Stephen Devereux and Meletu Getu (eds.), *Informal and Formal Social Protection Systems in Sub-Saharan Africa*. Kampala: Fountain Publishers, pp. 9–42.

ILO. (2010). *Decent Work Country Profile Tanzania (Mainland)*. Dar es Salaam: International Labor Office.

Kaijage, F. (2009). *Policy and Poverty in Tanzania: A Historical Perspective*. Distance learning unit for the Tanzania Diploma in Poverty Analysis. Module 3 unit 7. ESRF/REPOA, Tanzania.

Kanyandango, P. (1998). "The Role of Culture in Poverty Eradication". In D. Carabine and M. O'Reilly (eds.), *The Challenge of Eradicating Poverty in the World: An African Response*. Kampala: Uganda Martyrs University Press and Konrad Adenauer Foundation, pp. 119–152.

Kessy, F. (2014). *Assessing the Potential of Community Level Social Grants as a Promotive Social Protection Measure*. A paper presented in the Africa conference on social protection in Nairobi, Kenya organised by Partnership for Africa Social and Governance Research (PASGR) in November, 2014.

Oduro, A.D. (2010). *Formal and Informal Social Protection in Sub-Saharan Africa*. Background paper for the European Report on Development. Retrieved from: http://erd.eui.eu/media/BackgroundPapers

Okwany, A.; Ngutuku, E.; and Muhangi, A. (2011). *The Role of Indigenous Knowledge and Culture in Childcare in Africa: A Sociological Study of Several Communities in Kenya and Uganda*. New York: Edwin Mellen Press.

Raikes, P., and Gibbon, P. (1996). "Tanzania 1986–1994". In P. Engberg-Pedersen, P. Gibbon, P. Raikes, and L. Udsholt (eds.), *Limits of Adjustment in Africa: The Effects of Economic Liberalization, 1986–1994*. London: James Currey and Portsmouth (N.H.), Heinemann, pp. 215–307.

Risse, Thomas. (2011). "Governance in Areas of Limited Statehood: Introduction and Overview". In Thomas Risse (ed.), *Governance Without a State? Policies and Politics in Areas of Limited Statehood*. New York: Columbia University Press, pp. 1–35.

Sabates-Wheeler, R.; Devereux, S.; and Hodges, A. (2009) "Taking the long view: What does a child focus add to social protection?" IDS Bulletin 40.1, Brighton: IDS

Suchman, M.C. (1995). Managing Legitimacy: Strategic and Institutional Approaches. *Academy of Management Journal*, 203: 571–610.

Teshome, A. (2013). "Informal Social Protection in Ethiopia". In S. Deveraux and G. Melese (eds.), *Informal and Formal Social Protection in Sub-Saharan Africa*. Kampala: Foundation Publishers, pp. 95–119.

URT. (2008). National Social Protection Network.

URT. (2011). *National Social Protection Framework*. Dar es Salaam: Ministry of Finance and Economic Affairs.

Wuyts, M. (2006). *Developing Social Protection in Tanzania Within a Context of Generalized Insecurity*. REPOA Special Paper No.06.19. Dar: Mkuki na Nyota Publishers.

Yachkaschi, S. (2010). "Engaging with Community-based Organizations Lessons from Below: Capacity Development and Communities". In J. Ubels, N. Acquaye-Baddoo, and A. Fowler (eds.), *Capacity Development in Practice*. London: Earth Scan Ltd, pp. 194–207.

10 Conclusion and implications for public policy and governance theory
Possible but different

Nicholas Awortwi and Gregor Walter-Drop

Introduction

Structural Adjustment Programmes (SAPs) – the silver bullet of international economic wisdom in the 1980s – have brought both boom and burden to Africa. They triggered rapid and sustained economic growth in so many countries that the phenomenon is now called "Africa Rising". However, something else has grown just as much as GDP – the number and desperation of the poor and vulnerable. In Africa, that is not a small sub-set of unfortunate victims of change; it is often the majority of the population. Their condition is not "austerity" – it is destitution below the bottom lines of both human needs and human rights.

In this respect, SAPs may be credited with another positive: the delivery of proof that "trickle down" of new wealth does not work – at least not quickly, completely, or equitably enough to ensure even the most basic well-being for all, and for some, not even survival. Yet another equally extraordinary phenomenon has emerged. Every chapter in this book, and every study those chapters are based on across a diverse range of states and circumstances, come to a single and same overarching conclusion.

In the midst of unprecedented national economic growth, the first, last, and often only resort of the poorest is initiated, funded, organised, governed, and delivered most effectively by the poor themselves. This book has visited and profiled literally thousands of self-help projects that collectively achieve more than all their governments put together to meet what should be state obligations to poor and vulnerable citizens. They do so mostly without help or recognition, with extraordinary creativity and cost efficiency.

- Where? Everywhere in sub-Saharan Africa.
- When? Always.
- What? Respond to real need with what they have, in ways they can.
- Who? The people themselves.

- Why? Because limited states either cannot or choose not to adequately resource the state's obligation to social protection (SP).
- How? Community-based groups based on mutual trust and best-fit self-governance.

This book suggests that the impoverished masses must hope that "trickle up" will work and that at some point the economic elites and governments will look down at the grass roots to truly understand what SP is needed and learn from the lowliest of the low how it should be delivered. Community self-help groups deliver succour, sustenance, and survival to the poorest of the poor – in massive numbers – to compensate for limited statehood default, and they do the job remarkably well with extremely little.

The inescapable and overriding conclusion is this: if limited states cannot or will not directly support the poor and vulnerable, they should at least enable those who do. CBOs are helping the state do its job. It is time for the state to reciprocate.

The failure of the state is partly a resource issue. Even the rapidly growing GDPs are still relatively small, and the rapidly growing numbers of needy are relatively huge. That is a complex but numerically measurable challenge.

Other major impediments to state support for CBOs are less readily calculated: one is the fluctuating cause and consequence of endemic patronage politics; the other is state discomfort with CBOs' unconventional forms and styles of governance, which can only be judged by nuance, not audited accounts. That is the factor that this book has addressed: is the governance of CBOs too raw and random to be acceptable in a modern world? Should it disqualify them from state recognition and support?

This extensive research – eight studies in six countries – offers policy-makers an alternative thought: the governance of CBOs is indeed informal, but it is neither raw nor random. It ticks every box that defines the principles of what governance is for and what it should do. It is appropriate to the people's culture and context. It is effective.

CBOs' style and structure may not qualify as "best practice" in modern management terms, but this book has assessed their qualifications as "best fit" – not only acceptable, but arguably sacrosanct. Their idiosyncrasy is not a weakness in their operations; it is their essential strength. Government support could do more harm than good if it does not respect that.

Summary of the findings of the country studies

Social protection at the local level is a collective action without state involvement

Existing literature often describes CBO/self-help mechanisms as "coping strategies" because there is little confidence in their ability to sustain and move the vulnerable out of poverty. The eight case studies in this book clearly show that community-based mechanisms do deliver crucial and sustainable services using governance mechanisms appropriate to their circumstances and needs. These methods are informal but demonstrably effective. What matters perhaps most of all is the extent to which these organisations are seen by their communities to meet members' SP needs (without detrimental effect on anyone else) – not the informal nature and form of their governance.

Governance different without government

Even informal organisations fully meet – in their own way but to no less an extent – the definition of "governance" as the means by which social coordination is achieved (Lowndes and Skelcher, 1998). CBOs are effectively governed by norms of exchange and reciprocity. They may not use the "instruments" demanded by conventional "good governance", but they nevertheless honour the principles of accountability, safety, rule of law, participation, human rights, and effectiveness of public management. Indeed, they so excel in many of these respects as to outperform many much larger formal institutions and even governments themselves.

Self-governance structures, processes, and practices of NSAs are designed to fit the nature of their memberships, relationships, and services. Whereas mainstream conceptions of good governance emphasise "written" rules and other bureaucratic mechanisms, these do not feature as key tools in the running of small, informal, membership-based organisations at the community level. Instead, "trust" defines the operations and interactions between leaders and members/beneficiaries. Many don't write much, because most can't read much, but they have all the rules that they need, and every member knows them more thoroughly than any operations manual – through democratic decision, oral tradition, and an operating system that runs everything through regular plenary meetings, to a standard of accountability, transparency, and legitimacy beyond compare in any corporation or government department.

It is significant that larger NGOs – who much more closely comply with conventional and formal procedures – do not perform better than CBOs in real legitimacy, accountability, or service delivery. Indeed, their interventions, often driven by donor imperatives and remote control, can be anomalous to the perceptions, preferences, priorities, and real needs of the people they ostensibly exist to help.

So if government support for CBOs is to be contingent on "improved" CBO governance structures and processes, such efforts should build on the norms that are familiar within these organisations rather than displace them in the name of bureaucratic principles.

Non-state actors in social protection are not only safety nets but also developmental

About 60 per cent of NSAs are involved in promotive activities, even if their major objective is protective or preventive. Many have incorporated or transitioned into promotive services such as micro-finance, micro-health insurance, education, water and sanitation, agriculture, and economic empowerment (e.g. income-generating activities (IGAs)). They do all they can to incorporate the multi-faceted dimensions of vulnerability that beleaguer the poor.

Poor-to-poor funding mechanisms

Almost all – 92 per cent – of CBOs are self-funded through individual and membership contributions, and their beneficiaries are both members and needy non-members in their communities. There may be much to be learned from both the successes and failures of CBOs strategies and methods to optimise distribution of funding for SP nationally.

It is worth re-emphasising that there is a far greater risk and incidence of misapplication or diversion of funds at the state level than among local communities. The key to accountability lies in universal access to exact knowledge of where money is coming from and where it is going. And that knowledge depends not on the method of recording it, but on its unfailing communication to stakeholders: frequent, regular, and clear exchanges of ideas, feelings, intentions, and aspirations between members on anything and everything, using all the senses. States and donors that are worried about episodes of corruption in national agencies could learn much from the accountability mechanisms of small CBOs.

Comparative analysis of governance and service provision features of non-state actors in the six countries

Among the six countries, Ghana and Senegal have the highest scores on the Ibrahim Index of African governance indicators (accountability, safety and rule of law, participation, respect for humans rights). However, these two have the lowest percentages of NSA registration. See comparative governance indicators in relation to the percentage of NSAs registered with state authorities (see Table 10.1).

Clearly, registration of NSAs neither results from nor contributes to the governance ranking of a state.

CBOs are widespread in all the study countries, while the presence of international NGOs is negligible, irrespective of income per capita levels or degree of poverty (see Table 10.2).

Table 10.1 Governance indicators: Ibrahim Index of African Governance, 2015

Country	% of NSAs registered with national authority*	Overall governance score out of 100	Governance ranking	Accountability score (%)	Safety and rule of law (%)	Participation (%)	Human rights (%)	Public management (%)
Ghana	27	67.3	7th	56.3	70.6	80.1	79.6	50.9
Kenya	71	58.8	14th	44.8	53.8	65.7	57.3	56.5
Tanzania	54	56.7	18th	31.5	56.9	65.6	60.0	55.3
Senegal	42	62.4	9th	51.8	66.5	75.0	73.4	58.7
Uganda	58	54.6	19th	34.5	53.0	46.7	53.0	49.2
Ethiopia	45	48.6	31st	43.8	55.1	27.0	30.6	50.9

Source: Field data 2013

*

Table 10.2 Presence of non-state actors in the six countries

Country	Ratio of NSAs per population	CBOs (%)	FBOs (%)	District level NGOs (%)	National-level NGOs (%)	International NGOs (%)
Ghana	373	82.3	1.7	2.5	10.3	2.4
Kenya	452	81.5	6.8	2.5	5.3	3.9
Tanzania	911	89.4	4.7	4	1.2	0.5
Senegal	222	90.6	0.5	6.1	1.4	1.4
Uganda	146	87.7	1.5	4	4	2.8
Ethiopia	117	90.9	1.4	0.3	5.8	1.6
Average	**251**	**87.2**	**2.8**	**3.2**	**4.7**	**2.1**

There are interesting and sometimes extreme variations in the types of services (protective, preventive, promotive, or transformative) which predominate in each country. There is only one consistent pattern: the very low number of transformative services – readily explained because they require sophisticated skills, substantial resources, and national outreach to challenge entrenched cultural and political positions.

The logical expectation would be for protective services to dominate where poverty is deepest and where state assistance is most meagre; promotive services might lead where realistic opportunities are most available. The study results sometimes bear out that reasoning, and sometimes they don't (see Table 10.3).

The reasons for apparently random and even seemingly anomalous variations warrant further study and analysis, starting with (but not fully answered by) examination of each country's social and welfare indicators (see Tables 10.4a and 10.4b).

The low economic and social welfare indicators of Ethiopia mean collective action will be focused on protective services. Senegal has the lowest

Table 10.3 Types of social protection services provided by non-state actors[1]

Type of Service	Ethiopia	Uganda	Senegal	Tanzania	Kenya	Ghana	Average
Protective (%)	65.0	41.3	49.0	7.8	30.4	15.6	34.85
Preventive (%)	7.0	18.4	45.0	22.5	21.3	28.3	23.75
Promotive (%)	57.0	63.2	54.0	90.8	41.6	54.1	60.1
Transformative (%)	2.0	5.9	8.0	1.4	3.0	2.0	4.38

Source: Field data, 2013
[1] Many NSSPAs offer multiple types of services, thus the column sums are over 100.

Table 10.4a Economic and social welfare indicators

Country	GNI per capita (PPP$) 2014 (a)	Net ODA per capita (US$) (2013) (b)	Poverty headcount ratio at US$1.90 a day (based on 2011 PPP) (c)	Score IIAG welfare (%) (d)	Score IIAG sustainable economic opportunities (%) (d)	Score II2AG health (%) (d)
Ghana	3852	51	25.1	73.0	51.6	76.2
Kenya	2762	74	33.6	59.3	54.9	71.4
Tanzania	2411	68	46.6	59.9	51.3	79.6
Senegal	2188	69	37.98	59.7	51.3	79.6
Uganda	1613	46	33.24	64.3	47.8	70.3
Ethiopia	1428	40	33.54	64.0	46.9	70.1

Source: (a) UNDP HDI Report, 2015; (b) World Bank database; (c) Poverty Data World Bank; (d) 2015 Mo Ibrahim Index of African Governance (IIAG)

Table 10.4b Economic and social welfare indicators

Country	HDI 2014 rank (a)	% of pop. with access to improved drinking water (2015) (b)	Health expenditure per capita (US$) (b)	Policies for social inclusion/ equity 1 = low to 6 high (b)	Score IIAG welfare (%) (d)
Ghana	140	89	214	3.9	73.0
Kenya	145	63	101	3.7	59.3
Tanzania	151	56	126	3.8	59.9
Senegal	170	79	96	3.5	59.7
Uganda	163	79	146	3.7	64.3
Ethiopia	174	57	69	3.7	64.0

Source: (a) UNDP HDI Report, 2015; (b) World Bank database; (d) Mo Ibrahim Index of African Governance, 2015

score on policies for social inclusion and equity, which includes gender equality, equity of public resource use, building human resources, SP and labour, and policies and institutions for environmental sustainability. That explains why Senegal has nearly twice the average percentage of NSAs involved in transformative SP.

Conclusions

There are thousands of NSAs providing SP services in Africa, with the majority being CBOs. They deliver responsive SP interventions that are available and closer to the people at community level. They provide all sorts of assistance to their members and the community as a whole. This dependence of the poor on the benevolence of their fellow poor raises serious issues of social (in)justice at the state level.

The high number of unregistered CBOs calls into question the presumed superiority of conventional governance models that put government at the centre of welfare promotion. Of course, the legitimacy of the state includes guarantee of the welfare needs of the people, but it could be argued that welfare needs should not necessarily be delivered through public or state means. Herein lie a number of implications for both public policy and governance theory.

Public policy implications

The first policy issue is state recognition of CBOs and their role. The impact of this category of unregistered service providers is not well understood by many actors, including the state itself, which not infrequently tries to frustrate the very CBO systems that have sustained the poor.

One concrete issue in this regard concerns registration. The overwhelming majority of CBOs remain unregistered because the formal requirements are too difficult, because registration is seen as a means of control (rather than assistance), and because there are very few incentives to sign on. In Uganda, there is a concern that the Ministry of Internal Affairs uses registration to monitor and restrict NGOs and CBOs that campaign on human rights issues. In Kenya, a bill was tabled in November 2013 proposing that 70 per cent of their funding should come from within the country. In Ethiopia, NSSPAs are subject to (domestic) budget thresholds too low for them to do their work properly. If state recognition of CBOs demands registration systems, then the process has to be – and be seen to be – an entry ticket to support, not control. So far, efforts by states to expand SP services with support from donors have ignored the very CBOs that always have and still do most to sustain the poor.

The second public policy imperative should be integration of NSAs in national planning and budgeting. The money, time, and other material resources that individuals spend to cater for the vulnerable categories of the population – through CBOs – supplement government roles and budgets. Government welfare departments struggling against inadequate human resources, funding constraints, and exponential increase in the number of those in need should seek to "partner" (not replace or usurp) non-state SP actors who already mobilise more support and serve more people than the state itself. Even if state GDP and SP expand, the need for mutual support is not about to disappear. The whole coverage of state and other formal social security is less than 10 per cent in many countries. CBOs will continue to exist, and they will be essential to creating a comprehensive and responsive SP framework. Public policy must acknowledge and act on that.

So the third public policy imperative is to consider CBOs and NGOs as functional partners – encouraged by the state. There are already successful cases where NGOs use the services of small CBOs in HIV/AIDS awareness and other campaigns. The NGOs themselves provide services across the board (from protective to transformative), and they have access to much larger (externally provided) funds despite some drawbacks to their approach. They have the resources and status to exert leverage that is essential to transformative programmes. Transformative services are beyond the reach and scope of most CBOs, as they require larger funds and professional organisation capable of running campaigns, fighting lawsuits, and interacting with (central) government. NGOs should focus on what they do best: protective services (i.e. donor-funded emergency relief on a large scale) and transformative services (i.e. advocacy work). Collaboration of CBOs and

NGOs would be beneficial across all types of services (e.g. CBO knowledge should inform NGO action) but, operationally, the strengths of NGOs lie in protective and transformative services, while CBOs serve the members best in preventive and promotive services.

Fourth, once policy recognises CBOs as partners in development, this should come with opportunities for staff skills training, for networking, and for engaging with local government, as well as the opportunity to access additional funds. This has to be implemented in such a way that the very nature of CBOs that makes them so successful (small scale, trust relations, informality, immediate accountability to members, high responsibility to beneficiaries' demands) remains intact. CBOs' unique value will be lost if they are turned into something else. The proverbial butterfly has to be fed without touching its wings.

If community-based mutual organisations are forced to conform to more modern conventions through blanket regulation, they will dissent or disobey or disband. If they are encouraged (and enabled) to conform voluntarily, through skills support and practical incentives, no "enforcement" will be necessary. Their traditional practices persist because they work; they deliver the optimum cost benefit with the skills, time, materials, and funds which they are able to mobilise.

Great care should be taken not to undermine their informal governance methods, which make CBOs uniquely capable of knowing and responding to community and member needs with extreme accuracy and cost efficiency. Any edict which imposes rigid conventional governance mechanisms on self-help groups could be destructive, with significant political and welfare risks. The CBO system is not broken. It does not need to be fixed.

It is the rest of the national SP services system that needs to change: in its perception of informal governance mechanisms, in its respect for the essential importance of trust traditions, and in its willingness to engage CBOs – supportively – on a case-by-case community level for any intervention.

Finally, SP is a component of the bigger social policy that Africa needs. (Adesina, 2010; Bangura, 2010). The current programme of implementing SP in many African countries as short-term projects because of international donor support without clear state social policy is unhelpful. PASGR's ongoing study on the political economy of SP policy uptake in Uganda, Ghana, Kenya, Tanzania, Botswana, and Nigeria appears to show that some of these countries are implementing CT and other SP projects because they are partly funded by international donor community (Awortwi and Aiyede, 2017) and can be leveraged for political gain.

A decade ago, Tade (2006) proposed four key arguments to shape the construction of a comprehensive social policy in Africa. First, an all-embracing and integrated notion of social policy beyond mere delivery of social services; second, to ensure social policy is both thoughtful and practical, it must consider historical, political, and intellectual contexts; third, a viable social policy would need to promote a fundamental social justice perspective; and fourth, social policy is only practical and politically effective when it has active support from social and political movements and institutions. These agents would be carriers, promoters, and reinforcers of the policy.

Implementation of sustainable SP programmes – whether universal or means-tested, or starting from the ILO's proposed "social protection floor" – needs a comprehensive national social policy. Tade's arguments are as relevant today as they were ten years ago. Africa is rising, but it has not yet risen. Recent increases in unemployment and inequality are testimonies that the welfare role of the state is now more crucial than ever before. Social policy development and macro-economic development are inter-dependent, and both must embrace economic inclusion, social justice, citizenship, and rights, and build strong alliances between state and NSAs.

No country has achieved high development and greater provision of welfare to the citizens without both private sector leadership and state SP. The poor have and can do much for themselves through collective support, but their capacity is not yet adequate nor limitless. The state must participate to transform the prospects of the poor from being trapped by poverty to being liberated from poverty.

Implications for governance concepts

Governance consists of both structures and processes that enable production of collectively binding rules or goals. The essence of statehood is the ability to enforce collectively binding decisions (Borzel and Risse, 2010). The findings of these confirm that the absence (or weakness) of the state does not mean absence of governance. The rich landscape of non-state SP actors, especially CBOs, proves that CBOs are a classic example of non-hierarchical, horizontal social coordination as people truly govern themselves. Their central features are reminiscent of Ostrom (1990) work on the regulation of CPR. CBOs successfully rely on social cohesion and trust; their members share norms of reciprocity; monitoring and enforcement are minimal in either cost or necessity. Pooling is echoed in networking to exchange and sustain reciprocal support, knowledge, fundraising, and collective problem solving. Situations in which women assist each other reveal the value of cooperation instead of competition or hierarchy. Most remarkably, CBOs emerge in every context – even in the adverse conditions of an urban slum where social cohesion, trust, and common norms don't come easily. The potential for local self-governance is significantly higher than expected.

There is no anarchy at the community level where the state is absent (Wachhaus, 2014). When people have a common purpose, they connect. Below the state, people actively seek to govern themselves on their own collective terms. Their organisations and membership behaviour are structured by flow of information, resources, and accountability. They work to be the best they can be.

Left to their own devices, the poor will organise a functional contract among themselves. This does not come through spontaneous action as anarchists as Wachhaus, 2014 might assert. This informal contract controls human behaviour no less surely than bureaucratic institutions, but uses different tools: common motive, mutual trust, and peer pressure.

In Somalia, the absolute absence of a central government for more than two decades led to business groups, traditional authorities, civic groups, and international organisations (Menkhaus, 2006). Public law and order may not have been conducted in the conventional "good governance" sense, but NSAs did what they could to provide services to the communities. Clearly, studies in 30 districts in 5 countries show that even if there is no effective government, institutions develop; they are built around functions and then refine their efficiency.

State and NSAs need each other in SP programmes. Singularly, neither NSAs nor central government can assume absolute control; the best the government can do is to encourage diverse arrangements for coping with challenges that it lacks the capacity to solve. (Rosenau and Czempiel, 1992; Rhodes, 1996). Where state SP is limited or absent, the legitimacy of the state in that context becomes nebulous, and citizens will not readily surrender control of their effective measures to a government that had no measures.

The extremely widespread phenomenon of CBOs, one way or another, is likely to hold the key to reducing the enormous social risks many citizens of Africa face today.

References

Adesina, J. (2010). *Rethinking the Social Protection Paradigm: Social Policy in Africa's Development*. Paper prepared for the conference 'Promoting Resilience through Social Protection in Sub- Sahara Africa' organized by the European Union in Dakar, Senegal, 28–30 June, 2010.

Aina, Tade. (2006). *Reflections on Social Policy and Social Justice in Africa: Prospects and Challenges of Social Reconstruction and Transformation in Africa*. A paper presented at the 'Mijadala on Social Policy, Governance and Development in Kenya' sponsored by Development Policy Management Forum on 11 May 2006 at Holiday Inn, Nairobi.

Awortwi, N., and Aiyede, E.R. (2017). *Politics, Public Policy and Social Protection in Africa: Evidence from Cash Transfer Programmes*. London: Routledge.

Bangura, Yusuf. (2010). *Combating Poverty and Inequality: Structural Change, Social Policy and Politics*. Geneva: United Nations Publications.

Börzel, T.A., and Risse, T. (2010). Governance Without a State: Can It Work? *Regulation and Governance*, 4 (2): 113–134.

Lowndes, V., and Skelcher, C. (1998). The Dynamics of Multi-organizational Partnerships: An Analysis of Changing Modes of Governance. *Public Administration*, 76 (2): 313–333.

Menkhaus, K. (2006). Governance Without Government in Somalia: Spoilers, State Building, and the Politics of Coping. *International Security*, 31 (3): 74–106.

Mo Ibrahim Foundation. (2015). *Ibrahim Index of African Governance*.. Retrieved from: www.moibrahimfoundation.org/iiag/data-portal/

Ostrom, Elinor. (1990). *Governing the Commons: The Evolution of Institutions for Collective Action*. Cambridge, MA: Cambridge University Press.

Rhodes, R.A.W. (1996). The New Governance: Governing without Government. *Political Studies*, 44 (4): 652–667.

Rosenau, J.N., and Czempiel, E.-O. (eds.). (1992). *Governance Without Government: Order and Change in World Politics*. Cambridge: Cambridge University Press.

UNDP. (2015). *Human Development Index 2015*. Retrieved from: http://hdr.undp.org/en/data

United Nations Research Institute for Social Development. (2010). *Combating Poverty and Inequality: Structural Change, Social Policy and Politics*. Geneva: United Nations Publications.

Wachhaus, Aaron. (2014). Governance Beyond Government. *Administrative and Society*, 46 (5): 573–593.

Index

Note: Page numbers in *italics* indicate figures and tables.

accountability mechanisms: for burial societies in Uganda 78–9; downward, in services for children in Kenya 68; at local level 154; for mutual organisations in Ghana 46–7, 52, 53; for women's groups in Kenya 114
affinity of members of mutual associations 50–1
affordability of services, in Tanzania 146, *146*
Africa: comprehensive social policy for 159–60; demography of 56; extended family in 68; socialism in 137–8; social situation in 1–2; Structural Adjustment Programmes in 151; *see also specific countries*
African Child Policy Forum 56
African Union 44
associational life in Tanzania 138
associational membership in Ghana 87–8, 94–100, *95*, *96*, *97*
availability of services, in Tanzania 146, *147*

Bertelsmann Transformation Index 21n6
burial societies in Uganda: control, accountability, and transparency of 78–9; governance structure of 76–8; implementation lessons from 82–3; membership in 77–8; member views of performance of 79–81, *80*, *81*; overview 73, 74, 84; services provided by 76, *76*, 81–2; types of 75

case selection and method 8–9
cash transfer (CT) programmes: in Kenya 57, 110, 114; overview of 3, 13, 89; in Uganda 72
CBOs *see* community-based organisations
charities in Ethiopia 39
children, citizenship of 57–8
children in Kenya: assessment of impact of programmes for *65*, 65–6; education services for 59–60; governance of NSAs for 64–5; health and psychosocial support for 60–1; institutional care for 64; legal support for 63–4; micro-finance and livelihood enhancement activities to support 61–3; services provided to *58*; social protection for 67–8
Chronic Poverty Research Centre (CPRC) 118, 121
citizenship: of children 57–8; in Kenya 55–6, 67
civil society, strength of 4
collective action: of CBOs 138, 147–8; at local level 152–3; by women 107, 114, 115
community-based organisations (CBOs): effectiveness of 123; forms of 10–11; funding sources of 12, 66; governance

164 *Index*

of, in Tanzania 138–9, 141–4; internal governance of 14–15; limited statehood and 152; membership and beneficiaries of 13; outreach and capacity of 66–7; principal-agent dynamics of, in Tanzania 144–6; quality of services provided by, in Tanzania 146–8; state recognition of 157–8, 159; in Tanzania 136, 137, 138, 139–41, 148; unregistered 157, 158; *see also* burial societies in Uganda; mutual organisations in Ghana
community capacity building in Kenya 110
Cotonou Agreement 47
CPRC *see* Chronic Poverty Research Centre
CT programmes *see* cash transfer (CT) programmes

Debo 29
domestic violence: in Kenya 112; as negative coping strategy 121; in Uganda 119

economic empowerment programmes for women in Kenya *108*; assessment of 110–13; impact of 113–15; types of 106–10
education services for children 59–60
empowerment, defined 106
Ethiopia: case study of ISPOs in 30–1, *31*; Food Security Programme 25–6; Growth and Transformation Plan 9; informal social protection organisations in 27–30, 39–41; MDG indicators in *27*; National Social Protection Policy 2, 25; NSAs in 26–7; registration of NSAs in 158; state SP programmes in 26

faith-based organisations (FBOs) 13, 14
Fathers Foundation group 61, 64
female genital mutilation 108
functional partners, NSAs as 158–9
funding resources: for CBOs 12, 66; for CBOs in Tanzania 141–2, *142*; for mutual organisations in Ghana 52; poor-to-poor 154

Gadaa 29–30
gendered vulnerability to poverty and governance 120–4; *see also* women in Kenya; women in Uganda
gender sensitivity 123–4
gender specific, gender intensified, and gender imposed constraints 105, 121–2
Ghana: associational membership in 87–8, 94–100, *95*, *96*, *97*; Constitution of 44; extended family system in 45, 91; Growth and Poverty Reduction Strategy 9; living standards in 92; missionaries in 91; mutual organisations in 45–53; National Social Protection Strategy 2; old-age pension in 44–5; research design and methods 92–3; SP programmes in 91–2; vulnerability of individuals and households in 93–4, 99
governance: under conditions of limited statehood 5–8; gendered vulnerability to poverty and 120–4; "good-fit" or "best-fit" 84; implications for 160–1; informal, state acceptance of 152, 153, 159; self-governance, potential for 160–1; of SP, gender-sensitive 117
governance structure: of burial societies in Uganda 76–8; of CBOs in Tanzania 138–9, 141–4; internal, of NSSPs 13–15; of ISPOs in Ethiopia *37*, 37–9, *38*; of mutual organisations in Ghana 48; of NSAs in Kenya 64–5; of NSAs in Uganda 124–6; of self-help groups in Uganda 73–4
government, governance compared to 6

health and psychosocial support for children 60–1
hedging schemes, informal social 88–90
HIV/AIDS: children affected by 60–1, 62, 107–8; prevalence of, in Kenya 56
horizontal resource transmission 68

Ibrahim Index of African governance indicators 154, *155*
Iddir 28, 32, 33, 35, 38, 39
income-generation activities (IGAs): in Kenya 61, 109; in Uganda 74
informal social protection organisations (ISPOs): beneficiaries of *36*; case study of 30–1, *31*; charity work of 35–6; in Ethiopia 27–30, 39–41; forms and scope of 31–2, *32*; governance structures of *37*, 37–9, *38*; rural-urban split in collective action of 32–3, *33*; services provided by 33–4, *34*, *35*
institutional care for children 64
insurance, informal social hedging schemes as 89–90
integration of NSAs in national planning and budgeting 158
internal governance structures of NSSPs 13–15
International Labour Organisation 44
Iqqub 28–9, 31–2, 33, 38, 39
ISPOs *see* informal social protection organisations

Jitegemee CBO 142–3

Kenya: citizenship in 55–6, 67; Constitution of 55, 104; extended family system in 68; poverty in 107; programmes for children in 56–7; registration of NSAs in 158; SP definition in 57; state capacity in 104; Vision 2030 9; women's groups in *105*; *see also* children in Kenya; women in Kenya
Kind Women for Development Organisation 62, 64–5
K'Okumu self-help group 61
Kyakabeizi Twimukye Association 82

leadership of CBOs in Tanzania *143*, 143–4
legal support for children 63–4
legitimacy of CBOs 139
limited statehood: CBOs and 152; in Ghana 44; governance under conditions of 5–8; in Kenya 55,

Index 165

104; non-state actors and 117; in Tanzania 136
literacy levels in Ghana 51
livelihood enhancement activities in Kenya 61–3, 110, 113

Mahiber/Senbete/Jamaha 29, 32, 35, 38, 39
membership: in burial societies in Uganda 77–8; in CBOs in Tanzania 140; of NSAs and CBOs 12–13; *see also* associational membership in Ghana
merry-go-rounds 110, 113–14
micro-finance services in Kenya 61–2, 109–10
mutual organisations in Ghana: accountability mechanisms in 46–7; case selection *48*; drivers of reporting patterns among 50–2; funding for 52; governance structures of 48; overview 45, 52–3; reporting patterns among *49*, 49–50
MV Foundation, India 68

national planning and budgeting, integration of NSAs in 158
networking for synergies in Tanzania 147–8
non-governmental organisations (NGOs): funding sources of 12–13; performance of 153; as prime channel for transformative action 11–12; principal-agent relationships of 144–5; resources and leverage of 115; in Tanzania 141
non-state actors (NSAs): in Africa 157; case selection 9; comparative analysis of 154–7, *155*, *156*, *157*; defined 47; in Ethiopia 26–7; as functional partners 158–9; in Ghana 47–8; governance by 6–7; in Kenya 66–9, 105; limited statehood and role of 117; missions of 123; number and types of *10*, 10–11; reasons for joining 99; types of *11*; in Uganda 72–3, 83, 84–5, 120; *see also* community-based organisations; informal social protection organisations; mutual organisations

166 *Index*

in Ghana; non-governmental organisations
non-state social protection (NSSP): case selection and method 8–9; funding, membership, and beneficiaries of 12–13; internal governance and connection to state 13–15; theoretical framework of policy relevance 5–8; types of services 11–12, *12*
NSAs *see* non-state actors

Partnership for African Social and Governance Research (PASGR) 6, 159
Patience Pays Professional Organisation 125
poor-to-poor funding mechanisms 154
poverty: in Africa 151; in Tanzania 135
poverty of women: governance and 120–4; in Kenya 104–5, 118–19; in Uganda 117, 118–19
preventive services: of burial societies in Uganda 83; defined 8, 89; percentage of *156*
principal-agent dynamics of CBOs in Tanzania 144–6
promotive services: of burial societies in Uganda 82; defined 8, 89, 106; in Ethiopia 34; in Ghana 47; in Kenya 109–10, 114–15; NSAs involved in 154; percentage of *156*; in Uganda 126–7
protective services: defined 8, 89; in Ethiopia 33; in Ghana 47; percentage of *156*; in Uganda 126–7
proximity of services in Tanzania 147
public policy, implications for 157–60

registration of CBOs in Tanzania 141
risk-pool spreading 88, 89–90
Rwanda, National Social Protection Policy of 2

SAPs *see* Structural Adjustment Programmes
savings and credit initiatives in Uganda 126
school feeding programmes 59

self-governance, potential for 160–1
self-help groups: in Ethiopia 29–30; governance structure of 73–4; reliance on 151–2; *see also* associational membership in Ghana; burial societies in Uganda
Senegal: National Strategy for Social and Economic Development 9; Strategie Nationale de Protection Sociale en Maurritanie 2
skills training for women in Kenya 110
social protection (SP): citizenship approach to 69; comprehensive, for Africa 159–60; cost of and capacity for 3; defined 7; in legal systems 2; non-state providers of 4; in recovery programmes 2; state, coverage by 3; types of services 7–8; *see also* preventive services; promotive services; protective services; transformative services
Somalia, NSAs in 161
SP *see* social protection
state recognition of CBOs 157–8, 159
Structural Adjustment Programmes (SAPs) 151

table banking services 109–10
Tanzania: CBOs in 136, 137, 138, 139–41, 148; National Strategy for Growth and Poverty Reduction 8–9; socio-economic status of 135–6; *ujamaa* principle in 136, 137–8
transformative services: defined 8, 89; in Kenya 55, 114–15; percentage of *156*; for poverty 106, 122
"trickle down" of wealth 151, 152
trust: in burial group, and institutional sustainability 79; as "good-fit governance" 53; in NSAs 153, 160

Uganda: Constitution of 72, 119; economic status of 118; legal and policy context for SP in 119–20; non-state actors in 72–3; NSAs in 83, 84–5; Poverty Eradication Action Plan 9; registration of NSAs in 158; religious denominations in 75; state social protection in 72;

state SP services in 117; *see also* burial societies in Uganda; women in Uganda

ujamaa policy in Tanzania 136, 137–8

vertical resource transmission 68

women in Kenya: decision-making at household level 112, *112*; economic empowerment programme for 106–9, *108*; impact of SP services for 113–15; networking for 111–12; ownership of assets 113; participation in empowerment activities 111; promotive services for 109–10; SP services for 105–7; vulnerability to poverty 104–5, 118–19

women in Uganda: in decision-making positions in NSAs *127*, 127–8, 129–30; satisfaction with services of NSAs 129; SP initiatives for 124–9; vulnerability to poverty 117